BY DEGREES

Resilience, Relationships, and Success in Communication Graduate Studies

D1385257

BY DEGREES

Resilience, Relationships, and Success in Communication Graduate Studies

EDITORS

Betsy Wackernagel Bach

The University of Montana

Dawn O. Braithwaite

The University of Nebraska–Lincoln

Shiv Ganesh

The University of Texas at Austin

cognella®
SAN DIEGO

Bassim Hamadeh, CEO and Publisher
Todd R. Armstrong, Publisher
Michelle Piehl, Senior Project Editor
Sara Watkins, Developmental Editor
Alia Bales, Production Editor
Abbie Goveia, Junior Graphic Designer
Trey Soto, Licensing Specialist
Natalie Piccotti, Director of Marketing
Kassie Graves, Senior Vice President of Editorial
Jamie Giganti, Director of Academic Publishing

Cover and design image:

Copyright © 2018 iStockphoto LP/AlxeyPnferov.

Printed in the United States of America.

3970 Sorrento Valley Blvd., Ste. 500, San Diego, CA 92121

Betsy Wackernagel Bach

I am most thankful for Dawn and Shiv's collective willingness to engage in this process with me. I could not have worked with two better colleagues. I dedicate this book to all of the graduate students with whom I have worked throughout my career. I enjoyed mentoring and learning from you.

Dawn O. Braithwaite

I am extraordinarily grateful for the unwavering support of my professors, graduate school friends, and disciplinary colleagues who enriched my life and career. I dedicate this book to graduate students with whom I have worked, past and present, and for new generations of students who share a passion for understanding communication. This book is for you.

Shiv Ganesh

I would like to dedicate this book to all my friends who studied alongside me and to all those who I have had the privilege of teaching.

Contents

Preface

The three editors for this project mused about the possibilities for a book like this for a while, both together and separately. To be sure, there are plenty of resources out there for students who are interested in studying communication. There are any number of rankings of good programs, books about why graduate school is important, and websites on everything from the content of communication programs to how to write a thesis or dissertation well. So, for the three of us, imparting information about the content of graduate programs in communication studies was never the starting point for this book. We felt a sense of collective responsibility to articulate often tacit assumptions about what it takes to thrive and do well; make visible often hidden dynamics involved in navigating one's way through graduate school; and, critically, to consolidate multiple perspectives and resources on the subject. In addition, all three of us wanted to respond to what our own students have often told us: That there is (and perhaps has always been) a clear and urgent need to both discuss implicit norms and hidden curricula in all disciplines, ours included, and to challenge some commonplace myths about success.

Planning and undertaking this book at the present moment was particularly important. All three of us went through graduate school in the United States before the turn of the millennium, before digital technologies occupied the central place that they do in our lives today, before the most impactful pandemic in recent history hit us in 2020, before such significant political polarization, populism, and racism became flashpoint communication issues across the world, and before climate chaos acquired the urgency that it now has. At the same time, the range of people who study communication has mercifully increased to include more women, first-generation learners, and people of color, as well as a greater amount of diversity in gender identities, sexualities, age, and neurodiversity.

This was never a book we could have written on our own; rather, it was one around which we wanted to build a community of scholars. As we discussed how the project should proceed, we kept this goal in mind. In the end, we designed the volume to focus on four goals: (1) centering student voices; (2) highlighting diversity, inclusion, equity, and access; (3) shining a light on the international character of communication research and pedagogy; and (4) infusing each chapter with approaches to successfully navigating graduate studies: resilience, relationships, and success. We discuss these themes more fully in our introductory chapter for students, and we trust they are clear throughout the 15 chapters to follow.

The 21st-century academy is in many ways unrecognizable from academic life when we started our own graduate work, and we can expect flux to be constant in the years to come. What will not change, however, is the transformational character of good higher education and the place of communication as a key life force for good in the world. Historically, universities have always been sites of change, mobility, creativity, identity, and purpose. Our best chance of ensuring that this remains the case is to keep the doors of the academy as wide open as possible. Our hope is that this book will play a small part in that process.

Acknowledgments

This work was inspired by the first handbook for graduate student education in our discipline, Sherry Morreale and Pat Arneson's *Getting the Most from Your Graduate Education in Communication: A Student's Handbook*, published by the National Communication Association in 2008. It served graduate students well, and we are indebted to Sherry and Pat for pulling together this important resource. We used that volume as a starting place from which to conceptualize our ideas. We are also indebted to Krista Hoffmann-Longtin and Maria Brann for their 2019 NCA paper titled "'It's Hidden, After All:' A Modified Delphi Study Exploring Faculty and Students' Perceptions of a Graduate Professional Seminar in Communication." Their results provided us with important perspectives on what both faculty and graduate students expect from such a course.

Thanks also to Kendyl Barney, who reviewed the syllabi of 114 PhD and 24 MA graduate theory seminars, methods courses, and introduction to graduate studies seminars for course content relevant to being a successful graduate student. This work helped build the table of contents and provide subtopics for each chapter. Faculty members Sara Hayden, Jennifer Kruse, Jessy Ohl, Rebecca Rice, Sarah Riforgiate, and Heather Voorhees, as well as graduate students Kendyl Barney, Megan Cardwell, Robert D. Hall, Trevor Kauer, and Katjana Stutzer, carefully reviewed and commented on our proposed Table of Contents. We also deeply appreciate Xuan An Ho's thorough, efficient, and intelligent copyediting. Thank you to our longtime disciplinary colleague Todd Armstrong and to Michelle Piehl at Cognella for their editorial support for the project. Betsy, Dawn, and Shiv appreciated this opportunity to work together and with a stellar group of authors who care deeply about the experience and success of students.

Introduction for Students

Some readers of this book are considering graduate work in communication studies and are looking for more information about what graduate school and programs focused on communication studies are all about. Some of you are in master's programs already and thinking about whether you want to pursue a PhD in communication. Others are already in a graduate program and taking an introduction to graduate studies course. Still others may simply desire more information on the steps and strategies that will help you thrive as a graduate student. Perhaps you are facing challenges in your graduate program and are looking for help in navigating them. We designed this book to attend to these different needs and goals.

Each of us has our own personal story that led us to pursue graduate studies, and it is our hope that this book helps you write your own story. As far as the personal stories for the editors of this book, Betsy had earned a bachelor's degree in communication and was hired as a police officer to specialize in mediating domestic disputes. She enjoyed the work very much and returned to graduate school to learn more about interpersonal conflict. Dawn comes to the discipline through the debate team in high school. She always knew she wanted to be a teacher, and by the time she earned her bachelor's degree, she knew teaching and studying interpersonal communication was the direction she wanted to take with her life; graduate work was her natural next step. For Shiv, who has degrees in sociology, social work, and community organizing, communication was always a backdrop for whatever he was doing, so getting a PhD in the subject was both inevitable and allowed him to bring multiple interests in organizing, media, globalization, and justice together onto the same platform.

Like us, you have your own reasons for pursuing a graduate degree in communication. We imagine that we share a passion for understanding the role of communication in creating, legitimizing, enacting, and changing our personal, professional, and civic lives. It is hard to think of a more central pursuit to being human.

Once we decided to work on this book, we had to figure out what to include and asked a central question: What would be most helpful for students considering applying to or currently in a graduate program in communication studies? We started by reading existing resources and thinking about what had changed since they were written. We considered both our own experiences as graduate students and what we now see as faculty members. Next, we undertook an analysis of the topics included in introduction to graduate studies courses across communication master's and PhD programs. From there, we developed a list of chapters we thought would be helpful to include in the book, starting with an overview of what the discipline is about, then proceeding with how to successfully apply to a communication program, narratives, competencies, and strategies for navigating life in a graduate program, and preparing for the next steps after graduation. We shared this list of chapters and topics with a broad group of graduate students and listened to their feedback. In the end, we developed 15 chapters we wanted to see in the book and invited prominent scholars to author the chapters. We asked each chapter author to invite at least one current or recent graduate student to coauthor the chapter with them, as well as to add any other coauthors they thought would be helpful to the work.

We have four main goals that infuse *By Degrees: Resilience, Relationships, and Success in Communication Graduate Studies*. First, one of our most important goals is to make the perspectives and voices of graduate students central to this project and infused in each chapter. Each authorship team invited graduate students to reflect on their experiences and collected the quotations you will see featured in each chapter. Each of the chapters engages with issues, challenges, and insights experienced by graduate students. Perhaps more than any other element of this book, this is something about which we are immensely proud and excited. We hope the student voices will resonate with you; some will mirror your experiences, questions, and concerns, while others may provide new and different perspectives.

Second, we want to highlight issues of diversity, inclusion, equity, and access as serious and fundamental to graduate education. You will often see a single chapter dedicated to these issues in different books; however, we were committed to seeing these issues addressed meaningfully across the chapters. Taken together, the chapters in this book position diversity, equity, access, and inclusion not only as critical for excellence but, more importantly, also as fundamental social goods in and of themselves. We trust that you will see this commitment as you read the diverse selection of graduate student voices, especially in places where authors question and critique taken-for-granted practices that can create roadblocks for students

Third, while we understand that many of you are pursuing graduate studies within the United States, we want to stress the international character of communication research and pedagogy. In the United States, scholars tend to have a much more disciplinary view of communication, perhaps because of how the study of communication has been institutionalized into departments and colleges (see Chapter 2). It is important to understand that there is a strong and growing focus on communication outside the United States. Internationally, scholars are much more likely to take a field rather than a disciplinary view of communication and locate communication research and teaching in multiple places across the university, including in business schools, design and creative faculties, colleges focused in education, health, media, cultural studies, and/or sociology departments. Given how interconnected our world is, the number of international students who come to the United States, and, increasingly, the number of students in the United States who are pursuing academic careers outside of it, we made efforts to include perspectives and voices of people who teach and study communication outside the United States. As just one example, we wanted to highlight the institutional vocabularies involved; for example, outside the United States, universities use the term "postgraduate studies" rather than "graduate studies" and use the term "supervisor" or sometimes "guide" rather than the more North American label "advisor."

Fourth, we highlight three fundamental aspects to successfully approach navigating graduate school that you will see appear across all chapters: resilience, relationships, and success. You'll notice that these are reflected in the subtitle of the book. We start with resilience, as, in many ways, it is a master trope for this millennium. For our authors, resilience is not only just coping or surviving a graduate program; rather, resilience incorporates also thriving in the face of challenge or adversity that can accompany graduate studies. Resilience also implies agency and the ability to reflect, make choices, challenge, and sometimes resist power structures and discriminatory practices that can persist not only in academia but also in the world at large. We also want to stress that resilience is communal. That is, resilience is not only the property of individuals; it is a relational and cultural phenomenon as well.

We also seek to highlight the fundamental role that relationships play in your graduate school experience. As the philosopher Martin Buber put it: "In the beginning, there is the relation."[1] In relational communication we coproduce not only our personal and professional identities but also the sum total of our lives. Our chapter authors clearly recognize this and stress the convoy of people who will be part of your graduate program—in particular, your professors and costudents. For example, the formative role of mentorship in making decisions to go to graduate school and succeed in your program are featured in several chapters. All aspects of life in graduate school are deeply relational: faculty members, your graduate student peers in departments and across the campus, your students if you are teaching, colleagues you meet via professional associations, members of research collaborations, and those within different communities.

The idea that resilience and relationships involve thriving also implies success, the final theme that runs through this book. Throughout the chapters you will see that the authors explore issues of success in multiple ways, taking a hands-on approach in the form of pragmatic, creative, and inspirational advice, tips, and hacks. While our authors make it clear that success involves strategy and practice, in equal measure success also involves improvisation and creativity. The authors approach success as multidimensional, involving thriving with your coursework, scholarship, and teaching while also growing and transforming as a person. We also hope that you glean within the pages of this book that there is no single "right" outcome or "wrong" outcome of the journey through graduate studies and the stages to follow. Rather, the sum total of one's experiences through the journey makes it successful from a variety of pathways. Just as we came to graduate studies via different pathways and have taken our careers in different directions, all of us found our graduate education invigorating, challenging, and life-altering.

Interestingly, having four goals for this book carried over into identifying four segments around which we organized our chapters. The chapters are ordered to follow the life of a typical graduate student, ranging from the initial decision to enter the field through to the opportunities available

---

1   Buber, M. (1958). *I and Thou.* Macmillan Publishing.

once you've obtained your graduate degree. We wrote the first three chapters to inform you about whether a graduate program in communication is the *right fit* for you. In Chapter 1 we provide a history and overview of the discipline and describe the major areas of study and research to provide a context for you to understand the uniqueness of a graduate degree in communication. We wrote Chapter 2 to help you determine if graduate school is right for you. In this chapter we highlight the differences between master's and PhD programs and provide guidance on the application process. In Chapter 3 we offer narratives and graduate student commentary on the overall strategies they used to be successful in their pursuit of graduate education.

We focus the next set of chapters on succeeding once you are accepted into a graduate program. In Chapter 4 we identify and discuss important steps and tasks for moving through your graduate program in a timely manner, while in Chapter 5 we provide advice on how to select an advisor, one of the most important tasks in graduate education. The "coins of the realm" in graduate education are research, writing, sharing your work with others, and teaching, so in Chapters 6, 7, 8, and 9 we explore the process of planning and implementing research; communicating your ideas in writing; submitting, presenting, and publishing your research and creative activity; and learning to navigate the complexities of teaching coupled with balancing your role as both graduate student and instructor.

The authors of Chapters 10, 11, and 12 offer guidance for surviving and thriving in a graduate program. In Chapter 10 we identify personal resources for graduate students and provide suggestions for building strong working relationships with your peers, while in Chapter 11 we pinpoint and explore common roadblocks in graduate education and how to meet them head-on. In Chapter 12 we discuss how graduate students can grow and survive together to form a supportive graduate school experience.

In the last three chapters of this book we provide ideas, insights, and strategies for maximizing your graduate school experience as you complete your degree and enter the workforce. The authors of Chapter 13 propose many ideas for managing the academic job search across the different types of academic institutions. In Chapters 14 and 15 we turn to nonacademic life and highlight how to pursue careers outside of the academy. These chapters are devoted to master's and PhD students, respectively.

It is our sincere hope that you enjoy reading and learning from what is included in this volume as much as we enjoyed conceptualizing and writing it. We wish you all the best as you pursue your graduate education.

Providing the Intellectual Tools
Getting to Know the Discipline of Communication

Dawn O. Braithwaite

Tina M. Harris

Jessy J. Ohl

Trevor Kauer

We imagine you are reading this chapter because you are either considering applying to a graduate program in communication and want to get a sense of what the discipline is about, or you are already in a program and want to better understand why we teach and study communication in the ways we do. It would be hard to find scholars, practitioners, or community members who do not have an interest or claim some expertise in communication. So what makes a communication graduate degree a unique and worthwhile pursuit? Communication scholars Patrice Buzzanell and Donal Carbaugh (2009) reflected on this question and what binds the discipline together:

> Funding agencies like the National Science Foundation (NSF), the National Institutes of Health (NIH), the Social Science Research Council (SSRC), and so on read proposals and may ask what a communication study contributes to particular social issues that other stances of inquiry do not. A similar exigency is created by a call in many quarters for research teams from multiple disciplines to address a social problem such as AIDS, the removal of dams, environmental assessments, or security and privacy issues. ... Each such moment provides an opportunity for communication researchers to say what is distinctive about their communication research—its philosophy, theory, methodology, and/or findings. (p. 2)

Although members of the discipline do not speak with one voice about who "we" are, one thing we have in common is that the study of communication has always been a very practical one, both an art and a science, with the broad goal of "understanding and improving human relations" (Ehninger, 1968, p. 137).

What brings you to the discipline of communication? It could be the complexities of everyday conversation or the rich tapestry of communication theory. You may be attracted to the aesthetic, artistic, and performative aspects of communication or interested in nonprofit work or in industries related to communication. Like you, the authors of this chapter came to the discipline for many different reasons. Dawn's interest was sparked by a poster in her late 1960s middle school classroom that read, "Communication is the Beginning of Understanding." She recalls, "I started college when interpersonal communication courses were newly available and was drawn to answering practical questions about communication in close relationships." Tina realized that she did not feel represented in the research allegedly describing and explaining how all people communicate in different contexts and relationships. She recalls, "I started asking the questions that could/would give voice to the realities too often overlooked and marginalized." Jessy came to the communication discipline out of frustration with studying political science. He explains, "I was interested in power, influence, and persuasion, and these concerns found validation in communication. I also appreciate the discipline's core commitment to both research and teaching." For Trevor, the applied nature of communication inspires him to study and teach others how to live more fulfilling lives, stressing that "the research we conduct and the courses we teach produce a healthier, civically responsible, confident, and more eloquent society."

Whatever the reasons you are interested in the study of communication, we hope this chapter will help you think about this question and better understand the discipline of communication by focusing on (a) the roots and history of the discipline, (b) major journals in the discipline, (c) perspectives on the process of communication, and (d) the state and trends of the study of communication.

Roots and History of the Communication Discipline

It is natural to look at lists of college majors and assume that an area of study has always been there for students to choose. Yet every discipline of study started somewhere, sometime, and for particular reasons. Learning about the development of a discipline is helpful as you consider and pursue graduate work. It will help you better frame your interests and understand how and why the discipline took the paths it did. One doctoral student talked about how helpful it was to learn about the discipline's history:

> It takes the pressure off of your shoulders of not knowing what's going on. Sometimes as a graduate student, you feel like you are always out of the loop. Like there are always secrets that you have to face and overcome. When you have faculty who spend time situating you in your discipline and history, you can better navigate your future.

While the study of communication is an old enterprise, the academic discipline of communication is somewhat newer. The study of communication is often traced back to the ancient Greeks, but we can predate it back to Africa and China (Blake, 2009). Most early scholars and practitioners focused on the use of public speaking to persuade audiences. As you can see in Chapters 2 and 3, students can find graduate programs with different structures and foci across the globe, and envisioning your goals within different narratives will help you frame your own options and goals.

We begin our look at the modern study of communication in the United States starting in the 20th century. Around 1910, most university professors of rhetoric focused on building arguments and persuasive messages were teaching debate and public speaking primarily located in English departments; others were in theatre or communication disorders programs. These teachers were convinced that speech was different from a written essay; however, most English professors did not share this distinction. By 1913, the teachers of rhetoric and speech felt frustrated and disrespected. James O'Neill, the first president of what later was called the National Communication Association (NCA), spoke at the 1913 meeting of the National Council of Teachers of English (NCTE), recalling, "I claimed that about the only academically respectable work in public speaking was being done by teachers who were 'on their own,' ... [we needed] independent departments, an independent professional organization, a professional journal, teacher training, and graduate work" (O'Neill, 1989, p. 3). That year, 17 speech teachers walked out of the NCTE meeting and started their own association called the National Association of Academic Teachers of Public Speaking.

Braithwaite (2010) reflected on what this history tells us about ourselves, including:

- *We were born of rebellion.* Our founders were not satisfied with the status quo; they wanted change.

- *We were born of risk and sacrifice.* It would have been much safer and easier to stay in the English department and association than strike out and create something new.

- *We were born of the belief that there was something unique about speech.* Our founders knew speech was more than an English essay on its feet.

These early teachers of speech were tired of feeling isolated and wanted to be with people who valued speaking on its own terms.

Members of the association focused on determining the agenda for this new enterprise. Were they to be teachers or researchers (Cohen, 1994; Gehrke & Keith, 2014)? Today, we understand that communication professors can function as both; however, this was an important argument that would shape the discipline in the United States for many years. Graduate students entering the discipline today often appreciate the commitment to teaching as well as research. Recent graduate student Toni Morgan, PhD, reflects:

I appreciate understanding where we've been. Learning about the history of communication studies helped me feel even more passionate about teaching because that's why I pursued graduate work in the first place. Knowing that the early beginnings of communication studies emphasized teaching and pedagogy makes me even more excited to be in a field that centers student learning.

Those who thought the discipline should be solely about teaching did not see a need for research, and indeed, few had any research training anyway. Those advocating for research knew that scholarship would move the new discipline forward to achieve academic credibility. This was also a time in history when scientific inquiry was being stressed in universities and the broader cultural milieu. As the founders considered research, they also deliberated about whether or not research should be more *humanities based*, studying critical reflections on influential speeches, or focused instead on *social science*, where topics like speaker credibility, structure, or delivery were the research focus. From the beginning, the communication discipline has kept strong ties to disciplines such as English, sociology, education, psychology, anthropology, media studies, and political science. While some believe this to be a weakness of our discipline, your authors believe it is a testament to our inherent openness and interdisciplinarity, seeking the best ways to answer important questions about communication and society.

Leading up to the 1940s, faculty in speech departments were teaching public speaking, delivery, argumentation, and public address. During and following World War II, faculty added courses in small group discussion to understand and advance democracy, and those doing research began studying group interaction. Social scientists from the fields of psychology and sociology were studying persuasion and obedience to authority to understand atrocities that occurred during that war. Other social scientists were focused on how information was transmitted via mass media. Journalism and media programs and the Association for Education in Journalism and Mass Communication (AEJMC) started in 1912, which was around the same time as NCA (Eadie, 2008).

In the 1960s to 1980s, the discipline grew exponentially. In the United States, cultural struggles over civil rights, women's roles, the Vietnam War, interpersonal relationships, and technological advances brought forward scholars who taught and studied these issues. For example, Gerald Miller (1976) recalled, "Students themselves began to demand answers about how to relate communicatively with their acquaintances and close friends and romantic partners" (p. 10). Social scientists interested in communication joined rhetorical scholars in speech departments, bringing new research topics and using social science quantitative research methods (e.g., surveys and experimental methods) and, later, qualitative methods. By the mid-1970s to 1980s, they added new courses such as intercultural, organizational, interpersonal, and health communication. During this time, rhetoricians added courses such as communication and gender, social movements, and media and communication. At the same time these interests were developing in the United States, interest in communication, especially media, was developing internationally.

In the 1980s, most U.S. speech departments changed their names to "speech communication" and later to "communication" or "communication studies." You will find communication departments in different university colleges, such as arts & sciences, humanities, and liberal arts; behavioral sciences; or in units that include media studies and/or journalism. One clue about a program's focus is whether communication is pluralized, as "communications" most often signals a central focus in media, journalism, and/or technology (see Eadie, 2008). We realize this can be confusing at times; therefore, we advise that you study the composition and faculty to determine your best fit (see Chapter 2).

It is important to stress that the study of communication and the existence of communication programs has spread across the globe. For example, Rogers and Hart (2001) chronicled the roots and growth of international communication, development communication, and intercultural communication, explaining that all three share a focus on culture and communication within and across borders and "between unlike individuals" (p. 1). Scholarship and subsequent university-based programs developed in the early 1970s centered on mass media, beginning with studies of mass media systems and information flow and coming of age in the 1990s and beyond, with strong theoretical foci. International communication, development communication research, and academic programs feature a strong focus on mass media and "macro-level information exchanges between and within nations" (Rogers & Hart, 2008, p. 1). These academic programs are located in the United States and internationally and represent the majority of communication programs outside the United States. Intercultural communication had its roots in the more micro-focused interpersonal communication, beginning and located largely in the West. It started in programs with a strong social science focus and today has a strong presence in programs with a strong rhetorical and/or critical cultural approach in the discipline.

Over the last 15 years, we have seen tremendous growth in scholarship and programs taking critical approaches to studying communication, emphasizing social justice, power inequities, diversity, and inclusion. In the best of times, scholars with different research orientations and methods complement each other well. This blend of humanities (rhetoric and critical cultural studies) and social sciences represents many U.S. communication departments today. We believe that all of these approaches are important, and we encourage fruitful synergies between these different traditions. There are misunderstandings at times, as scholars do speak different research languages or have divergent perspectives on communication (Braithwaite, 2010, 2014).

How well these emphases function in any given program is undoubtedly a question to ask as you consider graduate work. We recommend programs that support a comprehensive, interdisciplinary, and global focus on contemporary challenges and opportunities regarding communication. A recent doctoral graduate from China explains her reasons for pursuing graduate education in communication:

A graduate degree in communication is important to me because I was able to use language(s) to describe, explain, and analyze abstract and complex relational processes on an interpersonal (relational dialectics, boundaries), organizational (action and structure), and sociocultural level. In China, it is believed that "communication" is a taken-for-granted or habitualized learning process for an individual to become a social being. My parents just told me, "You learn communication by talking properly and by observing and speaking to people around you." It sounded like an invisible, significant skill. But doing communication is not as easy as my cultural teaching. My graduate school education in the United States made me more conscious of every detail of communicative practice.

While the discipline of communication is broad, it is energizing to realize that there is an almost endless variety of topics you can study. Explore the breadth of the discipline in the wide variety of interest groups represented in communication associations, for example, the International Communication Association (ICA; see list of divisions and interest groups), the National Communication Association (see list of divisions, sections, and caucuses; https://www.natcom.org/about-nca/membership-and-interest-groups/nca-interest-groups), and the European Communication Research and Education Association (ECREA; https://ecrea.eu/Sections#sections). Search for international associations serving your interests, for example, the Center for Intercultural New Media Research (http://www.interculturalnewmedia.com/) or the Association for Chinese Communication Studies (http://www.chinesecommunication-studies.com/).

Major Journals in the Discipline

Becoming socialized into any academic discipline involves gaining familiarity with terminology, identifying established and emerging voices, and becoming informed about contemporary research trends. Getting to know the journals and book presses of the discipline allows you to see where your interests might fit and where you might make new contributions. Explore the different topics by visiting websites of journals, often published by communication associations. Study their tables of contents and reference lists at the end of articles to help you understand different topics that are studied. Look at the newest articles coming out to see topics being studied in different graduate programs. These steps will help you envision topics you may pursue in graduate courses and will help you trace where the faculty and graduate students in different programs are working and publishing.

While writing and publishing is discussed in Chapters 6, 7, and 8, our goal here is to help you learn about research journals. It takes time to recognize the vast and ever-growing number of outlets that publish communication research, but learning about each journal's tendencies, reputation, and commitments is vitally important to understanding the discipline. This is especially relevant when students embark on the often-mysterious process of publishing their own research. Each journal is designed to speak to diverse constituencies that can be challenging to recognize immediately. Some journals are tailored for specific research methodologies, while others take practical application as their primary means of evaluation. There are state, regional, national, and international journals and interdisciplinary journals that publish communication research. Some journals have a broader focus, and there are also reputable journals that focus on specific theoretical, pedagogical, and social concerns. Students should consult their academic mentors to learn which journals align with their professional interests and determine which potential "home" might be most appropriate for their research. Below is an abbreviated list of some important journals in the discipline, and our four regional journals, to help you become acquainted with the discipline and shape your future contributions.

- *Communication and Critical/Cultural Studies* (National Communication Association)

- *Communication Education* (National Communication Association)

- *Communication Monographs* (National Communication Association)

- *Critical Studies in Media Communication* (National Communication Association)

- *Journal of Applied Communication Research* (National Communication Association)

- *Journal of International and Intercultural Communication* (National Communication Association)

- *Quarterly Journal of Speech* (National Communication Association)

- *The Review of Communication* (National Communication Association)

- *Text and Performance Quarterly* (National Communication Association)

- *Journal of Communication* (International Communication Association)

- *Political Communication* (International Communication Association)

- *Health Communication*

- *The Howard Journal of Communications*

- *Human Communication Research* (International Communication Association)

- *Philosophy and Rhetoric*

- *Communication Quarterly* (Eastern Communication Association)

- *Western Journal of Communication* (Western Communication Association)

- *Communication Studies* (Central States Communication Association)

- *Southern Communication Journal* (Southern States Communication Association)

It is important to stress that there is an array of journals associated with international organizations and associations. Depending on your interests, you will find these journals important to your studies and can search for them given your specific foci.

We hope that a look at the wide variety of specialties represented in associations, programs, and journals will help you answer questions about your fit in the discipline and help you begin to envision your own place and potential contributions that start with graduate studies. To follow, we focus on different ways the process and study of communication is conceptualized and organized.

Perspectives on the Process of Communication

When scholars from other disciplines and laypersons discuss communication, they often focus on message transmission and exchange, clarity, and/or effectiveness. It is not unusual to hear people talk about how communication might break down or fail. While message transmission is important, this is a very limited view of communication. More useful and representative of the discipline is a view of communication processes by which humans create and reflect how relationships, groups, organizations, and cultures are shaped and defined and how persons interact and create social realities and personal identities in interaction within their social, cultural, and mediated contexts.

Scholars in the discipline study communication as a transactional process (see Braithwaite & Suter, in press), which has four implications for understanding the role of communication. First, communication is always an ongoing, dynamic process that is affecting and reflecting constant change. Whenever we study the communication process, we stop the process in artificial ways to analyze it. Second, communication occurs within complex and dynamic cultural and social contexts that frame interactions and relationships. Third, communication is the negotiation of shared meanings as persons create and coordinate social reality. Fourth, persons negotiate meanings on both content and relational levels, reflecting how persons metacommunicate via verbal and nonverbal cues about how messages should be interpreted and understood. In sum, we conceptualize communication as the symbolic, transactional process of creating and sharing meanings: the primary way humans develop, create, maintain, and alter identity (Baxter, 2014). Each of these goals is addressed by different paradigmatic approaches (Deetz, 2001), and to follow, we discuss effectual, constitutive, and critical perspectives.

Effectual Perspective:
Communication Patterns and Processes That Affect Outcomes

Communication scholars working from this first approach focus on the "effects of communication in shaping the world as we know it" (Baxter, 2014, p. 37), centering inquiry on communication processes, patterns, and variables that sculpt and influence experiences. Scholars taking an effects approach align with a social scientific perspective, examining functions of communication with the goal of producing generalizable explanations from testable hypotheses (Baxter, 2014).

Constitutive Perspective:
Communication as Constituting Relationships and Identities

Scholars taking a constitutive lens focus on identities and social realities as cocreated, negotiated, and changed through interaction. Craig (1999) argued that this constitutive turn was a unique contribution of the discipline. Scholars working from this approach also encouraged the discipline's turn toward the study of the communicative practices of postmodern or "nontraditional" relationships, for example, LGBTQ or multiethnic relationships, groups, organizations, or cultures whose members face challenges in explaining and legitimizing their relationships and identities and are especially reliant on interaction to do so.

Critical Perspective:
Integrating Issues of Power and Communication

In more recent years, scholars began undertaking critical scholarship that centers on communication and issues of power and ways that persons resist, critique, and transform relationships, groups, organizations, and cultures via interaction (Moore, 2017). This important work is especially responsive to cultural challenges being faced worldwide, for example, focusing on addressing racial and gender discrimination, economic and health disparities, and unequal access to opportunities and advancement. A recent doctoral graduate from Nigeria reflected on pursuing graduate studies from a critical focus:

> Graduate school helped me to develop further my critical consciousness (i.e., Paulo Freire's term for recognizing and analyzing systems of inequality so that one can take action) and express my perspective confidently in a variety of ways. On an intuitive level, I had always been aware that my way of seeing the world was markedly different. Unfortunately, academic circles can be exclusionary because if you do not express yourself in the dominant language, your perspective is disregarded or even criticized. Graduate school helped me to recognize and understand that but also gave me the intellectual tools to resist and disrupt it.

Each of these three perspectives is important, as they contribute to our understanding of communication and our experiences.

The State and Trends of the Study of Communication

As you familiarize yourself with the discipline and the structure of graduate programs, it helps to understand three complementary approaches to studying communication: (a) rhetorical and humanistic approaches, (b) social science approaches, and (c) critical and cultural approaches.

Rhetorical and Humanistic Approaches

The Western study of rhetoric is habitually tied to Greco-Roman ancient works and teachings, where the focus was on rhetoric as the art of persuasion. Scholars of communication in the 20th century attempted to bolster the nascent field's academic reputation by associating it with renowned figures who studied persuasion in extraordinary depth, including Aristotle, Isocrates, and Cicero, among others. By harkening back to Greco-Roman rhetorical theory and practice, scholars and teachers instituted an extensive lexicon and established a sense of shared disciplinary identity. Greco-Roman influence continues with rhetoric's ongoing interest in democracy, public address, and argumentation; however, canonizing this tradition has also been marked by systemic racial and gender exclusion.

From its early focus on orality, rhetoric eventually expanded to account for written, visual, mass-mediated, and digital processes of social influence. The 1950s and 1960s transformed the study of rhetoric due to the rise of the new medium of television, large-scale social protests for equality, and the emergence of Kenneth Burke. Burke's wild and polemic writing style encouraged a new generation of scholars to move "beyond the traditional bounds of rhetoric" (Burke, 1969, p. xxi) by theorizing identification, consubstantiality, transcendence, and the relationship between symbols and the material body. Three important turns in the field of rhetoric that extend Burke's scholarship are critical rhetoric, constitutive rhetoric, and invitational rhetoric. *Critical rhetoric* assumes not only that communication can be used as a weapon by the powerful but also that it is the responsibility of rhetorical critics to unmask and disrupt mechanisms of oppression (McKerrow, 1989). *Constitutive rhetoric* focuses on how discourse enables and forecloses the creation of individual and collective identities (Charland, 1987). *Invitational rhetoric* offers a feminist critique of persuasion in which understanding is embraced over change and domination (Foss & Griffin, 1995). For a field historically centered on public speaking, these developments helped solidify the contemporary period by making abundantly clear that the parameters of rhetoric were unnecessarily and problematically restricted.

The current study of rhetoric is guided by at least two overarching goals, one ancient and one contemporary. First, rhetoric's long-standing pedagogical commitment to the development of informed, engaged, and responsive contributors to democracy continues. Rhetoric classes are designed to build both fundamental skills of expression and the critical sensibilities necessary for social change. Collective problems demand collective solutions, and as the world grapples with the ravages of climate change, White supremacy, disease, and nuclear proliferation, the study of rhetoric is as relevant as ever. Second, a more recent goal within rhetoric is the honest and concerted confrontation with the discipline's colonial, anti-Black, and misogynistic history toward Black, Indigenous, and people of color (BIPOC). Calls for diversifying and decolonizing rhetoric are not new (Shome, 1996), but they received heightened attention following the research and activism surrounding the #CommmunicationSoWhite movement (Chakravartty et al., 2018). Despite, and in some cases, thanks to, the field's perfunctory Whiteness, Flores (2016) declares that "race is foundational to the work of rhetorical criticism and that any criticism void of this consideration is incomplete, partial, if not irresponsible" (p. 6). Both of these goals will test the resolve and relevance of rhetorical scholars and teachers in the years to come.

Social Science Approaches

The impetus for researchers, especially in the 20th century, was to focus on the science and empirical scholarship of postpositivism and the drawing of generalizable conclusions from data. This was a stark contrast to the work of humanistic and rhetorical scholars. Most of the early work was collecting data via survey and experimental methods imported from psychology and sociology and analyzing data via increasingly sophisticated quantitative methods. These social scientists seek to understand communication processes and patterns via causes and effects from an objective approach to produce generalizable explanations concerning how variables are interdependent. These scholars develop theories based on empirically derived propositions from testable hypotheses that describe, explain, and predict outcomes of communication behaviors. A robust set of research findings and theories were developed in several areas of the discipline, such as media, organizational, interpersonal, intercultural, and health communication. They imported theories from other disciplines and soon began to develop their own unique communication-based theories.

In the 1980s, some scholars adopted a *constitutive frame*, taking an interpretive turn using qualitative methods such as interviews and observation (ethnographic studies in particular contexts). Rather than seeking generalizable findings across contexts, interpretive scholars seek to understand social actors' points of view to understand how relationships, groups, organizations, and cultures are negotiated and changed in social practice. Interpretive scholars build theories of understanding that describe everyday communicative practices representing shared patterns of meaning (Baxter, 2014). For example, in organizational and intercultural communication, interpretive approaches were a natural fit and soon eclipsed effects scholarship in those areas of study. In other areas of the discipline, particularly in interpersonal communication, interpretive scholarship was resisted by many who espoused commitment to science, and it took longer for qualitative research to be an accepted research method (Braithwaite, 2014). Presently, there is a much stronger blend of perspectives, and more scholars are using a mixed-methods approach to research and theorizing. A current master's student explained:

> Communication theory has completely altered the way I view the world. I cannot consume media without thinking about whose interests the ideologies represented by dominant discourses serve. I can't have a conversation without thinking about the interpersonal communication theories I've learned and what our conversation is meaning/adding in our relational context. ... As soon as the light bulb flicks on about a particular theory, everything that that theory describes falls into place.

One exciting development in social science scholarship has been a greater focus on translational scholarship and theorizing (Frey, 2009; Seeger, 2009; Wethington et al., 2012). Early on, there was a greater gap between research and practice, stemming from the strong emphasis on knowledge generation and less value on application. The move of the *Journal of Applied Communication Research* to NCA in 1991 signaled value in making social improvements with scholarship. Health and risk and crisis communication scholars led the way in translational research, and there has been growth and concerted effort for both effects and constitutive work to be applied. More scholars are situating research in communities, focusing on local members' needs who function as the experts on their experiences.

The wider appearance and acceptance of interpretive scholarship and qualitative methods in social science and the desire to be responsive to important cultural changes have also helped open the door for critical approaches to communication inquiry within scholarly groups in the discipline that were not represented in social sciences. We are currently witnessing a greater diversity of scholars and scholarship, expanding more narrowly focused research topics, methods, theories, and perspectives.

Critical and Cultural Approaches

Critical and cultural approaches (CCA) "address how power and macro-historical, institutional, and economic structures shape and constrain interpersonal, intergroup, and mediated communication" (Hoops & Drzewiecka, 2017, para. 1). They are typically found in both humanities and social sciences. CCA is associated with the Frankfurt School of thought (Fuchs, 2016) and is a form of "emancipatory social philosophy" (p. 6) that "questions all thought and practices that justify or uphold domination and exploitation" (p. 9). There is an inherent desire by CCA researchers to create a fair and just society. Using these methods, scholars are better able to critique existing power structures and the artifacts used to produce them. Whether the goal is a critique of the media itself or the messages embedded therein, scholars engaging in these approaches attempt to facilitate change in the structure either on a societal and/or an individual level. This change is largely in the form of dismantling the existing power hierarchies that disenfranchise the less powerful who are also acknowledged as being "the oppressed." As Durham (2011) notes, the focus is "on the analysis of cultural artifacts and practices in relation to the social formations in which they exist" (para. 1).

CCA scholars are interested in human subjectivity and consciousness or the ways in which communication artifacts ultimately shape humans' understandings of and experiences with the world (Payne & Barbera, 2010). Of particular concern are the techniques the privileged use to preserve their power and ideologies (Wood, 2004). These approaches are both recognized as, and criticized for, having a Marxist leaning; however, given the many economic and social disparities existent throughout the world, they are critical for those committed to disrupting hegemony or the status quo. As such, the scholarship produced ultimately works to liberate those suffering because of these various forms of systemic oppression.

Since their inception, CCA scholars have had a tremendous impact on a plethora of disciplines, including communication. They have achieved the greater overarching goal of giving voice to marginalized groups and offering hope and liberation from systemic oppression. Communication scholars have either adapted existing theories or developed new theories to address systemic oppression due to race, gender, class, sexuality, ability, and other aspects of identity. Particularly noteworthy is critical race theory, Afrocentricity, and complicity theory. Critical race theory originated in legal studies and has been used by communication scholars to better understand the relationship between race, ethnicity, and communication (Orbe & Harris, 2015). Esteemed scholar Molefi Asante (2009) introduced scholars to Afrocentricity, which he describes as "a paradigm based on the idea that African people should reassert a sense of agency in order to achieve sanity" (para. 1). This theory and methodology were introduced because mainstream theories failed to explicitly acknowledge and address the racial and cultural realities of those of African descent. Communication scholar Mark McPhail (1991) extends the assumptions of Afrocentricity with complicity theory and challenges the belief that African Americans and European Americans have natural differences, which are typically negatively framed. In keeping with CCA, scholars using these theories direct their attention to power-based realities that perpetuate systemic oppression.

The strength of CCA scholarship is that it is action oriented, prioritizes facilitating change in the real world through theory and application, and is concerned with media control and ownership. At their very core, CCA are most appropriate and effective for scholars who believe that their work should have an impact outside of academia and in the "real world" per se. These strengths are also viewed as challenges, as some would consider CCA researchers as too political, lacking in scientific objectivity, and using questionable research methods. Collectively, these challenges attempt to frame CCA as being inherently biased and nonscientific, a critique with which we do not agree, as we have highlighted the many contributions of CCA scholars.

No brief chapter can represent the depth and breadth of the communication discipline or any discipline. However, our goal is to help expand your understanding of how and why the discipline evolved as it did and the different ways communication is conceptualized and studied. From our chapter and others in this book, we hope you will find resources to discover the many different topics you can pursue in your own work and consider how you wish to use your education after earning your communication graduate degree. Many different pathways are highlighted throughout this book. We want to stress that, while you may have a career goal in mind as you pursue your graduate work, it is not at all unusual for goals to change over time. It is also perfectly normal for students to enter the discipline in one particular emphasis and find a passion for other topics or perspectives during their coursework. We believe in the centrality of communication in our lives and that the discipline holds promise for those who study communication and employ this knowledge inside and outside of the academy.

For Further Thought and Reflection

1. Why did the 17 speech teachers leave the English group and form their own association in 1913? Once they left, what were their main debates and choices concerning the focus of the new discipline?

2. When you look at interest groups within communication associations, which of the topic areas interest you most, and why?

3. What are the unique contributions of the communication discipline when we conceptualize communication as more than simply transmitting messages?

4. What are three complementary approaches to studying communication discussed in the chapter? Which of these approaches interest you most, and why?

How Do You Find a Good Fit?

Applying to Master's and PhD Programs

Betsy Wackernagel Bach

Kendyl Barney

Mackensie Minniear

F inding a graduate program that best suits your needs and interests takes time and effort. For your success, you must investigate programs to find the best fit—a program that will provide you with academic, professional, and collegial support. In this chapter, we offer suggestions for choosing the right program, highlight differences between master's and PhD studies, and provide insight into the application process. We then explain how to ask for recommendation letters and identify decision criteria to accept offers you receive.

How Do I Learn About Graduate Programs?

First, it is critical to determine whether you want to make a short- or long-term commitment to school (Bach et al., 2008). Typically, master's studies takes two years; completing your PhD takes an average of four years. Suppose you are willing to pursue graduate work. In that case, the best place to learn about different graduate programs and what is involved in graduate studies is to quiz the professors from your undergraduate program. They all have advanced degrees in the discipline and are excellent sources of information. Discuss your plans with several instructors to learn more about the dedication required to succeed in graduate school. While conversing with professors about these topics can be intimidating, realize that they have been in your shoes before! We also encourage you to ask a few teaching assistants, who are also graduate students, about their experiences. They can guide you and provide suggestions.

If you plan to study in the United States, we recommend that you search the Doctoral Program Guide posted on the National Communication Association (NCA) website, our discipline's largest scholarly society. It is an excellent source of information. Not only are all 90 U.S. doctoral programs in the communication discipline listed, but other essential information is also provided.

NCA also provides lists of all master's programs at regionally accredited institutions. At this writing, there are 336 master's programs in communication. A state-by-state listing can be found on the NCA website. If you are interested in international PhD and master's granting institutions, we direct you to google "PhD studies" and use other keywords such as "international graduate programs in communication." You will find a number of links.

Finally, you might have read an article in one of your upper-division undergraduate classes that interested you. Learn where the author is teaching by Googling the program, see if it piques your interest, and add it to a list of possible schools you might apply to.

Choosing the Right Program

To find a program best suited for you, it is imperative to be an ethnographer. That is, it is essential to choose a program that best suits your needs, learn about the cultural context in which your program operates, and visit virtually or in person.

Identify Potential Faculty

First, think about what areas or topics of study interest you. You can think broadly, such as "organizational communication," but also think more specifically, such as "nonprofits" or "high-risk organizations." Try to brainstorm two to three different areas. For example, Mackensie knew she was broadly interested in family communication, and specifically in how families discuss identity and difference. After she pinpointed those ideas, she thought of different ways those areas might interact, such as looking at race and ethnicity or race and adoption. Once she had a few ideas, she sought out faculty who either had projects or research areas that reflected her interests or could enhance her scholarship. Try and find a balance of faculty who not only share your interests but can also help you conceptualize ideas in a new way and push you in ways you may not have considered.

Think About Advising

Consider what style of advising and support you may need from a program. Think about the type of relationship you are looking to cultivate with faculty members. Do you need someone who will keep you on task, or are you better working without deadlines? Again, you will never get everything you need from one person. Think about prioritizing a few things you may need from an advisor or having a faculty network. Know that faculty members—particularly those pre-tenure—move to other departments and campuses, so you should not apply to a program to study solely with one faculty member (see Chapter 5). As one recent PhD graduate noted,

> You don't want to be dependent on one person in case they move or leave. (Dr. Rebecca Rice, Assistant Professor, UNLV)

Determine the Cultural Context

Next, determine how much you want to prioritize the climate of the department, university, and geographic area, particularly if you have a traditionally marginalized identity. For example, attending a predominately White institution (PWI) can be difficult for Black, Indigenous, and students of color, particularly if you have attended racially diverse schools. It is essential to gauge not just the university writ large but also how it supports students and professors of color. Some departments or universities may be PWI but have special programs for connecting BIPOC graduate students with faculty mentors across departments. This is also true for other students who may not typically be represented due to sexual orientation, gender, or disability. It is okay to directly ask how the department, school, and surrounding area support marginalized groups. As a Black woman, Mackensie initially felt too intimidated to ask these types of questions. However, once she did, she found different support groups across campus in her PhD program, which helped her scholarship. Overall, if feeling safe and supported is a priority, make that clear, and let it guide your decision-making. Picking a school with mentors who can help you personally and professionally may supersede choosing a school solely for its reputation.

Consider the surrounding area. The state, country, or region you end up living in should not be your be-all and end-all. However, it can give you insight into what you may need to prioritize when seeking a department. Research resources and opportunities throughout the area. For example, does the city have the infrastructure for those who are disabled? Are there resources available that are vital for your self-care, such as support groups or a vibrant LGBTQIA+ community? Many states or areas that one would not typically think of being accepting can be, and vice versa!

Keep in mind that it is unlikely you will find a perfect area that matches all of your social identities, is affordable, and has faculty that have the same research area as you. It often comes down to prioritizing which of these is the most important to you. These priorities are going to be different for everyone, and that's okay!

Visit F2F or Virtually

A visit to each program(s) after you apply is optimal so that you can observe for yourself the program dynamics. That said, an in-person visit is not always possible, particularly for international students. In that case, a virtual visit could be arranged. Whatever your choice, departments have a faculty member designated as the Director of Graduate Studies (DGS). It is best to contact them to arrange a visit (some departments may not accommodate visits until you are accepted). Ask the DGS to help you arrange a virtual or F2F visit. Be sure to schedule meetings with the DGS and faculty with whom you'd like to work. We also encourage you to visit several classes or graduate seminars. It is there you will get an excellent idea of both what is required academically as well as faculty/student interaction firsthand. Also, ask to contact a graduate student who will also assist with your visit. Finally, and importantly for your finances, some master's programs and many PhD programs may provide top candidates funding to offset a visit's cost. You should ask the DGS if such monies are available to you.

If you visit, the Graduate Student Representative (GSR) and a group of fellow graduate students will likely coordinate your schedule. Make sure you interview the GSR, and also ask if you can spend informal time with them. Going on a "pub run" with graduate students is a great way to observe dynamics among the graduate students. For example, are they supportive of one another? Do they like to have fun? How do they talk about and to each other in an informal situation? Are they highly competitive or collegial? Do they call faculty by their first names or are they more formal, calling them "Dr."? It is essential that you also talk with current graduate students in a group and one-on-one to get their perspectives on the program (Bach et al., 2008). Of course, this can also be done virtually. From them, you will learn both what is required academically and gain insight into the informal department and graduate student culture—information that is crucial to your survival. One anonymous interviewee provided this critical information for interviewing current students:

> I remember very distinctly a discussion that I had with two graduate students from the department that was my top choice. They said that a student in the program had a reputation for stealing other students' ideas—and even data—peddling them as her own. They didn't like her, didn't trust her, but felt that they could do nothing because she was the department darling—any actions against her would come back to bite them. It was invaluable information to have. While I still applied to this department, it was no longer my first choice.

Feel free to interview graduate students about diversity issues, especially if attending a school that is accepting and supportive of your social identity is imperative to you. Ask direct questions like "How does the program support LGBTQIA+ students?" or "What opportunities are there for graduate students to connect with mentors of color?" These answers are critical. Always try to follow up with specifics. Even if graduate students or faculty members say their experience is excellent, ask them for tangible resources and direct examples to support their claims. Additionally, ask to be connected with students or scholars who share similar experiences. For example, it is fine to ask to talk directly with students who identify as LGBTQIA+. Straight or cisgender faculty and students can give you overall impressions but may lack the experiential knowledge that others would have.

You will get the most out of your virtual or F2F visit if you prepare ahead of time. Read about the university, the department, and the faculty. Reddit, YouTube, and the local newspaper will give you insight into the area. Even reading the student newspaper may show you relevant information about the campus climate. It's also important to google faculty members with whom you are interested in working and read, or at least review, one or two of their articles. We also suggest that you prepare a list of questions to ask, and ask the same questions during each program you visit, whether virtually or F2F.

Questions for the Director of Graduate Studies

The DGS will be able to tell you things about the program that other faculty might not know, such as the number of graduate students accepted, what previous students are doing, and specifics about scholarships for applicants of color, if they are available. In addition to the questions noted above, additional questions you might ask include:

- How long does it generally take for students to progress through the program?

- How many graduate students do you anticipate accepting for next year?

- What percentage of students applying are admitted?

- How are students funded—tuition waivers, scholarships, assistantships?

- If I teach, what are my responsibilities?

- What other forms of aid are available to students?

- What sort of funding is available to support graduate student research and mentoring, including travel to conferences?

- How many students finish the program, and what kinds of jobs do they take?

Questions for Faculty

When you meet with faculty, be sure to know their research areas, and show that you have read some of their work, as that will make a good impression and help you have a fruitful conversation. Also, be able to articulate, at least in general terms, what it is you would like to study, as many faculty will want to know how you will fit into the program. Talk in general, but informed, terms about your plans.

There are many questions that you can ask the faculty, and we offer these as essential:

- What research projects are you currently working on?

- May students work with you on research projects? How do you involve students in your research?

- Do you anticipate taking on more students to work with (as advisees, graduate researchers, etc.)? If so, what are your expectations?

- What are your former students doing now? Teaching? Research? Employment outside of the academy? (Bach et al., 2008)

Questions for Students

As noted above, it is also essential to learn how graduate students get along with each other. They will become your personal and professional cohort in the program and long into the future. Schools in North America typically have cohorts. In other areas of the world, this may not always be the case. Regardless, and if possible, identify both students who appear very involved in the program and students who seem more socially on the periphery to get multiple perspectives. We strongly encourage you to ask the following questions of numerous graduate students. These are the people with whom you will enjoy reuniting with over the years and will become lifelong friends:

- Why should I apply to this program? What makes it unique or different from other graduate programs? (Bach et al., 2008)

- What are faculty/student relationships like?

- What faculty do you work with? Why do you like working with them?

- Are faculty available outside of the classroom?

- What faculty would you avoid, and why?

- What are the out-of-class expectations? What events am I required to attend?

- Do graduate students generally get along with each other?

- Do graduate students collaborate on research?

- Are there department social events with just graduate students? Graduate students and faculty?

Conference Visits

If you can't afford a campus visit, you may wish to attend an academic conference. International, national, regional, or statewide conventions are a way for faculty and graduate students to present their research, learn about the newest teaching strategies, and network to ask many of the questions we identified above. Attending a convention is an excellent way to investigate specific graduate programs (see Chapter 8).

Master's or Doctorate?

Another decision is to determine if you should apply to a master's-only program or a combined master's and PhD program. There is no one size fits all, and choosing a program largely depends on your goals. There are benefits and challenges to each type of program, each with its own financial considerations.

Master's Only

There are several benefits to doing a master's-only program. A master's-only program is a great first step if you are not entirely sure you want an academic career, as other career trajectories are available to master's students (see Chapter 14). In a master's-only program, you often have more one-on-one time with professors, and you are not competing with PhD students for faculty attention or coveted teaching assistantships. Classes are typically smaller, and faculty get to know you well, which allows them to write more substantial and specific letters of recommendation. Moreover, if you decide to pursue a PhD, your master's thesis work can serve as an essential jumping-off point for starting new research in your doctoral studies. The experience gleaned from a master's program gives you a leg up in your PhD program.

However, there are still challenges in a master's-only program. Transitioning to a different PhD program in two years can lead to moving costs, which are often a burden on a graduate student's limited budget. Additionally, this also means that you may lose any community connections you have made during your master's program if you change geographic locations.

Combined Master's and PhD Programs

A combined master's and PhD program has several benefits. You gain exposure immediately to PhD-level coursework and expectations. Additionally, there is likely to be more ongoing research, greater expectations and opportunities to engage in research, and opportunity to establish significant faculty mentors.

If you stay at the same institution, there may be additional opportunities for teaching assistantships as well. TAs will often have the opportunity to teach more than introductory courses, so you can get more experience early on with stand-alone teaching or working with different instructors. Summer and online teaching are more readily available, and there also may be some funding for professional travel.

For those students who choose not to pursue an academic career, there also may be opportunities to collaborate with faculty on outside projects, such as training and consultation.

However, there are still challenges in moving to a combined program. First, combined programs tend to enroll more graduate students. Even a small combined program will typically have more people than a small master's program. This may be a shock if you have come from a small undergraduate program. Additionally, the pace of coursework may be much faster, as you often are completing PhD-level coursework. This can be very overwhelming for first-year graduate students. While this can help you acclimate to coursework expectations in the long run, it may be a very intense start to your academic program.

A final challenge is that advisers may prioritize PhD students. In combined master's and doctoral programs, advisors have multiple advisees and juggle more moving parts. This may mean less one-on-one time, which again is dependent on your advising needs. Of course, all benefits and challenges will vary based on the person, but these are critical things to consider.

Financial Considerations

Last, considering finances is a must. Most master's and PhD programs offer a monthly stipend in exchange for being a teaching or research assistant, which generally includes an in-state tuition waiver. As you will likely be joining a graduate program as an out-of-state or out-of-country student, make sure you find out if the compensation is commensurate with your residency status and what other fees the university will impose each semester.

A second consideration is to learn for how many years you will receive funding. Some master's programs will limit funding to only two years; PhD programs will typically offer you four years and the possibility of a fifth year, depending upon their department budget. Be sure to ask about the number of years of guaranteed funding.

The Application Process

Once you have sought out information about different programs, faculty, and assistantship opportunities, the time has come to begin applying. The application process includes several steps, which may look different depending on the institution. Generally speaking, the application process includes (a) narrowing down programs, (b) writing your curriculum vitae (CV), (c) writing your personal statement, (d) taking the Graduate Record Examination (GRE), (e) working with recommenders, and (f) tying it all together.

Step 1: Narrow Down Programs

Generally, we encourage applicants to apply to three to five programs for several reasons. As Sean, a PhD student at the University of Minnesota, explains:

> One or two might not accept you. Further, one or two might not be a good fit
> for a multitude of unseen reasons that may not be evident until you attend the
> program's visiting day for prospective students. These reasons include benefits
> offered by the university, the pay of the program relative to the cost of living,
> cost of student fees a semester, living arrangements, faculty that may not be
> aligned with diversity, the competitive or cooperative culture of the program, etc.

However, each application can take a significant amount of money, time, and energy. With application fees, sending transcripts, and sending GRE scores, the cost of applying to each program can add up quickly. Further, by adapting personal statements to each program, communicating with faculty in each department, and requesting multiple recommendations for each program, it is easy to get lost in the logistics of applying. Typically, the three-to-five application range tends to help domestic students be the most successful. If you are applying from outside the United States, we suggest applying for more.

Once you have narrowed down the programs, the next action we suggest is exploring each program's application requirements. You can locate this on each department's website. Some programs may require a diversity statement, while others will not. Some, but not all, programs in the United States will require Graduate Record Exam (GRE) scores. Pay close attention to what each program requires, and give yourself adequate time to fulfill these requirements.

It is also essential to be aware of application deadlines, especially if the schools you are applying to require the GRE. Different schools have different application deadlines. Some schools outside the United States even have rolling deadlines throughout the year.

Step 2: Write a Curriculum Vitae (CV)

A CV is a detailed summary of your educational and professional experience. Unlike a résumé, a CV does not have a limit regarding length. If you take a look at the CVs of faculty members at the institutions you're applying to (which we recommend you do), you will notice they might be upwards of 50 pages long. Indeed, your CV will be much shorter. Nonetheless, a CV is most commonly used to apply for academia; thus, CVs tend to focus more on experience and accomplishments related to your education.

Your CV should generally begin with your name and contact info, similar to that of a résumé. From there, it should contain the following information, if applicable:

- educational background

- awards or recognitions you have earned

- any research you have conducted in order of date completed (your projects, faculty projects assisted, etc.)

- teaching, instructional experience, teaching training received

- professional/volunteer work

- academic and professional affiliations

- languages spoken

Be sure to proofread and revise your CV. We suggest sending your CV to mentors and colleagues for constructive criticism.

Step 3: Write Your Personal Statement

The personal statement (also known as the letter of interest) is the most significant opportunity for the graduate selection committee at each university to learn more about you as a person. Your letter of interest gives you the chance to show them something more personal. Further, your letter of interest can help demonstrate not only why you want the program but also why the program should want you, helping them understand your fit with the program. As an anonymous master's student explains:

> The biggest advice for personal statements is understanding your story and being able to express it succinctly to others. Everybody has different reasons for going to graduate school and deciding to study what they study. The admissions committee doesn't know you, so your job is to sell yourself in terms of being a successful graduate student. I think the best way to conceptualize the personal statement is a cover letter in the sense that you're explaining why you're going to be a great researcher, which is backed by your professional experiences.

Graduate school, especially for full-time students and TA/RAs, can feel like a full-time job. Thus, your personal statement, like a cover letter, should explain why you are the best fit for the work at hand.

In your statement, we recommend you discuss your short- and long-term goals. How will the specific program you're applying to help you reach these goals? What are your scholarly interests? Are there particular faculty you may want to work with? Discuss your significant work, experiences, teachers, or aspects of your story that have led you to pursue graduate school.

Further, you may wish to discuss any experiences or aspects of your character that could outweigh weaknesses on your record, though without making excuses (Bach et al., 2008). For example, if you had to withdraw from a class in your junior year due to financial hardship, a loss in the family, or other circumstances, perhaps that is worth mentioning. Finally, if you apply for a TA or RA position, we suggest including some information regarding previous teaching or research experience. It is relatively common for PhD programs to request *evidence of teaching effectiveness*, which may include a list of courses taught with a summary of teaching evaluations for two or three classes. If you do not have teaching experience, explain that in your personal statement, and consider outlining other expertise you have related to teaching (e.g., peer tutoring, grading, or teaching training).

One of the biggest mistakes you can make is to send the same statement to each institution. These mass-produced personal statements are easily identifiable by the graduate admissions committee and can hurt your prospects for admission. Further, they may miss key content that specific programs request you include in your statement. In short, tailor each statement to the department.

Finally, once you have completed a draft of your personal statement, proofread and revise! Poor writing can hurt your credibility, as it can demonstrate a lack of care and attention to detail, especially for simple mistakes. Read your statement verbally to help you catch spelling and grammatical errors. Send drafts to a mentor or advisor and other colleagues to receive feedback on structure and content.

Step 4: Take the Graduate Record Examination (GRE)

The Educational Testing Service (ETS) offers the GRE for admission into universities in North America. Some graduate programs require applicants to take the GRE, while other programs do not. The GRE can be anxiety-provoking for many students. Keep in mind that it is only one part of your application; your personal statement and recommendations hold significant weight in your application, perhaps even more than your GRE scores.

The computer-based GRE is offered internationally. We suggest scheduling your GRE for several weeks, or even months, in advance so you can secure your reservation and have adequate time to prepare. Allot enough time for these documents to navigate paper mail and still arrive by the application deadline, especially if you are an international applicant.

Step 5: Work With Recommenders

You will be asked to include at least three recommendations with your application. Choose recommenders who can speak well to your academic capabilities and qualifications. Your professors have expertise in and relationships within the discipline that can help them advocate for you in such a way your employers may not be able to. While your work supervisor may be able to speak to your employability, they may not be able to address your fit for an academic program. For example, say you are still in the process of completing your master's degree while applying for a PhD program. Your advisor can explain your progress toward the degree; your work supervisor cannot.

Asking professors to write you a letter of recommendation can be intimidating. But, as Julia, a master's student from the University of Montana, explains:

> Chances are if you are applying for a graduate program, you were the kind of student professors liked to have in class. Let go of any notion that you don't deserve a letter of recommendation or that you were not a good enough student to have left an impression.

It is your unique background that makes you an asset to the academic community. Whether you were a first-generation undergraduate, nontraditional student, international student, or were not afforded certain academic privileges that others possessed, you still contributed to your classes in ways professors have certainly noticed. Asking your professors for recommendations will allow them to speak to the unique contributions you can make in a graduate program. Suppose you have been out of academia for several years. In that case, it may be helpful to remind your professors of who you are, the classes you took with them, and what work you have completed with them (consider sending a copy of a paper you wrote for them, for example). In any case, approach your recommenders with confidence, humility, and gratitude.

Once your recommenders have agreed to write for you, give them any materials they need to write you a strong recommendation. It will help to provide them with your CV, personal statement, transcripts, and so on. If there is anything specific you wish them to include, make that clear. For example, if you apply for a GTA position, you may want your recommender to discuss any teaching or peer-tutoring experience you have.

We suggest asking recommenders to tailor their letters to each institution. Tailored recommendations specify how and why you are a fit for each particular program rather than graduate school in general. To assist them with their letters, provide each recommender with information about the programs: Which faculty members do you hope to work with? What research areas does each program specialize in? What is each program looking for in a graduate student? By providing this information, it will be significantly easier for your recommenders to tailor your recommendations to each institution for which you are applying.

Be sure to let the recommender know when the deadline for each application is, and request their recommendation at least one month in advance. Give your recommenders specific instructions regarding the recommendation process for each particular program. Should they expect an email from the graduate program containing the recommendation form? Should they plan to mail or fax a printed and signed letter to the institution on their university's letterhead? Make these expectations clear. Finally, remind your recommenders four to five days before their recommendation is due. Do not worry about being a bother; recommenders can forget and will appreciate the reminder.

Step 6: Tie It All Together

Once you have researched each program's application requirements, written your personal statement and CV, and requested recommendations, you have completed the most challenging parts of the application process. You will often submit these documents through an online application portal through which you will also submit the application fee and upload any additional documents, such as a writing sample.

For international students, an additional consideration when putting applications together is difference in time zones. M.J., a PhD student from Korea, said an unexpected barrier in applying to programs was timing.

> Keeping track of the time difference between Korea and the United States was also another thing. I would stay up very late until 3 a.m. or 4 a.m. to send an email, for example.

Additionally, for international students, applying to not only more schools but also earlier is critical. M.J. recommends starting a year ahead of the application season, which is usually from November through January.

> [Starting] a year ahead of the applying season would be great, and [I] recommend they start as early as possible. ... There are many scores that you need to obtain to be competent and all different kinds of documents that you need to prepare in advance. To not feel overwhelmed and stressed out of tons of workload being piled up, it would be nice to start the process earlier.

Upon submitting all materials (including GRE scores and transcripts), contact the department in two or three days to confirm that they have arrived and if anything is missing from your application. Apply early enough so that you can correct any potential problems. Once you have confirmed the department's receipt of your materials, you have completed the application process! Now, we wait.

Making the Best Choice and Accepting Your Offer

There are many things to consider when deciding what program will work best for you. To aid in your decision-making, we have pulled together a list of what we perceive to be the most critical points to consider in Table 2.1, below.

Once you accept your offer, it is in your best interest to write a thank-you letter to each of your recommenders—and most faculty enjoy receiving a handwritten note of thanks for the time spent researching for and writing your recommendation letter. When you are accepted, your recommenders want to hear the good news, so be sure to inform them of your success!

What If I Don't Get an Offer?

Not everyone who applies to graduate school gets admitted early in the process or the first time around. While this is a blow to the ego, it can also provide a learning experience. Take this time to review your application, particularly your letter of interest, to see how it could be improved. We also recommend that you follow up with the graduate coordinator at the schools to which you applied to learn how you could improve your application. This is an excellent way to not only get feedback but also to let them know that you are interested in reapplying. Finally, we strongly suggest that you chat with those who wrote recommendation letters to get feedback on what you might do to strengthen your application for a second submission.

A lot of factors may play into your rejection from graduate programs. The scholar(s) you indicated you might prefer to work with might not be accepting new advisees or may be on sabbatical. The program may have received substantially more applicants than is typical, making the process more competitive. A rejection does not mean you are not a high-quality student. Remember, you do have something to offer. If you are not accepted the first time around, do not be discouraged from trying again! Likely, your application will be even stronger the next time around, having now engaged in the process before.

TABLE 2.1 **Questions to Ask When Considering an Offer**

	SCHOOL 1	SCHOOL 2	SCHOOL 3
Monetary Support			
1. Did you receive an offer of funding (a stipend)? How much?			
2. Does the funding come with a tuition waiver, and if so, is it in or out of state?			
3. For how many years is funding available?			
4. Are there funds for conference travel?			
5. Is other financial assistance, such as scholarships, grants, and so on, available?			
6. Is there funding for me to visit campus?			
Health Benefits			
1. Is there student insurance?			
2. What benefits are included? Vision? Dental?			
Teaching Assistantships			
1. Are there TAs available? Have I been offered one?			
2. What courses would I likely teach?			
3. Are there teaching opportunities other than introductory courses available?			
4. Does the department offer any training for TAs?			
5. Is summer teaching or support available?			

(Continued)

	SCHOOL 1	SCHOOL 2	SCHOOL 3
Research Assistantships			
1. Do any faculty have grants, and are there opportunities to assist them?			
2. Are there summer grant opportunities for students?			
Advising/Mentoring			
1. Can I select my own advisor/mentor, or is one selected for me?			
2. Can students collaborate in research with their faculty mentors?			
3. Are there faculty with whom I could work in an advisor/advisee relationship?			
Curriculum			
1. For PhD, how many credits from my master's degree will you transfer?			
2. How many graduate seminars are offered each term?			
3. How many of the courses counted for graduate credit also enroll undergraduate students?			
4. What are the capstone requirements of the program (comp exams, thesis or professional paper, dissertation)?			
Opportunities for Students			
1. Are there other opportunities available for graduate students, such as assisting with journal editing, professional service (NCA, regionals, etc.)?			
2. Are faculty available to supervise independent study or research?			
3. Are internships allowed?			
4. What opportunities are there for study abroad?			
Overall Fit			
1. Is this program a good fit for me?			
2. Is this a place where I can spend 2–5 years?			

For Further Thought and Reflection

1. Why is it important for you to pursue a graduate degree? What do you want to do with a graduate degree? How would a graduate program help you meet these goals?

2. What do you need to be successful as a graduate student? How can a graduate program and advisor contribute to your success?

3. Which type of graduate education would suit you best? A terminal master's program, or a master's/PhD program?

"I Have to Rechoose to Do This Every Single Day"

Beyond Narratives of Success in the Pursuit of Graduate School

Shiv Ganesh

Andrea Shute Zorn

V ery few people can claim to have clear and consistent explanations as to why they embarked on graduate studies in communication, and communication scholarship itself has an explanation as to why that might be the case (Hermann, 2008). As human beings, we are rationalizing beings much more than rational ones; we make sense of our intentions, practices, and beliefs only after enacting them. So the rationale for why we do something is likely to vary before, during, and after the act. So we believe that, should you choose to start postgraduate studies in communication, your reasoning behind your choice is not just an anticipatory task; rather, it is one you will keep revisiting for the rest of your life—revising, changing, improvising, and strengthening your reasons.

The two of us come to this chapter holding some experiences and values in common and diverging a great deal on others. Andrea and Shiv have both lived, worked, and studied in multiple countries, but there are plenty of differences between us; perhaps most visibly in our age, ethnicity, generational cohort, and gender. We teamed up for this project not only because we have known each other a long time, but also because we believe that the relatively global nature and wide range of our experiences may help tell a story about going to graduate school that expands dominant narratives about why people make that critical choice. And this, in fact, is the goal of our chapter.

Why is this goal important? Simply put, the field of communication studies has diversified considerably in the last century. Not only has communication turned out to be one of the most vital areas of contemporary practice, pedagogy, and research globally, but also the people who study and teach it are themselves becoming more diverse in terms of gender, sexuality, race, ethnicity, and age; and in this sense, it's a good time to enter communication studies. This is, of course, not to say that the field is inherently vibrant and diverse; rather, diversity and inclusion have become issues that the field has been forced to take more and more seriously. And as it does so, the reasons that people want to study communication will become much more complex, so it is crucial that we all are able to continually reflect on them.

So we hope that the template that we offer you will be useful not only for your initial decision-making, but also will be one that you can return to and use as a reflective framework every time you need to consider your standpoint, experience, and passions and why it is that you are learning, studying, researching, writing, teaching, or practicing communication (you can read more about the history and scope of the discipline in Chapter 1). Those reasons are likely to be substantively, sometimes radically, different depending upon your experiences, age, gender identity, race, class, ethnicity, sexuality, country of origin and residence, and, crucially, whether you are a first-, second-, or third-generation learner. Even though most of you are likely to be based in the United States, it is important for us to help you to cultivate a view of communication studies that is cognizant of its problematic history regarding issues of internationalization, diversity, equity, and access. Most of us still are not aware of how nationally specific the terms we use to describe graduate school can be. In fact, what we call "graduate studies" itself in North America is referred to as "postgraduate studies" in much of the rest of the world! We will use those two terms interchangeably hereafter.

As communication studies continues to globalize, as students in North America learn more about the study of communication in Europe, or as students in the Global North encounter more voices from the Global South, the need to understand these different but related histories will become ever stronger. To help with this, we reached out to and conversed with students in multiple parts of the world, including India, Australasia, and Europe, to obtain their perspectives on why they chose to embark on postgraduate studies. Their thoughts are interspersed throughout this chapter to help us challenge what we see as a globally dominant narrative that drives people's accounts of why they embark on postgraduate education. In this chapter, we have chosen to call this a *narrative of success*. In what follows, we present what we mean by that particular narrative and then discuss four additional narratives that were apparent in what other people told us about why they study and learn about communication, which resonated with our own experiences. Those narratives are: *opportunity, passion, challenge,* and *escape.* We discuss these various narratives in detail to provide you a template to help think through why you might want to study communication at the postgraduate level. As we do this, we will reference three longer accounts from current graduate students in different parts of the world to show how multiple narratives can intermingle in the same account.

Narratives of Success

What is a narrative of success? By this term we refer to reasons that people offer for graduate school that follow familiar social scripts for achievement. These achievements include traditional indices of career success, educational advancement, gender roles, work-life balance, cultural appropriateness, and so forth. Success narratives are deeply embedded in popular accounts about going to graduate school, so it is instructive to look at some examples.

A recent article in *Harvard Business Review* (Chamorro-Premuzic, 2020) stipulates that the number one reason to go to graduate school is "to bump up your salary potential" (para. 6). This claim is consistent with any number of advice columns on why students should try postgraduate studies, and no doubt you have read many of these yourself. Peterson's, the world-renowned guide on graduate school (for those of us who remember a world before the internet), offers 20 reasons to go to graduate school. They include: greater earning power, career advancement, educational enhancement (or credentialing), community and international recognition, and research opportunities, among many others. All these reasons underscore the idea of personal benefit and advancement in accordance with some sort of social script.

The narrative of success is something that both of us encountered and internalized when we thought about why we wanted to go to graduate school. Shiv says:

> I always knew I wanted to study communication and get a PhD, but once I had an offer of an assistantship from a few universities in the United States, I noticed that people around me reacted to me just a bit differently and treated me just a little bit more as a success. My parents had some qualms about what I would do with a social work degree, and in hindsight, I think they were relieved that I was doing something that seemed like it had better career prospects. So my narratives to friends and relatives about why I wanted to go to graduate school in the United States framed it as being a step up, something I wanted to do on my way to something bigger, better, and bolder ... an upwardly mobile and very respectable trajectory for a middle-class Indian male.

Andrea, whose father works in the communication discipline, says:

> From a young age I knew that university was the baseline expectation. So when I received a sports scholarship to get a BA over in the United States, I dreaded the thought of four more years at school. After freshman year I picked up anthropology and history classes, and my interest in education began to take precedence over sport. Going to graduate school became a regular conversation amongst my peers, and I already had a role model who had successfully been through it. My family's benchmark for success was professorship, and the decision seemed obvious, at the time.

Several people who wrote to us also echoed the success narrative in their stories, framing graduate school in instrumental terms, as a means to career advancement. One person said, "I needed the technical, conceptual, and practical understanding." Another initially made the decision to start postgraduate studies to get a better job, better salary, and to advance her career.

Interestingly, her decision was made during another recession, the Global Financial Crisis of 2007–2009, and it is consistent with commentary that suggests that people think about going to graduate school during a recession as a way to ride it out and upskill when they would not be that likely to get a better job anyway. External factors matter. We write this chapter when the world is in the midst of a pandemic, and unemployment levels have reached a peak unseen since the Great Depression in the 1930s (International Labour Organization, 2020). At the time of writing, we do not know how long lasting the current recession will be, but its sheer scale will, we believe, shape how people think of the place of graduate schools in their career advancement, and it is likely to have multiple, even contradictory, impacts upon people's decision to go to graduate school.

It's worth considering, also, the lure of an attractive career itself as a major part of the success narrative. Some participants spoke of specific aspects of communication practices, including journalism, public relations, and health communication, while others want an academic career. These sorts of career visualizations are a critical part of why anyone would consider graduate school, but it is important to remember that how we visualize careers is often drastically at odds with the reality of the career itself! L.L. Baird's (1973) classic College Senior Survey, now a huge, annual, national-level study of U.S. university graduates, talked of the image that graduating seniors had constructed of an academic career: "But more than anything, seniors thought professors are free—free as individuals, free from political pressure, free from narrow codes of social behavior, and free from the necessity of maintaining a pleasant facade" (pp. 60–61). Even a cursory look at the *Chronicle of Higher Education* or websites such as the Thesis Whisperer will tell you how unrealistic that view is and that academic careers, like any other, are shaped by all kinds of dysfunctional dynamics.

We are not saying that the success narrative is false, fake, or misleading. Inevitably, people actively think about self and career advancement when they consider graduate school, especially when they are likely to stretch themselves financially in order to attend. However, engaging with students from around the world showed us how the success narrative was immediately complicated. Some discussed finding new meaning from graduate school when they became disillusioned about their career prospects. In doing so, our participants began to mention all kinds of other reasons that were important to them, and we too realized how crucial it was to help potential graduate students reflect about the reasons they wanted to attend graduate school in multiple and complex terms. For that reason, we present four important narratives that we heard when people talked about graduate school: opportunity, passion, challenge, and escape.

MAL GREEN, NEW ZEALAND

My decision to enroll to do my master's in 1974 was determined by the providers of a scholarship I had. It was a New Zealand government scholarship that paid scholars a salary through their university studies at undergraduate and postgraduate levels. Then the student was required to teach for as long as the scholarship had been received

continued

continued

while at university. My [study schedule] preference was not allowed under the terms of the scholarship. I was equally fascinated with English language and literature as I was with modern Asian and Pacific history. In the end, history won by virtue of a high GPA for my final undergraduate history courses.

My intention was to teach for four years and return to do my PhD in history—I had the topic worked out, and my master's supervisor was lined up to take me on. Opportunities to pursue other interests in journalism and community youth work intervened, and the PhD plans were put aside. As a result of completing a graduate degree in theology in the 1980s and holding a professional teaching fellow role in a few seminaries, I began working on ideas for a PhD in theology. In the 1990s I had a topic worked out that combined my history and theology knowledge, had a supervisor lined up, and, despite numerous meetings with them, never managed to find time to get liftoff on it.

Fast-forward to 2016, and through a mutual friend, I was asked to do marketing for a postgraduate marketing course assessment (and more opportunities followed). A lecturer there challenged me to enroll for a PhD in communications as a way I could keep pursuing my twin passions for teaching at tertiary level and research and writing. Thus, my involvement in my current PhD program began.

Narratives of Opportunity

We understand opportunities as structured pathways that put people on career trajectories. We call them structured because they are available to us by way of our social positions, identities, and circumstances. Students we have spoken and corresponded with have described multiple opportunity structures that became available to them, including scholarship and financial opportunities, mentorship, and family support. Mal's account talks about his decision to get a master's degree being made for him by a scholarship provider, which determined the subjects he could take, although later, he talks about a challenge that a mentor laid down for him.

Mentorship, we find, is a recurring motif in both research and personal narratives. In fact, mentorship is particularly important when it comes to first-generation learners, those students who are either the first members in their family to attend university or the first to go to graduate school. For both of these groups, going to graduate school may not even be on their radar or something that they consider to be a meaningful life choice. Lunsford (2011) in particular has identified mentorship as being a crucial influence, saying that the role that an academic mentor plays is the single most important factor in helping a first-generation learner become interested in postgraduate studies.

That may or may not be the case; certainly, some of the stories we have heard and research we have read indicate the importance that family support plays in enabling people, especially first-generation learners, to take up postgraduate work. For instance, Robinson's (2013) influential essay "Spoketokenism," about Black women talking back to the academy, features an evocative and moving narrative from Lisa:

> I guess it goes back again to how I was raised.
>
> My mother always said: 'There's no such word as can't.'
>
> You make your mind up and you do it.
>
> You're going to have obstacles along the way, that's a given.
>
> But you don't sit there and say: 'Oh, woe is me, I can't do it.'
>
> So [her words] always gave me a framework for how I was going to pursue anything …
>
> I had my teachers' voices in my head telling me—you know:
>
> 'You're definitely going to be something. You're a great student.'
>
> So when I went to college, I had no fears of anything. (p. 163)

It is obvious that Lisa's mother was an inspirational and downright subversive influence. But families can also be opportunity structures in quasi-coercive ways. One person we talked with said: "Although I wanted to do a master's, I didn't have a choice per se. My parents funded my studies … and it was understood that I had to get a master's degree. It was a sort of 'contract.'" Conversely, Christine's story highlights how she felt inspired by her own children who actively confronted the racism of mainstream education. As she said, "If my kids can do it, then so can I."

Narratives of Passion

Another narrative that we heard both from people we engaged with and that emerged from our own conversations with each other had to do with the idea that we study communication because it is fascinating. Fascination, by definition, is not rational, but is premised upon emotional forces, attachment, habitus, and history. We call these accounts narratives of passion.

We both love communication because of what it achieves. Shiv, for instance, has always seen communication as *the* way to change the world and has loved that the word communication itself has afforded him access into entire worlds—sociology, politics, philosophy, literary criticism, anthropology, and even economics. It is in that sense that he identifies with the communication discipline: as quintessentially engaged not only in terms of research but also as a method and a means of procuring social change. Andrea, for her part, believes that communication is her passion because it is the most difficult and at the same time the simplest way to bridge the divide between two opposing forces, opinions, or thoughts. For her, communication studies helps us to recognize that we are all so different and yet still human—and that is why she loves it.

People we've talked to echo our sentiments, but some aren't quite sure why they are so passionate about studying communication. One person described their attachment simply by saying, "I just gravitated towards it." Others described their passion in terms of broad delight, saying, "I really enjoyed the experience and decided to continue with a PhD." Another even said: "I just wanted to be in university forever, and doing a PhD was the best way to do just that." Some were more specific, specifying that they found areas such as journalism or health communication fascinating and enjoyed learning and writing about them.

ASHLEY N. MACDONALD, UNITED STATES

In the department at my undergraduate institution, there is a wooden bench underneath a series of plaques of old, dead White dudes that donated a bunch of money to the college. There's gum stuck underneath it and a streak of Wite-Out across the last panel. I know this bench so well because I sat there for at least two hours trying to gather up the courage to turn in the form officially saying that I was dropping out of college. It was seemingly my only option in the face of owing my school $1,312.75. I don't know what made me get up and walk back to my dorm.

That lack of an answer or understanding is a running theme for me. When it comes to answering the question of why I decided on grad school rather than any number of other professional options, I don't actually have an answer. I don't know. I know what I've said in cover letters and statements of purpose. It's always something saccharine about representation, inspiration, and wanting to fix things. In a fit of what I would now label desperation, I trotted out the phrase "pedagogical kintsugi." Thinking of that idea now makes me slightly embarrassed that I ever said it in the first place. When I am trying to tell other people why they should choose me, the way that I explain myself seems so clear-cut. In reality, what made the decision for me has changed at every step.

I joke about it, which is probably why nobody ever takes me as seriously as they should, but I was not a "good student." I did not excel in high school or most of undergrad, and in fact, I was on academic probation twice because I failed multiple classes. When I say that this is not where I'm supposed to be, it isn't purely imposter syndrome speaking. I honestly don't know how I got here. Looking at where I came from, in particular, is why this feels foreign and wrong at times. I'm first-gen, and there is no precedent in my family for what it is that I am doing. I have had to find examples elsewhere, on social media, meeting people at conferences, and developing relationships with my mentors.

continued

continued

When I was encouraged by those people to keep going with my education, I knew that even if it would be difficult and wearing on my mental and physical health, it was the right decision to make. I like that I don't feel trapped, and I have a freedom of expression. I know that I get to do good work, and I have a sense of agency. I've found meaning in being a teacher and helping my students. I feel a duty to be an ethical teacher and to model to my students that ethical, caring teachers do exist. Being in academia is the best compromise between structure and creativity that I've found. Beyond that, I have an almost pathological need to fix things, and academia is very broken. But it is a puzzle that I refuse to put down without knowing in my bones that I tried as hard as I could. Even as I was facing something that is structured specifically against people like me, I still wanted to keep moving forward.

It's critical to identify your passion for communication not only because it is what will sustain you during your postgraduate studies or because it will underlie much of your intellectual engagement, but also because passion undergirds dysfunction and trauma as much as it underlies self-fulfillment. Ashley says that very powerfully in her narrative: "I love it, but I know it hurts me." It is really important not to consider passion as a kind of corporate speak, where you present yourself as being passionate in order to get employed; but it is crucial to be reflective about and consider what your passion for something might be—because being aware of it from the get-go might help you deal with troubling or challenging situations down the line, or even help you find an exit strategy if you need one.

CHRISTINE ELERS, NEW ZEALAND

It has been 20 years since I completed my Master of Laws with distinction from Waikato University, away from home. I did not want to embark upon a PhD. Instead, I returned home amongst my Iwi and learned knowledge and practices from Iwi elders and older Whānau members. It was a humbling experience serving my Marae, Iwi, and reconnecting with Whānau.

During this time, I had children [and] immersed myself in the Māori language in order to raise my children as Māori language speakers. Dr. Steve Elers is my brother. In 2018, Steve spoke about a research role and PhD opportunity at Massey and the difficulty finding a suitable candidate. He encouraged me to try and apply. I recalled the challenges I encountered as a law student, and I didn't want to repeat that. I also googled communication scholarship in Aotearoa and found there is an absence of Māori communication scholars. Steve was the only one. At least at law school there are Māori law lecturers. I tried to imagine what it would be like to be in the School of Communication, Journalism, and Marketing and the only Māori scholar is your brother.

continued

continued

The lack of Māori scholars was a red flag. To me that meant that the scholarship would be devoid of Māori content. Whiteness would be the default. I predicted that it would be a culture shock; it would be challenging and lonely.

My children changed from a Māori language immersion education to mainstream education. It definitely was a culture shock for them, challenging and lonely as well. They saw through the use of Māori culture as a tick-box experience. My son experienced racism for the first time. It felt like we took a step back into the 1970s. I realized that we had been living in a bubble. Living in a predominately Māori language speaking world, we were sheltered from the racism that is embedded in the education system and in Aotearoa. Sure, there were some gains in mainstream education (e.g., Māori students were considered priority learners due to the huge failings of the mainstream education system), so aspects of Māori culture were, on the face of it, incorporated into the curriculum. But as I said, my teenagers saw through it, and I was extremely proud of their analysis. It was then that I realized that it is not enough to remain in a bubble. To try to challenge hegemonic structures, issues have to be highlighted and fought in that space. Even when outnumbered. I thought if my kids can do it, then so can I. Even if I will be one of two Māori in the School of Communication at Massey University, I will be brave and step into that space, no matter how lonely or disempowering that it may feel.

Narratives of Challenge

Pursuing graduate school is a guaranteed social and personal challenge. The fourth narrative we discovered in our conversations highlights the daily struggles and labor that those pursuing graduate school perform so as to challenge themselves, the academy, and the world at large. Challenges might be to oneself—to overcome, deal with, or counter self-doubt or internalized bias; to the academy, for making it a more just and inclusive and equitable place; or to the world at large. For many communication students, it is a call to participate in social change and address the global issues facing us.

Two of the three featured accounts in this chapter discuss taking on this challenge as an active kind of self-disempowerment. Christine uses that very word to discuss struggles with White educational spaces; Ashley talks about ongoing hurt. It is essential to recognize that some may choose not to pursue graduate school because of the academy's history of privileging some forms of knowledge over others. So, why consider postgraduate study in communication, a discipline supposedly recognizing a fundamental human experience but less diverse than computer science, engineering, and the social sciences overall (Murthy, 2020)? For some, it is about creating alternative knowledge structures as a means of social survival.

Christine's excerpt highlights both her motivation and reluctance to enter the discipline of communication, where the only Māori scholar is her own brother. In Christine's words,

"Whiteness [is] the default." Calvente et al. (2020) define *Whiteness* as a "mythical norm to which we do not belong and of which assimilation is unacceptable" (p. 2). Inevitably, a person's standpoint and identity may make for additional challenges in graduate school and in life, but, in doing so, equips them to understand some aspects of the world more than others. Reflecting, knowing, and owning your narrative and reasons for pursuing an education is vital in developing resilience to challenges and in moving from invisible to visible with self-growth, agency, and knowledge.

Narratives of Escape

A final narrative that emerged from our discussions and engagement with current and recent graduate students was the idea that going back to university for further studies represented a form of escape, a getaway, retreat, or haven, sometimes desperately taken, from constraints, vicissitudes, and hardships. Certainly, there were elements of escape in both our journeys through our PhD programs. For Shiv, even though a PhD outwardly represented success, the journey to the United States was also a kind of escape from the career, social, and gender constraints that stem from heteropatriarchy, class, and caste—even though he couldn't quite articulate it in those terms at the time.

For some, graduate school is an escape from the mundane realities of their everyday life and the desire for new experiences. As one person said to us, "Graduate schools worldwide provide a (sometimes funded) way to experience new cultures." For others, the escape was more specifically related to work. Graduate school can be an escape from the difficulties of finding work. Other people we talked with also talked about starting postgraduate studies as an escape from work they were already performing: "Real-life work is draining and uninspiring," said one person. "The rat race is rarely meaningfully rewarding, other than financial," said another. Getting away from "regular" work, then, is an important reason that people go to graduate school.

For others, going to graduate school represents an escape from a multitude of oppressions, not just work. One of our respondents said bluntly that the real reason they started graduate school was because they did not want to get married. Both Andrea and Shiv have had many students for whom being at university is a form of freedom, a chance to experiment with oneself, craft their own identities, and achieve a measure of agency that had just not been accorded to them before by virtue of their gender, race, sexuality, and ethnicity.

That graduate school can be seen as a form of escape does not mean that it is a socially liberated Valhalla. On the contrary, it has its own set of unique dysfunctions and problems with race, class, and gender that can be shocking to a newcomer. Some people we engaged with were quite clear about that and saw going to graduate school as a compromise. In her narrative, Ashley says emphatically: "Being in academia is the best compromise between structure and creativity that I've found. Beyond that, I have an almost pathological need to fix things, and academia is very broken."

Common Obstacles and the Changing
Habitus of Communication Studies

We hope the five narratives we have presented in this chapter—success, opportunity, passion, challenge, and escape—will help you reflect deeply about whether or not you should go to graduate school to study communication. The three detailed accounts from Mal, Christine, and Ashley all indicate that there is no singular narrative logic that dominates any one story; there are multiple reasons why each of them made the initial choice—and keep making it every day—to study communication. The accounts also highlight the fact that reasons emerge over time and that there can be an entire lifespan that leads up to making the choice to study communication. And, conversely, there may be no clear reason at all. Above all, the accounts illustrate vividly how individuals try to find agency in a system that can be oppressive and made for someone else.

That in turn makes it important, in closing, to consider why people may choose to *not* go to graduate school. Our remit, in this chapter, was to prompt you to consider why to go in the first place, and while we hope that you are able to see yourself in the four narratives enough to help with that decision, we also ask you to consider why you might choose not to go to graduate school and how those reasons are embedded in your own identity, biography, culture, and history. In our view, there are four main reasons why students choose not to pursue postgraduate studies.

The first, and possibly the most debilitating is *imposter syndrome*—the very anxious feeling that you are not quite smart enough to go to university. We both continue to experience imposter syndrome regardless of how much we accomplish, and we know that the same is true for people across the discipline. We suspect that the fact that you picked up this book and are reading this chapter means that you're interested in communication—and if that's the case, you'll experience imposter syndrome at one stage or another. A good way to deal with such feelings of anxiety is to get feedback from supportive peers, family, mentors, and counselors. We've already said that the lack of mentorship is a major reason that people do not go to graduate school, so finding a mentor as you try to work your way through this process is critical.

A second reason is money. Graduate school can be expensive, and even if you have a scholarship or a paid assistantship, you will definitely not be making a lot of money while you are a graduate student. This is particularly the case in the United States, where PhD students are paid far less than their counterparts in Europe, or Australia and New Zealand. Money is a basic and intractable issue not only in communication studies but also in academics at large, and the only way to deal with and address the money question is to try to ensure that your postgraduate studies are funded. This is easier to do at the doctoral level than the master's, particularly if you are interested in a professional masterate.

A third critical obstacle has to do with cultural precedent and support. We both know people who were mocked for making the choice to go to graduate school for any number of stereotypical reasons—"It's not a real job!," "It's not masculine!," "It's an ivory tower!," "It's not worth the effort!" We were both fortunate enough to have mentors in our families and institutions who helped us make the choice—but that choice is compounded for first-generation students, when there is simply no cultural precedent or support or even a script that says that education is a good thing. Once again, we turn to the importance of mentorship by a professor as a means to work your way through this issue.

A final barrier to attending graduate school is structural, primarily international. For instance, it became increasingly difficult under the Trump administration for Chinese students and learners from the Global South to come to the United States. Some simply cannot set foot in the country because of their nationality, or access any funding for study or travel, and so they choose not to go to graduate school because structural factors are stacked against them. The International Communication Association, among other bodies, has been addressing the question of what it means to genuinely internationalize. In 2014 it developed a strategy to take the field beyond representation—that is, to ensure that people across the world were not only able to study and learn about communication but also to ensure that internationalization itself was a significant subject of study in communication and, crucially, to change the habitus of communication studies, that is, to change and shake up the ingrained White, Anglo American kinds of practices that underlie communication studies. Both of us believe that while we have done a lot in this regard, there is plenty more that we can all do together—and we truly hope that you will join us in this collective journey.

For Further Thought and Reflection

1. In the context of graduate school, what might success look like for you?

2. Putting success narratives aside, consider how each of the five suggested narratives (success, opportunity, passion, challenge, and escape) may describe your motivations for pursuing graduate school.

3. How might your wider community be impacted by your choice to step into an academic space?

4. What critical obstacles do you foresee requiring resilience in your choice to pursue graduate school?

Spanning the Abyss
Graduate Student Steps and Tasks

4

Randall A. Lake

Emma Frances Bloomfield

Beth L. Boser

Allegra Hardin

Barbara A. Pickering

> My Teacher gave a curious smile. "Look," he said, and with the word he went down on his hands and knees. I did the same (how it hurt my knees!) and presently saw that he had plucked a blade of grass. Using its thin end as a pointer, he made me see, after I had looked very closely, a crack in the soil so small that I could not have identified it without this aid.
>
> "I cannot be certain," he said, "that this *is* the crack ye came up through. But through a crack no bigger than that ye certainly came."
>
> "But—but," I gasped with a feeling of bewilderment not unlike terror. "I saw an infinite abyss. And cliffs towering up and up. And then *this* country on top of the cliffs."
>
> "Aye. But the voyage was not mere locomotion. That bus, and all you inside it, were increasing *in size*." (Lewis, 1973, p. 122)

C. S. Lewis's allegory of heaven and hell *The Great Divorce* serves equally as an allegory of graduate school. Graduate education can feel hellish in the moment; recognizing its heavenly aspects, which are real and more enduring, may require hindsight. We hope to help you calm the bewilderment and terror, span the abyss, and—eventually—appreciate the heights that you've attained.

Graduate programs in communication are unusually diverse. They differ substantively, in areas of expertise and programmatic strengths; structurally, in requirements, curriculum, financial support, and timetables; and culturally, in relationships among faculty, among students, between the two, and in their broader *ethoi*. Therefore, learning how things are done in your program is crucial: not only explicit rules and procedures but also tacit norms. The grapevine—including more senior students, others in your cohort, even alumni—is indispensable. (Don't believe everything you hear, though!) Regardless of program, however, graduate school differs dramatically from undergraduate education; by design, success will require much greater self-motivation and self-discipline.

Developing a Degree Calendar

Begin graduate study with its end in mind. A degree calendar that includes the following can assist in planning your program and keeping you on track.

Coursework and Other Milestones

Understand the requirements for mandatory, elective, and cognate (in a related field outside your department) courses. Know how many credits—of each type and overall—must be earned before you can take exams or begin your thesis/dissertation, and to complete the program.

Understand course sequencing. Required courses, which typically introduce foundational theories and methods, are offered regularly and usually taken early, often in the first year. Consult a schedule of classes, if available. There may be a standard course rotation or, at least, a tentative schedule for the immediate future. You also may be able to anticipate upcoming electives by ruling out those that were offered recently and by talking with the graduate director or your advisor. Be flexible. Accommodate courses that are offered intermittently, cover special topics, and offer opportunities to experience a particular professor's class for its own sake.

Consider whether courses work well together or should be taken at different times. Note any prerequisites, of course. Classes whose foci, theoretical orientations, or methods overlap may be less burdensome together than disparate ones that pull you in multiple directions (although the latter may offer welcome variety!).

> It is so much better to take summer classes if you have the option than take too many classes in one semester and be overwhelmed. Know how many courses you can manage at once before jumping in to plan your coursework. (Kylie Holman, MA, University of Nebraska Omaha)

Finally, consider university and departmental regulations and norms. How many credit hours are usually taken each term? How many are required for full-time status (on which international student visas, financial aid, health insurance, etc., may depend)? By what point should coursework be completed? When do students choose their advisor and/or form their guidance committees? When are comprehensive examinations taken? By what point must the thesis/dissertation be defended? Prospectively, your calendar should reflect "normal progress," however your institution defines it.

Life

Hopefully, your calendar will accommodate obligations to family, children, work, and so on. A single, 20-something, full-time, in-residence graduate teaching assistant's calendar may differ from that of a 40-something, working professional with a family who is taking the program online. Accommodating unforeseen disruptions, such as serious illness or death in the family, may require institutional dispensation (e.g., a leave of absence). Normal progress notwithstanding, paths to completion vary, so resist the temptation to compare yourself and your route to others.

Learning Schedule

A learning schedule is a timetable for completing specific tasks. It changes week to week and term to term, depending on your immediate goals and the time available for achieving them. Establish realistic timetables for completing projects. Multiply your initial estimate by time and a half! Effective time management skills are essential. Don't procrastinate (easier said than done), and allow ample time for revision and polish. Also, establish work boundaries. Rather than reacting habitually to looming deadlines, proactively schedule some free time. How (and how much) will change as your life changes.

> Self-care is really important to me, and taking time away from grad school helped bring balance to my life, which had a positive outcome on my mental health. I made sure to schedule my free time in my calendar, so I didn't feel guilty for taking time away from my studies. (Hayley Jurek, MA, University of Nebraska Omaha)

Finally, seek guidance as needed to stay on schedule. Working relationships with your professors are critical; take the initiative to reach out to them. Utilize their office hours. Request a meeting in advance, and set the agenda. Respect their own busy schedules by asking questions as specific as possible, and let them know that—and how—you've looked for answers elsewhere, without success. Professors help those who help themselves!

Thesis/Dissertation

Although we will say more below, here we want to stress the importance of developing a timeline for completion. Account for institutional expectations. If your stipend contains a year of support for dissertation work, use it! Also, account for other responsibilities and tasks. A time-consuming, emotionally challenging job search may impact your ability to write. Remember that your timeline is also your committee members', particularly its endpoint; everyone must agree to the oral defense. Hence, ask your advisor/chair: When should/must I finish? Should all members receive drafts as they are produced, or should other members receive chapters only after my chair has approved them? How many weeks should I allow for review and feedback? What should I be working on while waiting? Stick to your timeline as best you can, but don't beat yourself up if/when you fall behind.

Your Program of Study

A degree calendar establishes your path across the abyss and timeline for arrival. How should you spend all those days (and nights) en route? With what courses, professors, and experiences do you want to fill them, and why? You may even be required to formalize this schedule by filing a program of study (usually developed in conversation with your advisor) in your first semester or year.

In formulating a program of study, reflect on your interests, passions, and personal goals in entering your degree program. Are you pursuing graduate study for intellectual enrichment or professional development? What topics interest you? What issues concern you? Do you aspire to be a scholar in a major research university or a teacher in a liberal arts college, comprehensive university, or community college? Do you want to be a media guru in a prosocial NGO? When choosing electives, assess not only these interests and goals but also the future job market (unpredictable though it may be) and your employability.

The reasons that drew you to your program undoubtedly will inform ongoing choices of courses and faculty. However, don't be parochial. Coursework outside your immediate interests can deepen your understanding of the field and make you a better, more desirable colleague to a future faculty. You might even revise your interests and goals; your first idea in graduate school may not be your only or final one. One of us entered doctoral study in empirically oriented political communication and exited as a critical scholar of scientific and religious rhetorics.

Succeeding at Coursework

Some students earn bachelor's degrees at large research universities and attend mass lectures with hundreds of their closest friends. Others matriculate at colleges featuring small, discussion-oriented classes. Regardless, your graduate coursework will differ significantly in at least three ways.

Schedule

Full-time graduate students typically take three courses per term and may occasionally take even fewer. Courses typically meet less frequently, often once per week. Evening—even weekend—classes are more common. Courses aren't offered at multiple times during a term and may be offered only once while you are taking coursework, so either you will take a class when offered or possibly not at all. If you have an assistantship, you might teach a class at 8:00 a.m. and attend a seminar ending at 10:00 p.m., with little or nothing scheduled between. In short, your schedule will be largely out of your control and may vary dramatically from term to term—even from one day to the next. Vitally, don't mistake unscheduled time for free time. Compared with your college days, you will have much more free*dom* but much less free *time*!

Workload and Preparation

Graduate coursework is significantly more demanding. A doctoral student in the United States can expect to read approximately one book or five to 10 scholarly articles or chapters per course, per week. A master's student's workload may be somewhat lighter, or not. Managing such volume in three courses simultaneously can be challenging, even overwhelming. Moreover, whereas undergraduate textbooks summarize, synthesize, and simplify complex ideas, graduate students must make sense of theoretically dense, difficult, and even obtuse original sources.

> The amount of assigned reading is very different in the States than South Korea. In Korea, I used to have two to three articles per week, and you were expected to know every detail (more like deep reading). In the United States, it's more like you need to get an overall idea of the five to eight assigned readings. (anonymous PhD student, University of Southern California)

Hence, prioritizing may be advisable, at least occasionally. Difficult readings may require more time; required courses may matter more than elective ones (Azar, 2010). One reading strategy is to engage, first, a scholarly book's table of contents and introduction for a sense of its framework and main arguments; next, the conclusion, which will restate these arguments, explore implications, and suggest directions for future research; and, finally, specific chapters in depth (Sweeney, 2012). Reading for themes and key arguments that thread multiple works together is more efficient than sentence-by-sentence comprehension. One note-taking strategy is to compile a document that includes each reading's citation, abstract, key quotations, and your personal take.

> Treat coursework like a job. Because it IS your job. At the start of the semester when you first get a syllabus, sit down and write out all of your assignments and due dates into your calendar. I would do this and then work backwards to create my own timelines of when I should be working on pieces of the assignments ahead of their due dates. This also let me block out dates on my calendar where I knew I'd need extra time and prevented me from overcommitting on social engagements right in the middle of a bunch of assignments due simultaneously. (Amber Lynn Scott, PhD, University of Southern California)

Whatever your techniques, however, you will not effectively process 300 pages at once. Moreover, your objective is not comprehension alone but acquisition of a knowledge base from which to develop original ideas that can contribute to some ongoing scholarly conversation. Thus, question your readings. Dialogue with their authors, and relate their ideas to others. Consider how you might take the next step or approach the topic from an alternate perspective. Because ideas need time to percolate, work steadily and well in advance of that looming class session.

In the Classroom

Your professors will expect you to perform entry into this conversation: possibly, in regular reactions to and commentaries on assigned readings; commonly, in reports and presentations that synopsize and analyze related works; and, typically, in an original research paper of sufficient scope and quality to be accepted at an academic conference. Graduate coursework should be less about good grades and credentials than about intellectual exploration and discovery. Some seminar papers can birth your own research agenda and, with suitable revision, launch a promising career of conference participation and scholarly publication (see Chapter 8). Others may expand your horizons to an unfamiliar area of inquiry. Once you are a new assistant professor, your coursework may be useful in crafting syllabi, lesson plans, and content for your own undergraduate classes. Every graduate seminar contributes to your emergent expertise and identity in multiple ways.

> You'll hear a lot of people saying that every class paper should be turned into a journal article. Honestly, I think that's ridiculous. Sometimes the final paper is just trying to work out what you learned. It would definitely be a waste if you didn't create a publication from ANY classes that you took during your programme, but the key point is to learn which class papers are worth taking to the next level and which are fine to move on from. (Marcia Allison, PhD, University of Southern California)

As an undergraduate, perhaps you encountered the ideal of a community of learners in which instructor and students alike contribute mutually to their joint education. This ideal probably was realized partially at best. Classes of dozens or hundreds necessitate a lecture format in which students expect their instructor to make the material interesting and tell them everything they need to know. In most graduate courses, however, students will number in the single digits; even large classes seldom have more than 20. For these and other reasons, every student is expected to contribute meaningfully and consistently to each session. Anticipate that your classes will proceed primarily via discussion (although some professors interpret "discussion" to mean talking for three hours). Some professors don't direct discussion via questions, instead simply opening the floor to student questions and ideas. Moreover, in this seminar-style context, there's no place to hide!

This environment can be unsettling. Graduate school demands a strong sense of self-efficacy; it is important "to believe in [your] own abilities" (Stephanie, MA, University of Nevada, Las Vegas). Coming prepared with organized notes will build confidence even if you are prepared only to ask questions (sometimes, students' preparation and understanding are revealed better by their questions than their answers). But don't overcompensate. Showing off by dominating discussion will impress no one. Strive for periodic contributions that are appropriate within the flow of conversation.

> You have to be ready to proactively participate in class to exchange your ideas and confirm your knowledge. English can be a barrier at first, so be strategic about when to speak up. Usually, it's hard to chime in when the discussion is already ongoing, so try to speak first when the class is open for discussion. (anonymous PhD student, University of Southern California)

Relatedly, graduate classrooms are viewed primarily as fora for rigorous testing of ideas. You will be expected to critique others' ideas, including your professor's; rest assured that your own will receive equal scrutiny. More than unsettling, this environment may violate your cultural norms. Although high achievers (like graduate students)—especially Americans—may seem/be competitive, the graduate classroom should not be. Don't criticize an idea (let alone a person) to display your superiority. Conversely, don't become defensive or take disagreement personally. The best graduate education fosters a particular kind of humility: a recognition that, although some ideas may be (much) better than others, no one has a monopoly on those ideas. Each of us has much to learn. To this end, be open. You will encounter a vast array of thinkers and works, some familiar, many not. Don't prejudge. Your professor chose these materials for a reason, and each deserves to be engaged carefully and in good faith. Over time, some will become your intellectual allies; others, no doubt, will serve primarily as provocations and counterpoints. Still others will recede into irrelevance. But allies may be found in unexpected places, and what seems wrong or useless today may prove valuable tomorrow.

Finally, classrooms may reproduce social hierarchies and power relations. Members of underrepresented groups, especially, may encounter those who make them feel unwelcome. Many professors recognize and strive to mitigate these issues; for want of concern or skill, others, sadly, do not. Even when proactive efforts at inclusion are made, you may feel discouraged or unable to contribute, for instance, to a conversation that has pivoted from readings that interest you to others, including old-dead-White-men philosophers (Inglis & Steinfeld, 2000) to whom you haven't been exposed or may not relate. Don't let this experience create self-doubt. Had the faculty not valued your worth and ability, you would not have risen to the top of a highly competitive applicant pool. Reach out to trusted mentors, fellow students, and support services—both within your department and without—for reassurance and help in fostering resilience.

Comprehensive Exams

Unlike bachelor's degrees, one does not earn a master's or doctoral degree merely by earning sufficient course credits; instead, graduate programs incorporate some kind of culminating experience. Master's programs, especially, may culminate in various ways: a work-related, applied research project; training manual; documentary film; meta-analysis of literature in a specific area; or new course design, to name a few. Such diversity notwithstanding, very many master's and (nearly) all doctoral programs remain traditional in requiring a comprehensive examination and scholarly thesis/dissertation.

Upon completing coursework, most graduate students will undertake a series of comprehensive examinations: master's students typically near the end of their second, final year and doctoral students commonly sometime in their third or early in their fourth year. Protocols vary widely. Exams may be constructed, administered, and evaluated by faculty in various subfields or by each student's guidance committee. A committee member may pose questions or serve only as a reader who evaluates answers to others' questions. Students may answer some questions (typically regarding required courses) in common, or not. Students may write during a shared window of time, or not. Written exams may be followed by an oral defense, or not. They may be taken open or closed book. The number of questions and amount of time allowed vary. Students may have varying degrees of input into the exam's scope (defining the subjects to be examined, formulating reading lists, having input into question construction, or even having foreknowledge of questions), or none at all. Expectations for answers also vary. Answers in the closed-book format tend to resemble short essays, whereas answers in the open-book format may be expected to approximate full-fledged research papers, complete with quotations and references. To confuse matters even more, some departments are more transparent about their procedures and expectations than others. Differing preferences among advisors may even produce variability within a department.

Regardless, your department's protocols must adhere to rules established by your institution's graduate school. Even before exams commence, this authority typically regulates the size and composition of guidance (and thesis/dissertation) committees. Master's committees generally consist of two or three faculty from your department, possibly one from outside your department, and are chaired by your advisor. Doctoral committees commonly add one or two faculty, at least one of whom is from another PhD-granting department and acts as the university's representative to ensure that your department's process is both rigorous and fair. (Graduate school rules also may address the possibility of committee members from other universities in the United States or elsewhere.) Because guidance committees usually are integral to it, anticipate the exam process when forming your committee. Faculty who know you and with whom you have developed a positive working relationship in seminars and other contexts are better choices than strangers, no matter how famous. Graduate school parameters also govern the process's conclusion. Failure is uncommon but not unheard of. What counts as passing? Must your committee's decision be unanimous? If you pass most questions but not all, can unsatisfactory answers be rewritten? In a worst case, how many attempts are allowed?

Thus, becoming thoroughly familiar with the rules and practices in your university and department is essential. Early and often, consult your advisor, other guidance committee members, administrative staff, and senior students who have passed their exams (see Chapter 5 for more information on working with advisors and committees). If permitted, review previous students' questions and answers. Be aware that faculty commitments—conference travel, sabbaticals, and so on—may influence exam scheduling. Less tangibly, try to gauge your faculty's sense of the exam's purpose. Master's exams tend to be about demonstrating your comprehension of the totality of your coursework; answers tend to be expository. Doctoral students are expected, in addition, to display their facility in interpreting and evaluating others' work, thereby demonstrating the capacity for independent, critical thought that a dissertation will require; answers are expected to advance arguments.

Theses/Dissertations

Theses and dissertations are theoretically driven, individual research projects that contribute something original to our understanding of communication processes and events. They are fundamentally comparable, differing primarily in scope (dissertations being more ambitious). Even if you have written a master's thesis—which will be unlike anything you have written before—a doctoral dissertation will be unlike anything you have written before. Across all fields, roughly half of doctoral students never finish their degrees (Cassuto, 2013), and failure to scale the dissertation mountain is a major reason why. Professors aren't wicked demons intent on torture or perpetuating a cycle of abuse. If yours doubted your ability, you wouldn't have passed your exams and advanced to "candidacy" or ABD (all-but-dissertation) status. The dissertation is a rite of passage—an essential one. Although not all PhDs pursue academic careers, the foundational purpose of doctoral education is to preserve and perpetuate the academy, to train the next generation of teachers and scholars. Determining prospective faculty's capacity for original, independent, sustained intellectual work is, therefore, critical. Dissertations confirm—in a way that seminar papers and exams can't—that your professors' confidence in you was warranted. Further, if you invest the energy to convert it (see Germano, 2013), your dissertation can birth publications that jump-start or boost your scholarly career as a new assistant professor with a running tenure clock (Chapters 8 and 13 address these next steps).

Accordingly, selecting a topic, developing research questions, designing procedures, and—of course—completing the project will be your responsibility. This does not mean that you should work in isolation. Your committee (ordinarily, a three-person subset of your guidance committee), especially your advisor, will guide you in shaping the project and help you overcome roadblocks. It's crucial that everyone is on the same page. You don't want to devote hundreds of hours to a project that surprises them. For this reason, consultation at the planning stage is routinely formalized in a prospectus, which identifies the proposed topic, offers a rationale for study, reviews the relevant literature, details the methods to be used, and projects the study's significance. It is a blueprint that defines what is—and, importantly, is not—expected of you. Your committee's approval signifies their acceptance of these parameters, reducing the risk that major changes in scope or design will be demanded late in the game.

The kind and amount of guidance offered varies. Some advisors are more hands-on than others. Some may provide detailed templates for prospectuses and/or thesis/dissertations. Some may require regular meetings or other mileposts for progress. Even the most active advisor, however, will expect you to work substantially on your own; with most, you will be largely unsupervised once your prospectus has been approved. After all, this is a test of your ability to work independently. In addition, compared to the students in your advisor's courses, you will be out of sight, out of mind. Accordingly, obtaining guidance also will be primarily your responsibility.

The popular press offers much advice about how to climb this mountain (see also Chapter 9). One author (Bolker, 1998) even explains how to finish your dissertation in 15 minutes a day. If such advice works for you, count your lucky stars. We skeptics have seven broad suggestions, which will be outlined in the following sections.

Opportunity Knocks

Attitude matters. Approach your thesis/dissertation as an opportunity, not a hurdle. At the risk of shattering illusions, you'll never again have the opportunity to immerse yourself in the ferment of Big Ideas with so few competing responsibilities to distract and impede you.

Care

Although rewarding, much thesis/dissertation work is tedious. Writer's block is frustrating. To sustain you through the dreary times, choose a topic about which you truly care and want to say something—even if you don't yet know what you want, or what your data will permit you, to say.

Stand on the Shoulders of Giants

Other theses/dissertations have been written. Find exemplars that offer models and solutions to specific problems. Form matters more than subject or content: How is the study, and each chapter, organized? How is existing scholarship engaged, and how much is enough? Does it offer an argument or comprise a report? What are the components of the final chapter? Seek your committee's recommendations. Those authored by previous advisees can also reveal how your advisor likes things to be done.

Find Yourself

Discover and deploy your most productive writing practices. You may be a morning person or a night owl. You might spew first and edit later, in multiple drafts, or craft the perfect sentence in your head before committing its first word to "paper." You might relish routine or be given to bursts of creative energy. You may need background music or total silence. Everyone has habits, both good and bad. Practice the productive ones religiously, and remediate the unproductive ones as best you can.

> The best advice I heard about completing a thesis was, "Don't take six months to accomplish something that could be done in two weeks. Fail fast." (Allegra Hardin, MA, University of Nebraska Omaha)

Don't Be Afraid of Commitment

Your timetable for completion is a commitment to yourself. A writing tracker—recording how many words you write each day—can help you keep it. Tracking large units, such as chapters, may not feel like progress; tracking smaller increments can keep you motivated. The pomodoro technique (Cirillo, 2006, 2018) divides large projects into smaller units that can be completed in a distraction-free time frame. For example, you might spend 25 minutes on a task, followed by a 5-minute break to check your social media feeds or play with your dog. This is a *pomodoro*. After four pomodoros, you might take a longer, 20- to 30-minute break. Times can be adjusted to suit your needs.

If you answer only to yourself, though, the temptation to adopt a relaxed attitude toward your deadlines and excuse missed ones may be strong. Consider making public commitments to your advisor, whom you hope to impress rather than disappoint; your partner, with a special reward hanging in the balance; and/or other students. Creating a group scrum board (Pope-Ruark, 2017) is one way to track your progress collaboratively with your graduate cohort. Scrum boards have three columns marking what you need to do, what you are doing, and what is done (Figure 4.1). They can spur both accountability and the bonding that comes from commiserating over a shared experience as students pursue their individual writing targets in different locales.

FIGURE 4.1 Thesis/Project Progress Scrum Board. Photo by Allegra Hardin.

When your cohort gathers face to face, sharing what you have "nailed or failed" since the previous meeting can foster mutual support and problem-solving, reducing the feeling of isolation that often accompanies thesis/dissertation work. No cohort? No problem. Plentiful online writing communities hold authors accountable to one another while sharing trials and tribulations and celebrating triumphs.

Don't Leave Home Without It

If humanly possible, finish your thesis/dissertation while still in residence. The excitement of a new job and a real paycheck can be very enticing. Resist them unless absolutely necessary. Finishing a dissertation is orders of magnitude more difficult when you are saddled with the substantial responsibilities of a full-fledged faculty member while beginning a new life in a new place.

Don't Let Perfect Be the Enemy of Good

The best dissertation is a finished dissertation!

"Can I Plead the Fifth?": Oral Defenses

You probably never had to defend an undergraduate paper under direct questioning by your instructor, let alone multiple faculty. However, oral defenses are a signature feature of graduate education. There are three kinds, administered by your guidance or thesis/dissertation committee. In the United States, you may defend your written master's exams or project; you almost certainly will defend your written PhD exams and your master's and PhD prospectus and thesis/dissertation. *Exam defenses* probe the breadth and depth of your understanding of certain fields of inquiry. *Prospectus defenses* are comparatively collaborative, so expect questions, suggestions, and discussion aimed at shaping a project that is both sound and feasible. *Thesis/dissertation defenses* test your success in conducting original research that contributes to your field of inquiry.

The format and tenor of oral defenses vary dramatically. Some prospectus and thesis/dissertation defenses begin with a brief student presentation; some exam defenses begin by permitting the student to clarify, amplify, or emend written answers. Faculty might engage you sequentially or in conversational turn-taking. Some faculty are more aggressive questioners than others. The defense may continue for a set time or until committee members tacitly agree to conclude it. Therefore, clarify expectations with your advisor. Solicit insight from other students, especially those who also experienced your committee members in this setting. Prepare by honestly appraising your work, looking for weaknesses, anticipating questions, and developing responses. You could even rehearse responses out loud. Feedback from your committee—if they are willing—is invaluable.

Most students find these experiences to be stressful; unfortunately, a few let stress get the better of them. Remember that your committee wants you to succeed. Defenses don't resemble Jack McCoy's withering cross-examination on *Law and Order*. Some questions are asked because you can answer them. Some are asked because there is no answer. Even the toughest questions may be posed not to trip you up but to gauge how capably you participate in respectful scholarly disagreement. So don't be afraid to argue for a position contrary to your professor's or to express uncertainty, where appropriate. In a dissertation defense, remember that you are the expert on your study.

"Who Wants to Be an Academic?": Professional Degree Programs

Some graduate—especially master's—programs are designed for working professionals and aspirants to nonacademic careers in business, government, NGOs, and other sectors. (See Chapters 14 and 15 for additional information.) They may confer specialized degrees other than the MA or MS; for example, the School of Communication at the University of Southern California offers Master of Communication Management and Master of Public Diplomacy degrees.

Students in these programs often differ from "traditional" master's students. Their ages, work histories, and life experiences may be considerably more diverse. In universities that offer "progressive" degree programs (enabling students to earn both baccalaureate and master's degrees in a compressed time frame), your classmates could include undergraduates, working adults, and everyone in between.

Because they are designed to foster career preparation and advancement, structure, reputation, location, and alumni matter more in selecting a professional program than, for example, the opportunity to learn from Professor Renowned. A well-structured program—including curriculum, degree requirements, and schedule of course offerings—with clear goalposts will facilitate completion under your circumstances and the time that you have allotted. Reputation among (potential) employers will enhance your career opportunities. Work, family, and other considerations may rule out some locations. Well-placed alumni can bolster reputation (and thus the "value" of your degree) and may be more helpful in obtaining your own position than Professor Renowned's recommendation would be.

Because so many organizational settings require work in teams, courses in professional programs often feature group projects. Because they value mastery of existing knowledge for career preparation over generation of new knowledge, culminating experiences in professional programs also tend to differ. A comprehensive examination over coursework is unlikely; instead, a capstone course, the design and requirements of which are summative, may be required. Advanced, independent projects are common but typically apply knowledge to a real-world situation (actual or hypothetical) of the sort encountered by an employer, government agency, or other nonacademic audience. Just as an organization might task an employee with or contract with a consultant for specific work, students may have less responsibility (or freedom) to define their project, instead working within parameters set by others. Designing a messaging strategy for a state's Department of Public Health, urging residents to remain home during a pandemic, or developing a process for organizational culture change in an NGO might be examples.

Professional master's degrees generally are terminal, not prelude to doctoral study, primarily because most graduates have other life plans. In addition, though, admission to a doctoral program may be complicated by the widespread perception that professional master's programs are comparatively weak preparation for the pinnacle of academic study; graduates may even face a lingering suspicion that their professional degree signifies a lack of seriousness about academic study. Thus, if you hope or think you might want to pursue a future PhD, seek the most academically oriented path through your professional program. Professional degrees awarded by departments that also offer traditional academic degrees, including the PhD, are, generally speaking, more credible than those awarded by stand-alone, for-profit entities (to say nothing of unaccredited diploma mills). These programs also may present valuable opportunities to take part in more academically oriented activities. Seek opportunities to take elective courses in the doctoral curriculum, take courses from regular research faculty, participate in research-focused colloquia and other events, or volunteer for research teams. Highlight these activities when you apply to doctoral programs, and emphasize your intellectual interests. Letters of recommendation from your instructors will carry far more weight than one from your employer; especially valuable will be letters from the aforementioned research faculty who can speak to your motivation for academic study, your intellectual interests, and your capacity for original, independent thought and work.

Graduate education is unique. The route is unfamiliar, the climb steep. The trip is not for everyone; most don't board the bus. But riders who span the abyss enter a country in which their teachers become their colleagues and friends and to which, if they choose, they can shepherd riders of their own. Not quite heaven, perhaps, but not a bad gig here on Earth.

For Further Thought and Reflection

1. Why do you want to pursue a graduate degree? Are you highly motivated to undertake a challenging process?

2. How adaptable are you? Are you open to learning new ideas? Do you take feedback well and learn from it? Can you work effectively under pressure? What self-care practices could help you manage stress?

3. What are your typical work habits? Can you be productive on your own? What organizational and time management strategies work best? What habits might you need to avoid or cultivate?

4. What departmental, institutional, and other resources are available to assist you? Where and to whom can you turn for answers, advice, and support?

Work With Someone Who Seems Excited About Your Success

Building Advisor/Advisee Relationships

5

C. Kay Weaver

Bridget Reynolds Sheffer

The relationship between you and your research advisors has a profound impact on your experience as a graduate student. Advisors want their students to do well and thrive. Yet, in the context of students being recruited into graduate programs to generate research, publications, and income for educational institutions in large numbers, what constitutes a good advisor-advisee relationship has come under scrutiny, and we encourage you to enter this relationship well informed and prepared.

In this chapter, we provide guidance on choosing and working with an advisory committee, models of advisor/student relationships, negotiating the advising relationship and its power dynamics, and what to do when the relationship falters. Our aim is also to represent the varied experiences of graduate students as advisees. We therefore invited graduates of communication master's and doctoral programs from a range of backgrounds and demographics across Aotearoa New Zealand and the United States to respond to a set of questions about their experience of being supervised and what advice they would give prospective advisees in relation to finding and working with an advisory committee. Their responses inform this chapter, and we quote them extensively to provide examples of how graduate students have experienced their relationship with their supervisors. Since the type of master's or doctorate you study will directly affect the relationship you have with your advisors, in the next section we outline different types of master's and doctorate programs.

United States, European, and Australasian Graduate Programs: Terminologies and Expectations

Globally, two graduate school models dominate: the U.S. model, which is also the Canadian model, which includes coursework and a thesis at master's level and

57

coursework and a dissertation at doctorate level—and the European/Australasian model, which at master's level includes coursework and a thesis but at PhD level includes research thesis only and explicitly excludes coursework. In the European/Australasian context, there are other named doctorates, such as the Doctorate of Education (EdD) and the Doctorate of Business Administration (DBA), that do include coursework components—usually in the first year, followed by a second- and third-year thesis research and writing thesis focus. To complicate matters further, different international contexts use different nomenclature to describe the graduate program, the student, the supervisor, the supervision panel, the advisory committee, and the research paper. These are outlined in Table 5.1 below, and throughout this chapter we use the terminology of both models interchangeably.

TABLE 5.1 **Graduate Terminology by Regional Model**

E/A MODEL	U.S. MODEL
Supervisor	Advisor
Thesis *(PhD research paper)*	Dissertation *(PhD research paper)*
Dissertation *(Master's research paper)*	Thesis *(Master's research paper)*
Supervisory Panel	Advisory Committee
Supervision	Advisement

Note. These are the comparable differences in vocabulary between the European/Australasian model and the United States model.

Master's Programs

Internationally, master's programs in communication that include a research thesis, and which can variously come under the title of a Master of Communication, Master of Arts, or Master of Science, are very similar. These degrees usually take between 18 months and two years to complete and comprise coursework with specialized theoretical, methodological, and/or issues-based foci. They culminate in a research thesis that is expected to provide a critical investigation of a topic from clearly articulated theoretical and methodological frameworks. During the writing of this thesis, which can range in length from between 25,000 and 50,000 words, the student works with an advisory committee that guides and supervises their academic research practices. A master's thesis is usually examined and graded by at least one external examiner and internally by professors that may include members of the advisory panel. In some national contexts there has been a move away from using advisors as examiners to assure impartiality in the assessment process. In the United States, the examination of the master's thesis includes an oral examination; in other international contexts this is rarely the case.

There are master's programs in the United States, Europe, and Australasia that do not include a thesis or dissertation component. In these programs the student undertakes additional taught courses and completes a research project. There are also professional master's programs wholly comprised of taught courses. For those wanting to pursue a PhD, a master's that includes a research thesis or dissertation is commonly an entry requirement for admission into the doctorate program.

PhD Programs

At the doctorate level in the United States, for the first two to three years of study the student will undertake coursework that they are tested and graded on through oral and written exams. Only after completing and passing these comprehensive exams and demonstrating a deep understanding of their subject area does the U.S. PhD student go on to undertake their dissertation. In this context the creation of the supervisory committee is a negotiation process initiated by the student with potential supervisors as the dissertation stage approaches. The student then works with their committee to complete the dissertation. When the dissertation is submitted, the student orally defends their research to their advisory committee.

There are criticisms of how the U.S. model requires the supervisory committee to both supervise and examine the student's work, as this has the potential to result in a highly subjective and personalized, rather than objective and independent, assessment of the dissertation (Kehm, 2006, pp. 70–71). The other major criticism of the U.S. doctoral model is that it usually takes between four and eight years to complete the whole PhD program.

This compares with the European and Australasian model where the student is expected to have developed sufficient theoretical knowledge of their subject area and research methodologies through their undergraduate and master's qualifications as a prelude to entry into the PhD, where the doctorate is by research thesis only and ideally is completed in three to four years. The PhD thesis is usually examined by a panel comprised of up to two academics external to the university and sometimes an internal academic who was not on the supervision team. Before applying to study for a PhD by research thesis only, the student should attempt to engage with potential supervisors to explore their willingness to take the project on and their supervision styles and experience. We explain this in more detail below.

Selecting Your Advisor and Committee

When deciding where to study for a graduate program, whether at master's or doctorate level, you should research the college or department to assess if the courses offered and the research foci of the faculty are aligned with your interests. If you intend to study for a research-thesis-only doctorate in Europe or Australasia, your attention should be on the research interests of the academic staff. While ranking your preferred place of study, given that you might not be accepted there, you will need second and third options and, therefore, need to put time and effort into this preparatory research.

> First, realise you have choices. You don't have to do things or choose supervisors because other people are saying you need to take a particular course of action. Take your time to think about it carefully, and do lots of preparatory talking with all sorts of people and perspectives. It's not something to be rushed because it has lots of implications for a long time. Realise that you and your PhD are not totally dependent on your supervisors. There is a big part of the study and process which you, as a student, must own. (anonymous PhD student)

If you are studying for a master's degree or a doctorate qualification that includes coursework, it is while undertaking the taught courses that the advisee and advisor relationship begins through networking in the department/college. During this time, you learn about the faculty, their research interests, and whether they are taking advisees on. It may be that through engagement with you on a course, a faculty member will invite you to work with them on your thesis. You should still consider whether this is the best advisor for you; you need to be confident that the person has experience and knowledge of your research area and the supervision skills to support you to succeed, and you should talk about how you would work together. One of the graduate students who responded to our questionnaire offered this advice: "I would recommend finding someone with your desired shared expertise. Look for someone who has a reputation with balancing challenge and nurture" (Anonymous PhD student).

In countries where the doctorate is by thesis only, the potential supervisor plays a determining role in whether the student will be admitted to the PhD program. Consequently, it is important to make efforts to contact, build a rapport with, and, if you feel positive about the prospect, ask if a supervisor will support your application and work with you. Only one of the graduate students who answered our questionnaire said they were not given a choice about who would be their supervisor. It is also important to think about how you will engage with your supervision panel, and in this context it is valuable to understand some of the different models of advisee/advisor relationships, as we discuss next.

Models of Advisor/Advisee Relationships

When the modern doctorate degree originated in Germany in the early 19th century, there was one model of how the advisee and the advisor would interact:

The expectation was that a candidate or Doktorant would find himself a professor to act as a supervisor or Doktorvater (both were almost invariably male) and, with minimal input from the latter, successfully complete a major research project and produce a thesis which made an original contribution to knowledge and understanding of the discipline (Taylor et al., 2018, p. 47).

In this context, the advisor was positioned as the expert, "master" authority who oversaw the development of the student "apprentice." A variation on this is the *clone model* of advising, where the supervisor strives to produce a replica version of themselves both as a researcher and as a future potential supervisor of others.

In the master/apprentice clone/replica model of doctoral supervision, the parties involved generally do not talk about their relationship—the focus is on the student's development and conducting and writing up the research. This supervision model has been characterized as a kind of secret garden, black box, or "privatized practice, almost off bounds of collective reflections" (Denis et al., 2019, p. 31). Adding to the challenges that such a relationship can create for the student, the supervisor, by often being illusive and unavailable, can have a ghostlike presence in the process. Sadly, one of our graduate interviewees reported experiencing this with his supervision committee:

> I did not find my interactions with my supervisors to be a nurturing experience.
> ... I would often (half) joke with my spouse that all my supervisor tells me is
> "no" ... but I wasn't given enough instruction to figure out what I was doing
> wrong. ... I definitely didn't feel like I met with my supervisors enough. They
> too often seemed to be traveling, going to conferences, busy with teaching or
> research duties, and needed to end our meetings before I was ready because
> they needed to move on to the next thing on their schedule. (anonymous
> PhD student)

Communication departments should be concerned to receive this feedback given that over the last two decades, educational institutions have sought to be more accountable to students who invest considerable time and money in their graduate qualifications. Striving for such accountability has involved identifying and encouraging *best-practice supervision* models that acknowledge and respond to student needs. Consequently, postgraduate supervision and doctorate education have themselves become burgeoning academic fields of research with many conferences, journals, and books and edited collections dedicated to their analysis and discussion. This has also produced many resources that students themselves can refer to on how to succeed as a graduate research student (see Bain, 2004; Bastalich, 2017; McCulloch et al., 2016).

Today best-practice supervision is framed as a pedagogical relationship of professional mutual respect where colearning and coproduction of ideas occur. In this context the advisee is seen as a colleague in training to whom supervisors have responsibilities; they have a role in advocating for them, empowering them to succeed, and preparing them for the next stages of their career. Ideally, your experience would be like one of our respondents who explained: "My advisors pushed me to perform at a high standard ... through patient, insightful guidance. They helped me discover my potential, consider new perspectives, and otherwise grow as a student and a person" (anonymous PhD student).

Globally, there is more diversity in terms of age, gender, ethnicity, and race and increased first-generation learners among students in graduate programs than even 20 years ago. Universities have been comparatively slower to ensure diversity among their faculty. In an effort to fill this gap, most universities provide professional development training for advisors in working with students from different backgrounds and experience. Supervisors generally have many opportunities to learn about and develop skills to appropriately support and give feedback to their advisees and develop an "engaged, self-aware, and emotionally responsive practice" (Bastalich, 2017, p. 1150). You should expect your supervision panel to approach supervising in this way, though we are aware that too often advisors simply believe they know how to advise because they were successful as graduate students. You might want to inquire with your potential advisor about their supervision practice to assess just how self-aware they are of how they engage with students.

> The quality of my supervision was excellent. There was honesty and trust between all of us. I could rely on being told that my piece of work, decisions, or perspective were solid or needed more thought. All my three supervisors were diligent, and when they said they would provide feedback by a particular time/day, they did without fail. They made themselves available at any time and would make a big effort to accommodate times when quick decisions needed to be made. (anonymous PhD student, New Zealand)

From our participants' and our own experience, there are several characteristics that made a good supervisor or advisor: kindness, patience, and a willingness to mentor. One of our participants said, "Choose a kind person who gives you the room to grow." In contrast, when our participants talked about bad supervision, they spoke of apathy on the part of supervisors, with others reporting that supervisors were overly harsh. One participant explained:

> My MA ... panel was made of one woman and two men. ... The woman was very hard on me. She wanted me to read more, write more, and work more in the department. At my defence, she did not want me to pass because I didn't use APA well enough. The men signed off on my degree and persuaded the woman to sign off on the condition that I would improve my APA knowledge. (anonymous PhD student)

This comment also points to the need to consider gender issues in your panel constitution—might you feel more comfortable working with female or male advisors or a combination of both? In the next section we talk about how you can go about trying to establish this kind of healthy, best-practice relationship with your supervision panel and establishing expectations in relation to meetings and feedback.

Negotiating the Advising Relationship

Supervision Agreements

When you begin working with your supervision panel, it is important to establish a clear understanding of the institutional expectations, if any, in terms of how often you will meet; if there are formal milestones to achieve in particular time frames, progress reporting or annual evaluations; and what your final research dissertation or thesis is expected to contain and demonstrate about you as a researcher. It is also important to discuss how you will work with your whole committee. Will you meet with all of your panel members together or separately? How will you ensure consistency of advice and feedback? It can feel daunting to initiate discussions about these matters as a new research student working with a committee who you may assume has experience and knowledge about their roles and about dissertations and theses. However, doing so will help set the scene and tone of your advisee/advisor relationship from the outset.

Developing agreements about how you will work with your supervisors early on will make a difference to your relationship, your resiliency, and your likelihood of success. To support these conversations, some institutions and advisers provide a learning agreement document to work through, with some requiring these to be completed and copies kept by all parties for later referral. These agreements, which can be extensive in content—covering issues from the regularity of advisor/advisee meetings, time frames for feedback, hours the student is expected to devote to study per week, ethics and academic integrity expectations, intellectual property sharing, the student's right to request alternative supervision—can help you understand and develop a checklist of institutional requirements in relation to your research project and manage your own and your committee's expectations of you. If your institution does not have one of these, examples can be found online and in the literature (see, for example, Taylor et al., 2018, p. 75).

Meetings

In the early stages of your advisee/advisor relationship, you should establish how often you will meet with your advisor and committee. Regular, meaningful meetings are vital to your progress, and developing an action list out of those meetings holds you accountable and helps your supervisors keep track of what you are working on. When the authors of this chapter worked together, for the first year we met every two weeks, and Bridget would write up the notes from our meetings. She then made a to-do list and spent the next weeks working through that list. Occasionally, Bridget would record the meetings for later review. As Bridget progressed, the meetings happened less often. This pattern of meeting every one or two weeks for the first six months of the research project and then meeting less frequently was common across most of the graduates we interviewed. One of our respondents explained:

> I was fortunate because my advisor was a recent PhD graduate who knew what it was like to be a doctoral student. … I did most of my dissertation remotely, so we would have periodic meetings over Skype. He would return comments on my chapters within three to four weeks, and I would make the revisions. We did not meet weekly, just as needed when there was an issue that would arise. (anonymous PhD student)

This respondent also raises the issue of gaining feedback and seemed happy to wait three to four weeks for that feedback, which seems a little long to us.

Feedback

Waiting for feedback can be nerve-racking for graduate advisees, and whilst the ideal is that supervisors give feedback that thoughtfully assesses and guides the advisee on how to improve and develop their work, frustration with feedback was common among our participants. One said, "The feedback was not nurturing and more transactional. … Thinking back … sincere guidance and feedback and honesty regarding my subject matter would have been beneficial" (anonymous MA student).

There are practical ways to solicit meaningful feedback from an advisor. These include being clear about what kind of draft you are submitting for review—a planning draft and draft for thorough review or a near-completed final section of work, chapter, or full thesis. We suggest that advisees and advisors explicitly clarify expectations about feedback in terms of institutional and/or realistic turnaround times, types of feedback (e.g., oral, written, in track changes, hard copy annotations), what action is expected in response to feedback and when, and whether and how feedback can be directly used and incorporated into the text. Establishing common ground around these issues might have helped one of our respondents to avoid some frustrations: "My supervisor … didn't help me when I ran into challenges with understanding … opposing viewpoints. Feedback was only provided on the writing that was submitted. It would have been helpful to get feedback more often along the way" (anonymous PhD student). We suggest that if this student's committee had seen their role as "personally supporting the candidate through the slings and arrows of life as a researcher" (Taylor et al., 2018, p. 79), they might have reached better outcomes.

Ultimately, success in your graduate research venture involves achieving independence from your committee in the confidence that your thesis demonstrates your own ability to develop and undertake a substantive piece of original research. Your relationship with your committee should evolve as the project progresses with you becoming less reliant on your advisors and more reliant on your own ability to critically assess and evaluate your own work. Toward the end of the process, you should feel that you own the project and are confident in defending it. Some advisees might have the confidence to adopt this sense of ownership of their relationship with their advisors early on, especially if you come to your project with already-developed self-efficacy, resiliency, and ability to self-manage. You should, however, always be prepared to listen to the advice of your advisers and balance self-efficacy with the ability to consider others' viewpoints and perspectives.

> I was given total control throughout the life of the whole PhD, meaning it was up to me to decide how often we met and the agenda of these meetings. Being the kind of person who likes autonomy and freedom, this aspect of our relationship worked very well for me, and indeed for all of us. I managed all the meetings, and it was my own expectation to come to the meetings with sufficient work or questions to make them worthwhile. (anonymous PhD student, Texas, United States)

You may have noticed quotes from graduate students in this chapter that encourage you to develop resilience as well as self-efficacy as a researcher. To enhance your own resilience—your ability to manage and bounce back from challenging situations—we encourage you to negotiate your relationships with your advisors in a way that builds mutual trust and consistency of understanding of expectations. Engaging in healthy, proactive, resilience-building behaviors creates a foundation that can ground us when challenges arise. Learning how to interact with your advisors in this way may take time as you get to know each other and your respective communication styles and behaviors. You also need to think about how power will be vested in this relationship, which we turn to discuss now.

Power in Advising Relationships

Power is inevitably invested in advisor/advisee relationships, and it is normal for that power dynamic to change and adapt as the advisee evolves to become an independent researcher. Understanding how different types of power function, from "power over," "power with," and "power to," can help you to reflect on how the advisee/advisor relationship is operating, to what ends, and in whose interests.

Power Over

The traditional dyadic master/apprentice advisor/advisee relationship comprising a hierarchical vertical power over relationship is now regarded as far from ideal. However, many still adopt this hierarchical power over approach to advising, as evidenced by one of our participants who stated: "The longer I worked on my project, the more it felt like I was working to meet his internal agenda rather than meet my own goals and accomplishments." Reflecting on their experience, this same participant suggested that a "weekly touch-point, sincere guidance and feedback, and honesty regarding my subject matter would have been beneficial. Working with me to select a topic meaningful to me would have been better than being assigned to a topic" (anonymous PhD student). This provides valuable insights into how to avoid becoming subject to a supervisor's assumed power and authority.

Power With

Today supervisors are expected to be more accountable for their student's academic well-being, learning, and development. This accountability helps keep power in balance, and power can be used for positive outcomes, especially as we consider the power-with dynamic. Robertson (2017) explains, "Power may be seen as emancipatory and productive, supportive of individual and team agency" (p. 361). For example, one of our interviewees said, "The sole reason I chose my committee chair was she held significant *power within* the department, and she was therefore the most prudent person to lead the committee because she could (and often did) use her clout to minimize obstacles and steamroll objections or difference of opinion" (Anonymous, MA). In this case, the student used power dynamics in the department to advance their education. Additional power-with examples would be flattening the traditional vertical power dynamic of higher education by working on research together to submit to conferences or to publication. Being cojoined in such a power dynamic also provides you, as the advisee, with the power to learn how to submit to conferences or to publications.

Power To

In the case of power-to dynamics, you want to find supervisors who provide you with power to improve and think for yourself. One of our interviewees was grateful that their supervisor was a recent PhD graduate. The supervisor showed sensitivity and generosity toward the student about the pressures of being a graduate student. This provided space in the relationship to explore ideas and make mistakes. Finding a supervisor who gives you the power to make mistakes is critical, as this provides the opportunity to learn, change, grow, and become resilient to what might otherwise seem to be insurmountable challenges.

Much of the literature on supervision observes "that the supervision relationship is infused with desire, fantasy, unresolved transferences, [intimacy,] and power" (Bastalich, 2017, p. 1153). Let's break this down. In graduate work—from the supervisor's perspective—the desire and fantasy is for you to be an outstanding student who works hard, seeks to research and publish, and represents the supervisors and your institution well. Unresolved transferences are situations in which your supervisor may hope for you to reach heights beyond what they have achieved. In many ways, an excellent supervisor wants you to use them as a stepping stone to move into greater experiences and discoveries. To provide this, they need to have power—expert power—to get you where you and they want you to go. This means they need to know what your interests are and what you would like to achieve. One of our participants gave advice about this in the following terms: "Get to know the faculty as people, not just by their résumés or areas of expertise. I built my committee based on the sincerity and interest of the individuals in actually helping me and nurturing me" (anonymous PhD student).

As an advisee, you should also consider how you might infuse the relationship with your advisers with power and how, while this might be seductive, it is unhealthy, as you cede your agency and emotions to the other person. This can reduce your resilience and result in exhaustion as you try to favorably influence how you are perceived. Female students have been found to be more vulnerable to these issues (Devine & Hunter, 2017) due to the gender-inflected, conventionally masculine context of academia. For these reasons, it is important to reflect on the boundaries in the advisee/advisor relationship.

Boundaries are important for the educational and research experience, and these include personal relationship boundaries. Always remember—sexual intimacy between an advisee and advisor is not permissible; neither is bullying or any form of harassment. If there is anything that leaves you feeling uncomfortable, it is critical that it is reported to the proper channels at your institution. Each institution has a designated processes to handle harassment and sexual misconduct complaints. In our experience, it is better to report; you will not be judged negatively, and you may well save another student from suffering a similar experience.

One way to create boundaries is by getting emotional distance from the situation; stepping away and also talking to others about your experiences provides an opportunity to bring some objectivity to your thinking. These boundaries are also important to your being able to work through the range of challenges that come with graduate research. In the next section, we specifically address some of the difficulties you might experience in your advising relationship and how to manage these.

Difficulties in Advising Relationships

It is rare for a graduate advisee to have a perfect ride and not to experience some difficulties with their advisors. These difficulties can come in many forms, from struggling with the style of supervision to not getting timely feedback on work, getting no feedback, feeling aggrieved about the feedback, and/or being told by that you are not achieving in terms of quality and/or quantity of output.

Sometimes, as Bridget found, challenges can be a result of your own approach to the thesis project. Bridget had an expectation that she would be perfect in her writing, learning, and research. It was difficult for her to process through this self-talk. She ended up working with a life coach and a psychological therapist to finish up her PhD thesis.

It can be healthy to work through difficulties, as it helps the student experience, learn about, and manage conflict and develop resilience and self-efficacy. However, with the power in the advisor/advisee relationship being on the side of the advisor, it can feel challenging for the advisee to work through these problems. A common theme among the graduates we talked to was that when they experienced challenges, they internalized the problem. One said: "Road-blocks included not liking the topic of my thesis, feeling like I was working towards his agenda rather than my own, and feeling a lack of guidance. ... My writing, work, and mental well-being suffered" (Anonymous, MA). Another said: "The biggest roadblock was figuring out how to succeed. ... My supervisors didn't make me feel I was doing well, or even belonged. ... I never figured out how to interact with my supervisors!" (anonymous PhD student).

Processes for Managing Conflict

Having a supervision agreement or contract and discussing this when embarking on the advisee/advisor process is valuable, as it can provide an opportunity to talk about how future conflicts can be handled prior to the conflict actually occurring. This means that processes can be established while all parties are in a positive frame rather than when they are in the emotional turmoil of a disagreement. When difficulties arise, consider what strategies you might employ to overcome these.

> One of the most significant challenges was that one supervisor did not communicate with emails. This led to the obvious challenges for me such as obtaining feedback and planning meetings but was also easy to (mis)interpret as lack of interest. I eventually learnt his weekly schedule and went to his office in person with a list of requirements and hard copies. I had to plan this in an effort not to forget to do it! (anonymous PhD student)

The first person to talk to if you are experiencing difficulties with an advisor is that person. In the communication disciplines we are fortunate in usually having some awareness of important communication techniques, such as active listening, demonstrating concern, deferring judgment and waiting to disclose your opinion, paraphrasing to show understanding, and responding and giving feedback appropriately. These are good skills for both the advisee and advisor to practice with each other and, if managed with emotional intelligence by both parties, can support identification of the problem and possible solutions.

Formal Processes

If an advisee is unable to resolve a problem with their advisor and it is the relationship with the advisor that is the problem, recourse to more formal processes may be necessary. The advisee should identify who is responsible for managing advisors in a department or college. This might be a graduate convenor, chair of department, or associate dean graduate. Talking through the issues and seeking advice from these people can assist to raise the matter again with the advisor, or it might be decided that it is appropriate for another person to help resolve the problem by acting as a mediator or support person in discussions. If the advisor-advisee relationship is not serving its purpose, the best action is for a change of supervision; providing all parties accept the situation and another supervisor can be found to take over the advising, the process is usually a matter of completing some forms and having these signed off. The challenge here is, of course, that a new advisor or committee might not think that work already completed is adequate or in line with their expectations or direction they think the research, or the methodologies, should have taken. This can then involve some pivoting and reorienting of the project to ensure a successful outcome.

Concluding Remarks

Wherever you undertake your research thesis or dissertation, the challenges and benefits of working in an advisee/adviser relationship have the potential to be very similar, though different models of advising may predominate in different contexts. If you enter this relationship with realistic expectations and an understanding of the challenges and power dynamics that you have the potential to experience, you will be more resilient and able to take more ownership of your project than if you enter the relationship without having given thought to how it might unfold.

There are challenges in working and relating with others in any situation. Yet your relationship with your advisor is crucial to your development as a research student. Advisors have already proven themselves to be credible and skilled researchers, and they have valuable knowledge and experience to impart to graduate advisees. For an advisee, it is important to assess what you need from your supervision committee and how the knowledge and experience they have can best be imparted to you. Your advisers will have an idea about how to do this, but we encourage you to establish a position of agency in this relationship so you can play a role in determining what it looks and feels like, how it progresses, and how you achieve success out of it.

For Further Thought and Reflection

1. What type of qualities do you need in advisors to help you to grow? Do you know yourself well enough to know what you need? In other situations in your life, what characteristics did others exhibit that helped you improve as a person and/or as an academic?

2. Each advisor/advisee relationship will be unique. What can you do to gauge how you might relate to your advisor, and how they might relate to you, before formally agreeing to work together?

3. Imagine you are having your first meeting with your advisory committee. Placing yourself in a position of agency, what would you like to come away from that meeting with in terms of having established your expectations of your committee and their expectations of you?

4. What will you do when you reach difficulties in working with your advisor? Consider what informal and formal resources you can draw on to help you to successfully navigate these difficulties.

Do Something You're Passionate About

Planning and Carrying Out Research

Sarah J. Tracy

Cris J. Tietsort

Laura V. Martinez

A cademic research provides the opportunity to explore big questions, expand understanding of our social worlds, and create scholarship that meaningfully advances our passions and commitments. At the same time, learning research methods can sometimes feel overwhelming, and excitement can occasionally give way to anxiety. In this chapter, we offer tips and recommendations for graduate students as they plan and carry out their research. We believe research can not only be personally rewarding but also serves to create better and more just social worlds. Our hope is to help alleviate some of the uncertainty that accompanies research so that graduate students remain committed and resilient.

We draw from our collective 30-year history of experience in research methods and communication studies, relevant literature, and conversations with four other graduate students. One of the hallmarks of good research is being transparent about subjective researcher positions (Tracy, 2010). The student voices included in this essay include two of the authors (Cris and Laura) as well as four others who generously offered their insight (thank you Reslie Cortés, Emi Hashi, Corey Reutlinger, and Andee Zorn). Together, this group comprises a mix of students who identify as White, Latinx, Asian, female, male, disabled, cisgender, heterosexual, and queer. These voices range across the spectrum of critical, postmodern/poststructural/postcolonial, interpretive, and postpositivist paradigms, including a range of communication subdisciplines. What's more, they practice diverse methods, such as qualitative, quantitative, archival, and/or rhetorical.

Throughout this essay, we survey nine core topics related to conceptualizing, planning, and executing research. Central themes running throughout the research process include apprenticeship, collaboration, resilience, and a strong commitment to justice, difference, and ethics. Each section provides practical action steps, and we close the chapter with several reflective questions that may help guide students as they embark on their research adventures.

Scholarly Traditions for Inquiry

As soon as they begin, graduate students are typically presented with readings and courses focused on scholarly traditions, each of which have different preferred ways of viewing reality, building (or deconstructing) knowledge, and values about what kinds of academic studies are most important. A common way of sorting through paradigms is to place them roughly in the camps of positivism, interpretivism, critical, and postmodern/poststructural/postcolonial (Tracy, 2020). Relatedly, students are introduced to different subareas of the discipline, such as activism and social justice; media studies; rhetoric; and interpersonal, intercultural, and organizational communication. So, how do graduate students go about choosing a scholarly tradition?

First, we suggest openness to different approaches and subdisciplines. "Don't feel like you have to silo yourself," Reslie encourages. Especially early in graduate school, it makes sense to take courses across a range of methodologies, paradigms, and topics. Corey affirmed, "Messy it up!" Read widely and pay attention to the subjectivities, backgrounds, and paradigms of the authors of your studies. Western European postmodern paradigmatic research (e.g., Deetz, 1998) offers one viewpoint on justice, while an Indigenous Afrocentric postcolonial paradigm (e.g., Cruz, 2014) offers quite another. It is unfortunately all too easy to silo one's reading, not only to certain paradigms but also to that authored by dominant group members. A purposeful intention toward broad and diverse reading nuances and complicates your thinking, which ultimately serves to strengthen your overall research foundation. Also, incorporating a range of standpoints is a key way for research to be justice-focused, in both process and product.

As students walk the path of learning and finding scholarly traditions, they are wise to look for those "aha" moments, make their choices consciously, and pay attention to their research questions and curiosities. You might also think about advice Andee recalled from her postgraduate supervisor: "Pick something that I would want to read at night when I was tired." Ultimately, it can be painful to focus and specialize, which feels like walking through a single door. However, it's useful to learn a range of scholarly traditions first and keep leaning in even if it starts to feel laborious. As Cris reflects:

> Paradigms can feel a bit constraining, but don't forget the heart of what you're doing. Not only are you trying to understand key philosophical foundations that inform your research, but you're also discovering what you believe about the world and how it works. No single paradigm may fit, but you still need to understand your convictions and how they inform your work.

By continuing to lean into the complexity of paradigms, not only will you emerge with a greater foundation for your philosophical convictions, but you'll also come to appreciate the offerings of other academic areas.

Developing a Topic

As you focus on your core topic, we recommend asking yourself three key questions: (a) what am I curious about; (b) what is a problem or dilemma in the world or literature that I want my research to ameliorate, dismantle, or illuminate; and (c) to what kinds of people do I want my research to be a contribution? The first asks you to be self-reflexive and hone in on the puzzles in the world that sustain your passion. The second asks you to look out to the world and to others' scholarship to see where your research could make a difference. And the third question encourages careful thinking about the kind of scholarly community you want to join and how you might extend or complicate that work. To help answer these questions, it's very useful to think inter- and trans-disciplinarily, as the same curiosities, problems, and contributions are going to be seen very differently depending on where you stand. For example, whereas many research methods suggest the importance of specific rules and procedures, González's (2000) "four seasons of ethnography" framework suggests that it's important to know who created and validated the rules and encourage researchers to ask questions that validate traditionally marginalized standpoints. Thus, if there is an injustice that you want to dismantle, it could be that some disciplines do not even acknowledge this phenomenon, let alone find it worthwhile to study. In such a case, keep searching for your scholarly comrades.

The students we spoke with landed upon their core topics in a variety of ways. Though research projects in graduate classes can at times feel like busywork, Emi argues that there is great value in being "forced to sit down and brainstorm with research ideas"—even when doing so, as Laura said, "pushes you outside of your comfort zone." Along the way, it is valuable to take note of things you learn that surprise or befuddle. Andee admitted that, "It was kind of a shock to me that women didn't rule the world. … I was like, I am quite interested in women's leadership and why New Zealand doesn't have very many women leaders." This shock helped Andee determine her thesis topic. Furthermore, sometimes students know their topic intuitively by just connecting with some mentors more than others. As Corey said, "The moment that I [took] the module with Amira [DeLaGarza], it became clear that this was very much my area. … This was me. And this was the space to grow."

Developing Skills and Using Research Methods

Research skills, from multiple regression to deconstructionism, are all craft practices. As such, they require moving beyond "knowing about" a certain body of literature, something that

Aristotle would call episteme, to encompassing how-to skills (techne) and phronesis, a practical wisdom that can only be built by immersed contextual judgment (Flybvjerg, 2001). Whereas episteme will help us understand abstractly what constitutes a survey, for instance, techne is needed to design a survey, and phronesis is fundamental for understanding when a survey is an appropriate research method. And whereas abstract knowledge can often be learned on one's own by reading books, techne and phronesis benefit from contextual immersion, apprenticing, and learning by doing (Tracy & Donovan, 2018).

When considering research methods, many students wonder whether they should learn qualitative, quantitative, rhetorical, or a mixture of all three. Qualitative methods include interviewing, fieldwork, and interaction with other human beings, often in real time. Rhetorical methods pay close attention to archival or real-time texts and may include investigation of historical documents, political speeches, or social media exchanges. Quantitative methods typically make use of experimental and survey designs and employ measurement and statistics to develop mathematical models and predictions. Some researchers choose one method over the other, whereas others choose a mix. Case in point: Kim (2018) conducted qualitative interviews, textual analysis of online interactions, and content analysis to examine social media use at work. If in doubt, Laura suggests that students "do all of the methods." Certainly, the more tools you learn, the better you will be equipped to tackle a range of projects and questions. Of course, if you know a certain type of method is the best fit for your skills and topic, then dive deep.

Research questions that begin with terms like "how," "why," or "in what ways" are usually better suited for qualitative research. If you are more interested in questions of correlation and causation, or if your questions begin with "how much" or "to what extent," then quantitative methods are likely going to be most useful. And much communication research, especially that emanating from critical, cultural, performative, and rhetorical traditions, begins with a purpose statement rather than an empirical question.

We also recommend simply paying attention to methods that feel right. If you want to understand how people self-describe the effects of a certain phenomenon, then quantitative surveys may be most appropriate. If you like to design situations where you can observe and test a certain phenomenon in a controlled setting, then experiments may be an ideal method. If you are fascinated with language in use, then rhetorical and textual analyses will be of interest. And if making meaning from an array of embodied subjective performances appeals to you, then we would encourage you to venture into the world of field methods.

In addition to taking lots of classes, students highly valued the opportunity to practice the method via an actual project. Emi said,

> Statistics aren't easily learned by reading or even watching videos. You have to do it. Until you've actually worked with your own data and conducted the analyses from start to finish, you won't truly be comfortable. Having faculty to mentor you during that process is invaluable.

Indeed, reading about regression is very different from planning and executing regression in a study. We encourage graduate students to actively reach out to their professors and to not be afraid to ask for help.

Along the way, students should give themselves time and permission to tinker, play, and fail. As Cris said, "Get your hands dirty, [and] don't be afraid of messing it up because we all mess it up early on." Skill acquisition requires that people are willing to experiment, fail, pick themselves up, and try again (Dreyfus & Dreyfus, 2005). This cycle is to be expected and celebrated rather than feared and denigrated. Certainly, there will be dead ends, pit stops, and breakdowns along the way, but these are necessary methodological breakthroughs that lead to expertise. So worry less about doing it "right," and instead just jump in, and be compassionate with yourself along the way.

Crafting Research Questions and Hypotheses

Students often wonder about when in the process of research they are supposed to develop the study's question or hypothesis. Quantitative research benefits when students carefully delineate variables, read the literature, and apply theory so they can develop informed hypotheses (hunches) and then test these hypotheses by laying them deductively onto their own study. In such studies, Laura mentioned that it is very helpful to consider desired outcomes and contributions in advance, and have these guide the sampling and research design process.

Qualitative research, in contrast, requires researchers to begin more broadly, pay attention to the unfolding material with an open mind, and make conclusions through induction (e.g., gathering lots of small parts of data to then lead to a larger conclusion). Often, qualitative research questions start out as the very broad "What is going on here?" and then repeatedly update and change to fit the particularities of the scene. In this way, qualitative research questions are as much a result of the study as they are a precursor of it.

Rhetorical and performance research often begins with a particular text or argument rather than an empirical question. For example, rhetoricians may choose to analyze the confirmation hearings of a supreme court justice, a certain type of tattoo or body piercing, or a viral YouTube video and then make arguments about what these texts served to accomplish in the world. Or performance scholars may craft an ethno-drama that brings into sharp relief a certain phenomenon of interest, whether that is racial injustice, trauma, or personal transformation.

Of course, most researchers rely on a combination of approaches to land upon their research questions, purposes, and hypotheses. One way to do so is by using abduction and working iteratively between larger universal theories and smaller details of a specific study (Thornberg & Charmaz, 2014). Emi shared, "Even when you're 'supposed' to start with a research question," it doesn't always play out that way. Thinking abductively means that students benefit in paying attention both to phenomena of interest as well as returning to the literature and talking about hunches and emerging findings with mentors. As Corey mentioned, it's better to enter research without holding tight to one's assumptions. He recommended that students allow themselves "space to [notice] what is missing. ... What hasn't been really studied in this phenomenon, and where do we need to go next?" Andee also shared about adapting her focus over the life of the research project:

> It's important to have research questions in your head as you go into a big project. Otherwise, you're not going to be narrowed. But also, as I'm talking to [my participants], it's a constantly changing context. So, I'm finding other questions that ... are far more interesting. A large part of research is just [to] constantly question what you are asking and what they're talking about and if your research questions are even important to the context.

Writing and revising research questions and hypotheses is like any other research methods skill. Dive in. Practice. Apprentice. Learn from the experience. Repeat.

Navigating the University Institutional Review Board (IRB)

Universities in many countries have human subject protections and institutional review boards (IRBs) that try to ensure that research participants are not unduly coerced, understand the study's risks, and have freedom to refuse to be involved in the study. These research boards were ostensibly designed to protect human subjects from unethical action. However, many people question the wholly ethical purpose of review boards or view them as merely posing unnecessary research hurdles (Tracy, 2020). The stringency of institutional review depends on the ethical risks of the study; for example, observing people in public carries much less risk than working with populations with diminished ability to consent, such as children, prison inmates, or those that do not speak the same language as the researcher.

So how should you navigate IRB? First, complete any training required by your institution for certification. Most universities will require students to work under the supervision of a faculty member and list that person as a coinvestigator. Students new to research are wise to choose a low-risk study initially to get some experience and receive an expedited approval. As you fill out IRB forms and paperwork, it is useful to examine models of past successful applications. Many universities also post samples of informed consent forms and recruitment scripts. We recommend that students make the most of these models as needed for their project. Remember that these boards are primarily interested in the study's effects on participants. As Laura said, you don't need "crazy amounts of details about communication theory"; the boards just need to ensure that the research is not going to cause undue harm.

IRBs typically will ask for one or more rounds of modifications on the initial application. Their requested clarifications are not designed, as Cris said, to "shut you down." Likewise, Laura said, "Don't think of it as a huge, scary monster." When IRB recommendations or requests don't make sense, we recommend you talk with your faculty supervisor and then, if needed, get on the phone with IRB, and talk through the study and how it might be modified to meet concerns. Often, you'll find they just need simple clarifications rather than major overhauls.

Most students shared relatively positive experiences with IRB, but certain types of research require extra attention. Reslie offered some tips that are especially important to consider when conducting research in different countries. When interviewing participants in a language other than that which is native to the IRB, Reslie said, "You're going to have to submit your materials, get approval for the materials (e.g., recruitment scripts and consent forms), and then translate and then get the translations approved." This extra work will likely require more time and insight, so heed Andee's advice about IRB to "ask for help … and get on to it early!"

Carrying Out the Study

You have written your research questions and have permission from your mentors and IRB to carry out your study. For many people the next part of conducting research is the most exciting. This is the time that we are able to answer those pressing questions, expand the body of knowledge, or complicate problematic assumptions that have led to unjust outcomes. Despite the exhilarating promise of carrying out a study, this is also a phase in research that can feel most uncertain and vulnerable. Being in the field—whether that field is conducting an experiment in a laboratory, engaging in virtual interviews, or traveling to engage in fieldwork—is the hot, intense, "summer" season of research (González, 2000).

A key part of any research study including human participants is recruitment. Resilience is critical in this process (Buzzanell, 2017), where one has to get used to asking, getting rejected, and trying again. Reslie explained her process:

> You have to really build up some courage to recruit on site. Mostly … I just had to walk up to people, to complete strangers, and talk to them. You have to learn how to be rejected, and be okay with it and not take it personally and to ask again. Maybe they're busy. Maybe they don't have time. Maybe they don't have the resources. And so, if you can, offer them flexibility and resources.

Further, researchers may find themselves having to adjust their recruitment criteria if they are unable to access the desired population. As Corey said, "You need to be able to cast a wide net of what you want initially, and if you need to change once you figure out that your net doesn't capture the right fish, then you can change your net to capture a different pool or go to a different lake." It is common for researchers to modify or amend their IRB applications or iteratively modify their studies along the way. The following tips may help in carrying out the research.

Pragmatically, one of the biggest mistakes that researchers make during participant recruitment is failing to take their participants' perspective. Incentives such as child care or a gift card can certainly help facilitate participation. However, it's even more important to hook into participant interests from the beginning. All too often, researchers send out emails and social media messages asserting, "I need …" and followed by a multiparagraph, jargon-laden informed consent and procedural document. Although family and friends may care about the researcher's personal needs, researchers should instead focus on participants' concerns.

As such, consider initial recruitment messages that begin with a question that speaks to potential participants. For example, "Are you a single parent struggling with child care? You are invited to share your story for a study examining the ways that workplaces can better facilitate their support of single-parent employees." This type of message puts the emphasis on the participant rather than the researcher ("you" rather than "I") and links to potential participants' concerns. When participants respond, it's important to provide full details on risks, logistics, and informed consent—and to be prompt in scheduling. Provide specifics on when, where, and how. Follow up. Try to use the participant's preferred communication channel.

Carrying out a study is more than just the summer of data collection, as González (2000) suggests in her "four seasons" epistemology. Eventually, one must exit the field. During this time, it is normal to wonder whether you have enough data, asked the right questions, or examined the appropriate texts. As you enter into the "winter" season of analysis and writing, know it can often feel cold and solitary. However, this is also an exciting time for developing research conclusions.

Working With Data and Developing Conclusions

Most graduate-level research goes beyond exemplifying or testing established theory to developing conclusions that *extend* or *complicate* theory. Developing conclusions and building theory are creative and artistic endeavors that may just as easily emerge when engaging in mundane activities like taking a walk as they do through rational linear thinking. Cris indicated how his best theoretical insights begin "bubbling around, and then boom!" come together when he goes for a run.

Although mundane activities like long runs may serve as individual theorizing incubators, Laura emphasized the importance of also collaboratively reviewing data as a practice for moving beyond individual biases or tunnel vision. Indeed, working with others provides access to their theorizing in motion. It could be as simple as a coauthor continuing to ask you: "Why is this interesting?"

If you need further structure for developing conclusions, we encourage claim-making heuristics and writing activities, such as creating typologies, naming metaphors for new phenomena, identifying surprising aspects of the project, and crafting living hypotheses (Huffman & Tracy, 2017; Swedberg, 2016). It's important to remember that writing and talking are key parts of developing conclusions. Researchers do not "write up" already developed conclusions. Rather, conclusions are developed through communicating, drafting, and rewriting.

Similar to devising research questions, it's important to remain flexible when developing conclusions. As Reslie said, "I think we can get a little arrogant and think that we already see patterns." Marinating in the data is a good way to avoid presumptive arrogance. Andee described the value of transcribing and listening repeatedly to data as a method for moving toward claims and conclusions. This process forced her to hear "that information multiple times before I even got to reading it."

Being very close to the data—through multiple listenings, readings, transcribing, and analysis—provides motivation for devising conclusions that are important to participants. Additionally, researchers can valuably engage in member reflections by sharing their tentative interpretations with research participants or other interested stakeholders (Tracy, 2010). As Corey noted, "Let the data guide you into spaces where interpretation is a possibility and then have it confirmed by members." Researchers can valuably incorporate this research step into their IRB application from the beginning. Simultaneously, it makes sense to be reading and exposing yourself to theories and conceptual frameworks external to the project at hand. Reslie said, "Take some time to try different schemas. … Exposing yourself to a variety of different literature is really helpful. Even if it's … science fiction." Indeed, the juxtaposition of different literatures and schools of thought sparks creativity and novel insight.

Reflecting on a diverse range of literature sharpens conclusions. Citational diversity in terms of race, sexuality, and abilities serves to challenge assumed views of communication and prompts conclusions that have been marginalized in the past (Ballard et al., 2020). What's more, incorporation of a variety of voices is one small move toward rectifying the imbalance and underrepresentation of race in the production of knowledge (Chakravartty et al., 2018). Most researchers agree that one's subjective identity substantially affects the research at hand. Reslie shared how reading widely, across disciplines and including a range of languages (e.g., Marte, 2008), offered rich, critical, and compassionate viewpoints that were instrumental in her research. "If you're bilingual, and are doing work in Latinidad at all, and you're not citing scholars in Spanish, you're leaving yourself a really big gap."

Engaging Ethical Research Practices

As researchers, we place ethics as central to the research process and understand that ethical considerations come in a number of different forms, including procedural, situational, relational, and exiting ethics (Tracy, 2010). IRBs are an example of procedural ethics, which refer to ethical choices dictated as necessary by larger governing bodies. Situational ethics are those required in a specific context or culture. Relational ethics focus on caring for participants as whole people, and exiting ethics ask that we as researchers consider how we appropriately extricate ourselves from a research endeavor and/or share our research with interested stakeholders.

A primary challenge we face in ethically enacting research is addressing the multiplicity of our stakeholders, including participants, potential readers, the larger scholarly community, and ourselves as researchers. IRBs are primarily focused on protecting research participants in the course of data collection (and protecting the university from being sued). However, even if the data collection does not immediately harm the participants, the eventual publication may serve as an act of ethnocentrism and colonialism (Bhattacharya, 2009). As researchers, we often encounter competing ethical tensions that must be navigated wisely.

When we asked students about the most important stakeholders in their research, they agreed that, although they certainly considered faculty supervisory committees, eventual readers, and potential grant funders, their most important ethical priorities were research participants and those who may practically benefit from the research. Corey said,

> It's not about trying to advance research. It's never about that. It's about trying to advance humanity and about trying to advance better relationships. Because at the end of the day ... the primary stakeholders are always going to be the people that benefit from the practical side of what we do.

Reslie shared that "participants are the most important thing to protect," a conviction that is fueling her development of a trauma-sensitive methodology that attends to how research may trigger and further trauma.

Protecting research participants is especially important when they are relatively low in power. As Andee said, "They're trusting me with this story." Researchers can mitigate their power relative to participants by "reminding them that they're the expert of their own experiences" as Andee continued. Understandably, graduate students often do not feel all that powerful. In fact, they may feel vulnerable and low on the hierarchy. However, as Cris said, "I think most of the time, we do have a lot of power. And I think we need to stay mindful of that."

Collaborative Work With Faculty

A recurring theme throughout this chapter has been the importance of apprenticeship. The students we spoke with agreed that collaborating with peers and faculty was crucial for learning and practicing the nuts and bolts of research design, implementation, analysis, and writing. Such collaborations not only pragmatically help students to "get more publications" but also spark their curiosity and help foster intellectual growth, research experience, and skills. Andee said, "I love bouncing ideas off of people. Especially with [academic publishing] standards, I think collaboration is almost necessary for survival." Corey cautioned, "Doing your own research can be exhausting and taxing" and explained how collaboration can be an opportunity to breathe, share, and receive acknowledgment for your own contributions.

How can students spark a collaboration? Students can purposefully enroll for a course or attend research colloquia. Students can even directly say something to a faculty member along these lines: "I would like to work with you. If there are projects that come your way where you would like to collaborate, will you let me know?" While saying this might seem awkward or forward, faculty usually appreciate the opportunity to talk about their research even when they are busy or mentoring multiple other students. Emi notes the importance of moving beyond the threat of social comparison:

> When you see someone else working with faculty on a project, you might worry that means there's no room for you. It feels like that person is competition. You might wonder if they like that person better, or if that person was presented an opportunity you weren't. But maybe, they just asked to collaborate.

And students should also bring up their own interests with faculty. Graduate students are often reading the latest literature, and faculty tend to welcome hearing about new research trajectories that might complicate or extend those with which they are already familiar.

Each research partnership is different, and students are wise to examine the faculty member's collaboration reputation. A scan of a faculty member's curriculum vitae should indicate the scope of their former supervision of research assistants, special independent readings courses, coauthored conference papers, and coauthored publications. It can be useful to reach out to these students and ask about their experience. How were they treated? What type of input did they provide on the project? Did they perceive they were provided with proper credit?

Even though the students we spoke with largely found joy and inspiration in coauthoring, collaboration can sometimes be challenging. Key concerns include: (a) data ownership, (b) necessary permissions for writing papers, and (c) determining authorship. To navigate these concerns, first, we encourage reading up on the ethics of collaboration (e.g., Fine & Kurdek, 1993). It's important to build a relationship that is not just based on a simple exchange of academic commodities. As Andee said, "Make sure [faculty] know that you are interested in learning." Second, we encourage open and early conversations to ensure you are clear and comfortable about expectations before starting a project. Reflect on crafting boundaries, and be realistic with the time and effort you can contribute. Third, we recommend being in touch frequently with collaborators. If you haven't heard from them in a while, check in, and show interest in them beyond the task at hand. Likewise, if you cannot follow through on a deadline, realize that you may be in good company. Rather than avoiding, be clear about the situation and how to move the project to the next stages. Fourth, know that some faculty engage in bad collaboration behavior. If you feel you are being taken advantage of, this warrants talking with another mentor (such as a graduate director or departmental chair) and seeking their input about potential next actions.

Moving Forward With Planning and Carrying Out Research

Hopefully, this chapter has helped reduce some uncertainty about the research process. However, your greatest learning will happen as you actually dive into your own research projects. As you do, we offer a core piece of advice: Continue to chase your passion. Research can be a challenging process, and remaining focused on your core commitments will help you remain resilient. Such focus will also help you craft your individual scholarly identity. Coming to a deep understanding of who you are as a scholar and how your work is a reflection of your commitments in the world is a key part of a sustainable research program.

In conclusion, remember that research is a process. As Corey said, "Recognize that small goals are the things that you can be proud of and that you don't have to have everything figured out." Celebrate small victories. Be okay with nonsignificant findings. Even if you find something that feels minor, know that this is still a contribution. If we hope to expand our theoretical knowledge and advocate for a more just world, we must do so one step at a time.

For Further Thought and Reflection

1. What curiosities and questions do you have about the world? How do these show up in your research questions?

2. What paradigms most resonate with you? What might these paradigms be obscuring and privileging?

3. How will your research topic enter into an ongoing academic conversation in the communication discipline? How does your research contribute to or critique this conversation?

4. Where might diverse voices and scholarship challenge, complicate, or nuance your thinking and research on a particular question? How might you proactively seek out diverse voices and participants in your studies?

5. What parts of the research process bring you the most joy? The most concern? How have you found avenues or resources for resilience during research challenges?

A Process of Discovery

Finding Your Groove as a Writer

7

Lisa Keränen

Andrew Gilmore

A colleague's social media post caught our attention. Nathan Johnson, a well-published scholar of rhetoric and media, wrote, "I'm not sure if this is common, but I mostly want to spend my time reading rather than writing. Or vacuuming. Or doing laundry. Or taking out the garbage. Or herding squirrels." The post resonated because there are many times when we, too, feel like doing anything but writing. Lisa has been known to declare "I hate writing," and even as she says it, she knows this sentiment is not quite true. Like many academics, she may sometimes procrastinate by cleaning, cooking, exercising, or caring for plants, but once she gets into a project, she quite enjoys it, especially when it is collaborative. Andy has been known to procrastinate by alphabetizing his music collection, suddenly remembering that he enjoys baking, and caring for Lisa's plants when she is out of town, but once he starts, he, too, enjoys writing. The most successful graduate students and faculty members make time to write regularly and find ways to imbue the practice with mindfulness and, on a good day, even joy and pleasure. Finding your groove as a writer is an important skill for graduate school and beyond.

Some graduate degree programs leave expectations for graduate-level writing unstated, assuming (erroneously) that disciplinary standards are readily evident and widely shared. Badenhorst et al. (2012) explain that universities, departments, and disciplines "have ways of structuring writing (genres), ways of doing research, ways of asking questions, and ways of using language"; instead of being stated openly, these "hidden requirements" can feel like "secret handshakes" or impenetrable codes to the uninitiated (p. 64). In this chapter, we attempt to make explicit some of the assumptions of graduate-level writing to facilitate your growth as a writer, as well as to encourage a mindful, creative, and structured approach that allows you to see writing as part of the routine work of both graduate study and professional life. We'll begin by outlining four tools that will help you develop as a writer, review the basics

3

of making an argument and justifying your research, and conclude with an overview of citation practices, style guides, and collaboration.

Developing Tools as a Writer

The reasons you are asked to write in graduate school are to refine your thinking, share ideas with wider audiences, and contribute to a knowledge community (Booth et al., 2008). Writing provides a way for readers to understand, assess, and engage with your ideas. Four primary tools will help you grow as a scholarly writer: adopting a writerly attitude, understanding the scholarly process, finding your voice, and making time to write.

Adopting a Writerly Attitude

Adjectives like "anxiety, distress, suffering, agony, and even torture" sometimes characterize learners' attitudes toward writing in graduate school (Badenhorst et al., 2012, p. 63). If language shapes our social reality, then reframing the writing process can help overcome roadblocks. Behavioral psychologist Robert Boice (2000) spent decades of his career studying academic writing, observing faculty write in real time. Although his insights applied to faculty, we believe they hold true for many writers. In one study, Boice compared the productivity of faculty who stored up writing for major chunks of time, engaging in practices of mindless writing, to those who built in a structure for at least 30 minutes of writing per day using practices of mindful writing, which involved moderating emotions and engaging in intentional activity. Boice found that mindless writing, "working intermittently in long stretches, in postures of physical tension, and experiencing cycles of euphoria and despair—produced considerably fewer pages of publishable scholarly prose over the course of a year" than mindful writing (Elfenbein, 2015, para. 7; see also Boice, 1989, 1997, 2000). Boice's data consistently showed that writing steadily over time was more effective than intermittent bursts. Boice's research led him to advocate an everything-in-moderation approach to writing along the lines of the adage "slow and steady wins the race". Even critiques of Boice (e.g., Sword, 2016) note that positivity, resilience, and attention to the craft of writing strengthen the development of writing skills and products overall. By approaching writing with a genuine sense of curiosity at the process of discovery, it can become a regular practice instead of an occasional and pressure-filled binge activity.

In addition to mindful and steady writing, adopting a writerly attitude entails openly soliciting and being responsive to feedback. We firmly believe that writing is made stronger when more people engage with your drafting and revision process. If peer review is not built into your required assignments, we recommend trading papers with others to offer and receive critique in advance of turning in the assignment. Your advisor or faculty member should never be the first person reading your prose. If faculty members are not assigning scaffolded writing assignments that incorporate feedback or revision into the assignment, consider asking them or other peers for feedback on drafts or portions of writing along the way.

Finally, adopting a writerly frame of mind means not being overly critical or overly attached to your prose. While some writers spend hours agonizing over each word, others are their own worst critics and slash and burn entire drafts, starting new drafts from scratch each time they sit down to write. Neither of these practices will serve you well. We recommend outlining your main points, writing quickly, and revising later, without being overly attached to your word choice in the early drafts. The initial and primary focus should be on the macro level—ensuring a clear structure, coherent focus, and evidence for all claims. Is there a central argument maintained throughout the essay? Do all the parts of your paper align? Only when the broader argument and structure are in place should you worry about the micro level of syntax, grammar, and spelling, as Rudong Zhang, a Communication University of China PhD candidate, discovered when writing in a non-native language.

> I am a native Chinese speaker who studied for a year in the United States. Writing in English was never easy for me. When I first wrote in English, I always focused on vocabulary and grammar. However, the truth was that a better structure would have helped me convey my point better than worrying about specific word choices. It would have been faster too, but it took time to develop confidence. You also have to learn the cultural differences in writing papers. In China, the expectations are more descriptive, so I had to learn about U.S. expectations.

Understanding the Scholarly Process

As the second half of Rudong's quotation explains, learning expectations are an important part of becoming a writer. At its core, graduate work involves identifying problems, posing questions, situating your projects within a scholarly literature, making and defending arguments, and assessing ideas. Foss and Waters (2007) distinguish between writing as a reporter and writing as a scholar. While writing as a reporter entails re-presenting existing knowledge, writing as a scholar involves offering unique insights gleaned from research or investigation. Instead of merely rehearsing others' arguments, scholarly writers are also expected to contribute to the development of knowledge. While some graduate-level assignments may ask for reportorial writing, by and large, the expectations for graduate-level writing include the ability to make and maintain an original argument in a clear, polished, and largely error-free professional, first- or third-person voice while synthesizing and building upon other scholarly sources.

Consider, by way of example, the differences between a popular health magazine article and the scholarly journal article that informed it. The popular health magazine article will be short, include plentiful visual images, use everyday language, and lack specific, cited scholarly references. The scholarly article will typically be longer, use specialized language, often follow a conventional format (introduction, methods, results, discussion, known as IMRaD or IMRD), include data tables and figures, and include a list of references or works cited. The popular article is most likely to have been written by a journalist or generalist, while the scholarly article is typically written by a specialist, an expert in their research area. The scholarly article also most likely underwent peer review, a process involving experts who evaluate a manuscript anonymously and recommend for or against publication based on its quality and contributions to the field. Peer review is not a perfect practice, but the idea that manuscripts are improved by having experts weigh in on them is sound.

Understanding the scholarly process also involves knowing the generic and audience expectations for your writing. *Genres* are recurrent and recognizable types of writing that contain similar organizational, substantive, and stylistic patterns (e.g., Bazerman, 2009). In higher education, literature reviews, research proposals, conference papers, journal articles, grant proposals, translational essays, and blog posts constitute distinct genres or types of writing that have unique rules and expectations. Research papers entail aligning a research method with data and analysis tools, discussing the data, and arriving at conclusions that contribute new knowledge to the field. They tend to proceed in a recognizable pattern with similar moves (Graff et al., 2016).

As you read examples from different scholarly genres, pay attention to how they are structured, how they argue, what counts as evidence, and how they use language, voice, tone, and visuals. A good exercise is to sit down and explicitly compare an article from a science or social science journal alongside one from a humanities article. What differences do you see between them? How are they differently organized? How are their arguments formulated?

Academic research and writing skills can also be transferred to nonacademic settings and can strengthen the writing you do in other areas. For University of Marland PhD student Sean Rhodes, writing for graduate school improved the movie reviews he regularly writes.

> Scholarly writing has helped me to more critically assess the movies I watch, and it has given me the language to actually discuss and contextualize what I'm seeing on screen. The language of academia and some of the structure of the writing lends itself to being able to push people to think about the media they consume rather than just to see it as "good" or "bad." I learned to see each film as a complex artifact with a message and a meaning. I think it's more important to help someone understand those messages than simply focusing on whether they think they'll have a good time. Critique helps someone contextualize what they're experiencing and gives them the ability to discuss movies in more nuanced ways than they would've otherwise. I don't think I'd have learned to think more dynamically without the helpful aid of academic writing.

Finding Your Voice as a Scholar and Writer

Some writers work hard to sound like what they think a scholar should be. This practice can sometimes produce an antiseptic disembodied social science voice, a clone of a beloved mentor or academic hero, or an ill-advised tango with a thesaurus. We recommend avoiding all three of these tendencies. As you grow as a writer, you will develop the confidence and skills to let your own voice shine through your prose. Although some publication outlets still require a somewhat dispassionate voice from above, many increasingly encourage a distinctive authorial presence. Graduate-level writing may not be the place to offer your unsupported opinions, personal preferences, or tangents, but your unique use of language will add flair and animate your writing.

Writing in a scholarly way involves merging your own interests with the expectations of your field. Badenhorst et al. (2012) maintain that academic writing can be alienating and "other" newcomers by encouraging writing that lacks history, context, narrative, and the writer's voice. They developed an intervention that encouraged creative expression to allow "students to write their own stories, their own narratives, to contextualize their own experience, and to link their personal identities to their researcher identities" (Badenhorst et al., 2012, p. 76). By reading their personal narrative writing aloud, participants began to hear their own voice as opposed to a disembodied, ventriloquized academic voice, which many had become accustomed to using in their writing. Interested readers should consult Badenhorst et al. (2012) and practice their exercise. Of course, as other chapters in this book emphasize, it helps to have a passion for your topic.

Writing can present varied opportunities, barriers, and challenges to learners depending on their unique background and identity, including their writing skills and past educational experiences, disciplinary knowledge, emotions and attitudes about writing, familial and financial support structures, and sense of inclusion or belonging in their academic community. As Rudong's earlier quotation illustrated, some learners can face additional challenges learning to write in a second, third, or fourth language on top of acclimating to new expectations for graduate school writing, a situation that is magnified by transcultural differences in writing norms and expectations. Returning students can sometimes face concerns about how the demands of their current career will differ from graduate school expectations or how graduate school itself is so vastly different from the paths taken by their family and friends. Ali Nassiri, a recent master's student who started his graduate education in the Philippines, noted how his broadcast journalism background required a different genre of writing—"a more descriptive style, including adjectives"—than faculty expected in his United States communication studies classes. Calling his process of discovery the "eternal struggles of a broadcast student in the Land of Communication," he described navigating the tension between his personal and journalistic styles of writing and writing that was acceptable to different communication faculty members. In addition to accommodating faculty preferences, some learners have emotions and attitudes about writing that serve as barriers to writing, and still others may struggle with imposter syndrome, doubting that they possess the skills or smarts to be in graduate school. A final set of barriers may include a lack of family or financial support or a sense of alienation from mainstream academic culture.

Gaining new skills takes time and patience, including a willingness to take risks and mess up along the way, and numerous resources exist to help learners navigate various writing barriers and challenges. Campus resources, such as writing centers, English Speakers of Other Languages (ESOL) support teams, and other student services can help learners to overcome writing challenges. So, too, can organizations and voluntary associations that provide mentorship, resources, and support to learners of particular identities. Finding the right mentor and supportive peer group can prove invaluable. Another important part of seeking writing assistance is to enact a *growth mindset* that sees new skill acquisition as possible and desirable instead of a *fixed mindset* that suggests change is not possible. By acknowledging the barriers and seeking guidance, assistance, and community, learners can begin to overcome their writing challenges through ongoing reflection, conversation, and practice. For some learners, a writing group can help acquire new habits, as Emily Amedée, a PhD candidate at Colorado State University, explains.

> Four years ago, I found myself at a summer "Show Up and Write" retreat. After years of working outside academia, the return to graduate school amplified my insecurity around writing. The first rule of struggling as an academic writer is you don't talk about struggling as an academic writer. On the heels of a high-strung and anxiety-laced year of writing, I needed help. "Hi. I am Emily, and I am a binge writer." Group writing, for me, served as a guided meditation. I benefited from learning and working through the common failures and follies that many writers experience (e.g., procrastination, not sufficiently blocking out time, losing momentum, etc.). Over time, I was able to sustain my writing practice independently, and I became quicker to recognize when I was falling into old habits. I may now write in isolation, but I also now have the skills to keep writing.

Making Time

Good writing rarely happens overnight. Professional writers often say that it can take anywhere from three to 10 drafts of a manuscript to reach a final product. If this much redrafting sounds daunting, it helps to think of your writing projects in terms of smaller chunks. "Writing a paragraph explaining the rationale" of your study is much easier than "writing a paper for graduate seminar." "Revising an introduction" in one session is more manageable than tackling "an entire draft." Foss and Waters (2008) offer guidelines for breaking your writing into smaller, manageable tasks, while Belcher (2009) explains the parts of writing a scholarly article. Many apps can also help you break your writing projects into smaller chunks and allocate time for them on your calendar. Ask your cohort and faculty members for their recommendations of apps, and be sure to block out time on your calendar for reading, reviewing, synthesizing, drafting, revising, and polishing.

Making Arguments in Your Writing

One of the marks of scholarly writing is being able to make and sustain an argument throughout an essay. What is meant by "an argument," however, often remains unstated. For most research papers, your argument consists of the answer to your research question or the findings of your test of your hypothesis. For a literature review, the argument captures the essence of your categorization of the literature and may include its gaps and areas for future investigation. For an article critique, the argument encapsulates your assessment of the strengths and areas to be strengthened of the article.

Consider these two arguments from two essays published in recent issues of *Communication Education*:

- "Participants [in the interview study] revealed that they feel chronically misunderstood by their communication partners" (Bernaisse, 2020, p. 1).

- "The traditional student construct, rooted in citizenship and whiteness-centering discourse, exacerbates student precarity" (Bahrainwala, 2020, p. 257).

The first argument presented the central finding from interview data of people with an autism spectrum disorder [ASD] who were asked about their communication concerns and their communication with instructors. It broadly answered the research question: "What concerns do young people with ASD report about their interactions?" The body of the paper elaborated the specific ways that students felt misunderstood. The second argument offered a rhetorical analysis of the idea of the "traditional student" and made a claim about the harms the idea of the traditional student can do to students who work, support family, are people with disabilities, and who are minoritized learners. In the first essay, supporting evidence came from the voices of the participants themselves in response to interview questions; their responses were organized into themes, and the snippets of their answers served as evidence of the themes. In the second argument, evidence of precarity, that is, of experiencing ongoing financial or wage insecurity, originated from student wage data and demographics, while evidence of the traditional student concept emerged from unpacking its historical assumptions and association with discourses of immigration and citizenship.

The alignment of your research question, method, and literature review terms can help you sharpen your argument as you answer your research question. Figure 7.1 contains an example of an aligned hypothetical research project.

In the following figure, you will note the strong relations among the research question, key terms, data, method, and significance.

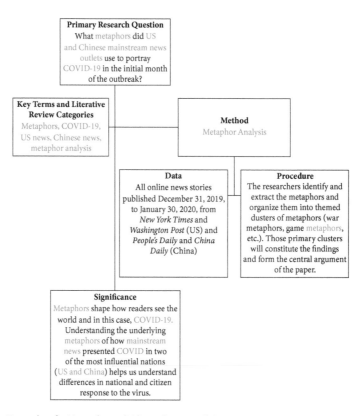

FIGURE 7.1 Example of a Hypothetical Aligned Research Project

Writing an Abstract and Key Terms

Abstracts

After typing thousands of words onto your computer screen, you might think that writing the 100 or 250 words for an abstract would be easy. Writing an abstract, however, can feel like an arduous process. But being able to concisely summarize the key components, argument, method, and findings of your study is an important skill, and the good news is that writing an abstract can, in fact, help you to check that you have done what you set out to do. Writing an abstract will help you to answer a number of questions, including (a) are your argument and research question(s) clear; (b) have you answered your research question(s); (c) do you have enough evidence; (d) is your method clear; and (e) is too much or too little going on in your essay? Writing an abstract (and key terms) is advantageous when writing an essay or term paper for a class or seminar, even if doing so is not an explicit requirement for the assignment. Just like every other element of your essay, your abstract should go through multiple revisions and reflect research alignment.

The length of your abstract depends on a number of elements, including your chosen citation style guide, the conference or journal to which you might send your essay, your professor's preference, or the purpose of your essay (e.g., thesis and dissertation abstracts are often longer). The goal of an abstract is for somebody who is unfamiliar with your study to be able to read the abstract and gain a clear sense of what you have done, how you did it, and what you found. One easy formula for constructing a social science abstract is to include one sentence for each of the following: purpose, method, results, discussion, and conclusion or implications.

Key Terms

In addition to your abstract, your essay will also need a number of key terms. Once your essay is published (even if this is online on your own website), it will be indexed in databases and search engines. The key terms you choose will determine if people can find your work. Consequently, while you often only need around five key terms (this number might change depending on the conference, interest group/division, or journal), these terms should be considered very carefully.

We recommend a number of strategies for deciding on your all-important key terms. First, in social science research, your key terms will often come from your research question and form the main categories in a literature review. Alternately, you can scan your essay or do a search in your word processor for the most common words used throughout your essay. Another approach (although not foolproof) is to take your abstract and try to reduce it into a single sentence or two, then underline or bold the important/key words. Your key terms should cover the general subject matter that you are writing about, without being too broad. So what is your essay about? One way to test your key terms is to put them into your library database or Google Scholar. Do essays similar to yours appear? If so, you are probably choosing appropriate key terms.

Developing the Rationale for the Study

A key argument you need to make in graduate-level writing is to explain why your topic merits investigation. You must, in short, argue for its significance. This "so-what" question supplies the why of your analysis and is sometimes called the justification, the significance, the problem, the need, or the rationale. Regardless of its name, this argument addresses the reasons that your analysis needs to be conducted. Often, the reason is practical (a problem exists in the world that research can help alleviate), personal (your experience leads you to want to understand), or conceptual/theoretical (scholars do not understand an aspect of the topic). A health communication study of interventions to discourage opioid abuse might connect the study to the practical need to reduce the number of people who abuse fentanyl. A rhetorical analysis of #BlackLivesMatter protests might connect to the conceptual need to understand how social media can be used to promote positive social change. In scholarly writing, the rationale is often couched in terms of a scholarly conversation, something that is a problem or puzzle in the literature. Even when the topic has deep personal significance to you, your readers will appreciate when you explain why it matters to them.

Foss and Waters (2008) make clear that just because no one has written about your topic before doesn't mean it's worth writing about. Beginning scholars can sometimes find it difficult to develop a rationale for their study because they have not been steeped in the literature. Booth and his coauthors (2008, p. 51) have developed a statement that helps supply the "so what":

1. Topic: I am studying _____

2. Question: because I want to find out what/why/how _____

3. Significance: in order to help my reader understand _____.

Answers to the third question can form the basis for a rationale.

Using Literature to Develop an Argument

Scholarly arguments must be supported by evidence. To better understand the common moves of how to integrate literature into your argument, we recommend reading Graff et al. (2015) and Booth et al. (2008). In general, though, much of the body of your paper will consist of analysis using evidence from your research or from the texts or artifacts under investigation. In the example from Figure 7.1, the evidence of the central claim about metaphors in U.S. and Chinese mainstream news coverage will be examples from the news stories themselves that demonstrate each metaphorical pattern.

There are several types of sources you can use to support your argument. While primary sources are firsthand or eyewitness accounts, reflections, and recollections of an event or topic, a secondary source is one step removed from an event or topic. Rather than providing a personal account, secondary sources evaluate, analyze, and interpret information from primary sources about an event that has already occurred. The distinction between primary and secondary sources, however, is not always obvious. For example, an autoethnography published in a peer-reviewed journal could be classed as a primary source, as it provides a firsthand account of an event/experience. Online content can also prove to be tricky to evaluate, and the context in which something is published or written should always be considered. One question to ask yourself when trying to distinguish between a primary or secondary source is "Is this a firsthand account, or is it drawing from other people's experience?"

TABLE 7.1 Types of Sources

PRIMARY SOURCES	SECONDARY SOURCES	TERTIARY SOURCES
Interviews	* Peer-reviewed journal articles	* Dictionaries/Encyclopedias
Observations	* Textbooks	Guidebooks
Surveys and questionnaires	* Online sources (use cautiously)	Manuals
Speeches		* Online sources (use cautiously)
Photographs		
Historical and legal documents		
Archive material		
Personal correspondence (including letters and diary entries)		
Government documents		
Works of art and literature		
Newspaper/Magazine articles		
* Online sources (use cautiously)		

These sources can straddle multiple columns.

Citation Styles and Academic Integrity

Style manuals offer guidelines for how to format papers, citations, and references. They are markers of belonging to a particular scholarly community. Historically, in the United States, many social science communication scholars have preferred the style guide of the American Psychological Association (APA), while rhetorical scholars often write in Chicago style (CMS). The style manual of the Modern Language Association (MLA) is another commonly used style for communication scholars who publish in humanities journals. Internationally, other styles may be preferred. In graduate seminars, your choice of a style may be determined by faculty preference, while some faculty may ask you to use any style you want as long as you use it properly. Beginning writers often underestimate how much being able to properly cite their sources speaks to their credibility.

As you learn about writing as a graduate student, it is important to become well educated on the standards and expectations for the highest levels of academic honesty, especially when it comes to using and citing sources of information and the words of others. The ethical principles of transparency, respect for others, and fairness dictate that you make sure you are thoroughly familiar with and know how to use and cite sources. It is also essential you understand what constitutes plagiarism (see for example COPE, 2019; Roig 2015), remembering that you can also plagiarize your own previous work (this is called *self-plagiarism* and sometimes, if you publish similar works, *duplicative* or *dual publication*). Another serious ethical breach, called *contract cheating*, involves hiring someone else to do your academic work and writing.

The term *research integrity* involves honesty and transparency in conducting academic inquiry and in writing about/communicating your results. It encompasses a set of standards for how to treat others with respect, openly credit the work of others, and act honestly and openly through all phases of academic life. By contrast, the term *research misconduct* includes *fabrication* (making up data, results, or sources), falsification (altering or changing data, results, or sources), *plagiarism* (using or copying someone else's ideas, text, or images/artwork without proper attribution), or any other behaviors that deviate from widely accepted standards in your academic community. Research misconduct can occur at any stage of inquiry, from writing a proposal to communicating research results to borrowing someone else's ideas during an anonymous peer review process. Ethical lapses, whether intentional or not, can negatively impact your reputation and career. Serious lapses can even end academic and professional careers. Being clear, accurate, and skillful when quoting and paraphrasing are critically important, as are avoiding sloppiness in notetaking and attribution. For a guide to ethical writing that discusses how to avoid improper writing and research practices and that includes examples of how to paraphrase and attribute ethically, see Roig (2015).

Choosing a Style

When beginning a piece of writing, it helps to have a target audience in mind. While this might seem premature (and you might not initially have any intention of submitting a piece to a conference or publication), this process will ensure that you start out using the style that is accepted by that audience. If you have an outlet in mind, starting with the correct citation style will save you time and inconvenience. Also, selecting a future possible publication outlet can help you with your literature review (you can cite previous work that has been published by the journal), abstract, and key terms. Moreover, by looking at the editorial board of the journal, you can gauge who your essay might be sent to during the peer-review process. For seminar papers, you may wish to have a target conference in mind. Bear in mind a paper will need to undergo rigorous revision from a seminar paper to a conference paper to a publication. Many writers underestimate how much revision is required to move from first draft to final publication. While many professors will list their preferred style guide in their syllabus, other professors are open to you using a different style if you advocate your position, such as your plans to submit to a particular conference.

Researching a Style

Each conference call and journal website lists important information for authors, including the required citation style. Submitting an essay that uses APA to a journal that requires Chicago, for example, communicates a lack of audience adaptation and professional know-how. Some editors will "desk reject" manuscripts that do not conform to the journal's style, sending them back unread to the author.

Cite as You Go

While you might be tempted to include loose citation notes as you write, going back and fixing these after the essay is finished is time-consuming. Moreover (and this has happened to us), in the midst of writing, you may think that your loose citation notes will be enough to help you find the source again and cite it fully a few weeks down the line, but this isn't always the case! If you really don't want to work on citations while you are writing, plan to set aside a small amount of time at the end of each writing session to fix citations.

Citation Managers

Although citation managers like Zotero and EndNote can be helpful with organization and timesaving, these programs are not always perfect. If using a citation manager, be sure to still carefully proofread and check each citation before you submit your essay. Your graduate program will likely have recommendations based on campus library compatibility.

Writing Collaboratively

Often, graduate students who work with faculty and other graduate students find such partnerships enriching and highly productive. Because we believe that the best work results from a convergence of minds, we encourage this practice. Utah PhD candidate Madison Krall explains how her writing group has allowed her to develop and grow as a researcher while publishing in several top-ranked venues.

> My writing group experience has taught me, first and foremost, that kindness and expressions of appreciation set the tone for any successful research group. Acknowledging everyone's contributions fosters stability within the group and sets the scene for positive interactions in the future. Second, a research group must clearly outline author expectations before beginning new projects. Because membership changes, it is vital that groups thoughtfully orchestrate how everyone's projects will integrate second, third, fourth, etc., authors into the unfolding process of research and manuscript writing. I recommend graduate student members share any grievances about author order with the faculty leader early on so roles can be reassigned. Finally, make sure at least one member regularly checks in with everyone regarding project progress throughout the year. Since most of us work on several research projects at once, frequent communication helps folks feel supported while they complete their first-author project.

1. Writing is an exercise. Do a little bit each day or on a regular schedule, and it becomes easier. Avoiding the binge and purge model of writing allows you to do your best work slowly over time.

2. Schedule blocks of time in your calendar to write and make them sacred. If you aren't feeling in the mood some day and can't overcome it, at least work on your references list or take notes.

3. Just start by typing anything. It will help you get in the groove. (Andy begins by "sightless typing"—turning the brightness down on his laptop so that he can't see his screen. He writes for 10 or 15 minutes, then turns up the brightness again to see what he has. Yes, the screen will be full of spelling and grammatical errors, but it is a great starting point. This method means you are writing without judging yourself. Lisa begins by typing in quotations from other scholars she thinks she may want to use, and once she starts typing them, she finds she can write.)

4. If you are not sure how to get into a scholarly voice, read a few journal articles related to your topic, and adopt a similar style that still lets your voice shine through.

5. Proofread your work carefully on paper before turning it in. Better yet, print it out and have others proofread it for you. Reading a print version is important because it helps find errors easily missed on a screen.

6. Remember that planning your essay or outlining a section of the essay or working on citations is still part of the writing process.

7. Accountability can help those who tend to prioritize other projects. Find a friend, family member, app, or colleague to help keep you on track, or join a writing group.

8. Many writers do not know exactly what their argument will be until they finish the first draft. Be sure to go back and polish your second draft by aligning all the pieces of the draft with the argument you discovered during the drafting process.

9. Be kind to yourself and your drafts.

10. Make writing *the* sole priority during your scheduled writing time. Turn off your Wi-Fi, close extra browser windows and social media, and invite family members to give you space. If children, partners, family, and pets can't or won't leave you alone, arrange for some solo writing time.

FIGURE 7.2   Lisa and Andy's Top 10 Writing Hacks

Like Madison, we firmly believe that those who begin collaboration should do so following an explicit—and, ideally, documented—agreement about the roles, expectations, ethical norms, and best practices for working as a team member. A number of rubrics and guidance documents explain processes for determining authorship credit and assigning the order of authors as well as resolving author conflicts; we recommend Committee on Publishing Ethics (COPE, 2019).

As we drafted, redrafted, revised, and polished this chapter, we endeavored to follow our own advice. Were we perfect about writing each day? Not always. But we wrote regularly enough with a mindful attitude that led to on-time completion with time enough for revision and reframing. We recognize, however, that writing is not a one-size-fits-all set of prescriptions, and what we offer is merely what works for us, as outlined in Figure 7.2. We wish you luck on the journey to discovering your own habits and techniques as you grow and evolve as a writer.

For Further Thought and Reflection

1. Choose a metaphor that best describes your writing process. What are the benefits and drawbacks of this metaphor? What might be a more productive and useful metaphor?

2. Describe your ideal writing session. What promotes your best writing?

3. What are the biggest barriers to your writing? What psychological and physical steps can you take to remove them?

4. What commitments can you make to yourselves and your classmates to make the craft of writing a regular practice?

8

"Yikes! What Do I Do Now?"

Advice for Graduate Students Sharing Their Work

Ronald L. Jackson II

Celnisha Dangerfield

The graduate experience is a grand experiment that exposes us to the existing breadth of disciplinary knowledge while simultaneously creating incubators of new ideas to shape the world. Students are taught to challenge themselves and the ideas of others and are also invited to become conduits for change. While undergraduate education is mostly sharing your work with a single faculty member, graduate education provides opportunities to branch out and share your work with others in your program, in your discipline through conference and publications, and in your communities through translating scholarship for those who would benefit. Somewhere along the way though, for many graduate students, imposter syndrome creeps in—causing some students to question whether they have chosen the right path, whether they belong, or whether they have the ability to make meaningful contributions to the discipline. Left questioning how or where to move next, some find themselves flailing, trying to compensate for feelings of inadequacy, comparing themselves to their peers, submitting underprepared work, or, in the most extreme cases, feeling as though they have been rendered mute. Anxiety, insecurity, and fear keep some from sharing their work with others, limiting or canceling the possibility of impact. The key to increasing output and to instilling the confidence to share one's work is in demystifying the process of presenting at conferences and publishing one's work.

Graduate student life is riddled with uncertainty. There is so much newness to adapt to, and students report feeling overwhelmed by the expectation to learn rapidly and then apply what they have learned just as quickly. From the time one enters into a master's degree program and receives a first-semester syllabus with an end-of-semester literature review assignment, the heightened anxiety begins. The imposter syndrome creeps in, and students wonder whether they missed a presemester seminar on literature reviews. They are told that literature reviews are a staple in a graduate student's intellectual diet, but they still do not know what a literature review is. It is as though it is a hidden curriculum, a competency that is an unwritten expectation of all graduate students but is rarely formally taught. There will always be some challenges to progress, but guidance along the way helps ensure students make better use of the time spent in their graduate program, leading to the production of high-caliber work that positively impacts the discipline.

For those choosing to pursue a career in academia, success necessarily involves sharing your work with others. Admittedly, this can be a scary prospect, whether you are sharing your work in a conference presentation or as a publication. There may be broad-based insecurity about exposing your writing and ideas to scrutiny or even a lack of clarity about the steps necessary to navigate the process; however, the importance of sharing should overrule those concerns. The dedicated researcher must push past uncertainty to reach career goals, to impact the discipline, and to ensure others get exposure to the work produced. Within this chapter we discuss two primary ways people tend to share their work within academe—presenting at professional conferences and publishing one's work.

Professional Conferences: A Prime Launching Pad

One of the easiest ways to begin sharing your work outside of the classroom is through academic conference participation. Far more than a space for socializing and "hanging out," conferences provide opportunities for intellectual compatibility. They tend to be affirming spaces, which is powerfully important, especially when your work is subsumed under a specialized area of study that is not largely represented in your graduate department. Beyond that, the opportunity to connect with other scholars with similar interests fosters intellectual stimulation and engenders the development of new creative spaces.

A conference should be considered worthwhile to you if it enhances your academic experience now and helps you advance your long-term career goals too. Networking is a prime example. Far more than just hanging out or attending parties, networking gives graduate students the opportunity to glean from more seasoned scholars in the field while fostering relationships with peers across the discipline. Some students new to academic conferences may initially worry about not knowing anyone and wanting to find a sense of community. When sharing one's work, newcomers will often find that audience members will want to learn more and even want to get to know the presenters better. In that way sharing one's work can be a great start to building community.

Camaraderie develops as you commune with others, but it can also lead to assistance in finding other graduate programs for master's students, post-doc opportunities, and jobs, not to mention help finding (and securing access to) important resources like people, texts, and all kinds of other pertinent information. Again, knowing your desired destination should drive every other decision you make in this process, including which conferences to attend, how many to attend, and whether or not the benefits (short and long term) outweigh the costs associated with attendance. Over time, consistent attendance at conferences produces exponential benefits, which means a strategic financial and social investment early in your career could continue to pay strong dividends long after the conference event ends.

There are a lot of conference options out there, and this could make choosing the right one(s) a bit overwhelming. Just remember the best conference fit for you will vary based on your area of study, mentoring needs, location, and career goals. Do your research, and confer with faculty mentors to find the unique mix of conferences that will help you get the most out of your graduate experience. This can be especially important for international students who have the added responsibility of getting adjusted not only to the university and profession but also to the country and its way of doing things.

Before getting into the details, it is important to give voice to graduate students who experience anxieties around sharing their work at professional conferences. Here are two students who share their own personal standpoints. First, Staci, a first-year doctoral student at University of Pennsylvania, states:

> As a graduate student I would have to say when I go to present at conferences most of my anxieties come from thinking about how the tools and methods I use as a Black feminist researcher will be regarded. I wonder whether they will be valued. Although I see the validity and utility of Black feminist ethnography, for example, I also get that it can sometimes be read as lacking methodological or conceptual rigor. This is often because these methods may not be widely taught in other graduate programs. Anyhow, that concerns me as I prepare to convey my ideas through this lens.

Staci's perspective is an important one. One thing first-timers wonder is whether they will fit in or whether their work will be valued. Staci's angst subsided once she attended a national conference and found that what she thought was a narrow niche in the field was not so narrow after all. As previously mentioned, intellectual compatibility is certainly one of the advantages of attending professional conferences.

Alice, a second-year master's student at University of Cincinnati, is an international student from China. She shared her perspective as well:

> When I think about presenting my work at a professional conference, I worry about whether the largely American audience will value my perspective. Am I going to be the weirdo on the panel? Are they going to judge me for what I am thinking, and do so based on their biases? Will people expect me to represent all of China? As a Chinese student this topic is really sensitive.

Alice's comments reflect a genuine concern shared by many international students. In a politically charged national milieu, the question of immigration and international citizenship is at the forefront of national media. It makes sense that Alice would be concerned about how biases might intercept the audience's regard for her perspective. She has been surprised to learn that the major associations like the National Communication Association (NCA) and International Communication Association (ICA) have a substantial number of non-U.S. members and even have interest groups that are aligned with various continental cultural perspectives. This alleviated some of the anxiety about being treated differently.

Deciding which conference is right for you is important, but there are still several more points to consider when preparing to share your work there. Let's examine each step of the conference experience from submission to presentation.

Submission Considerations

Submission for a conference usually takes place four to eight months before the conferences. The process begins with knowing where and when to submit. This is why being familiar with the types of conferences early on is important. Discerning the best home for your work minimizes the likelihood of conference-hopping just for the sake of securing an acceptance, ensures that one's efforts are concentrated towards the most beneficial outlets, and decreases the likelihood of work being rejected merely because the conference (or division of a conference) chosen is not the ideal outlet for your submission. Familiarity with specific conferences also allows you to track calls for events and publications related to your specific area of study or that are most closely aligned with your professional goals.

A helpful strategy here is paying attention to the listing of upcoming conferences, calls, and announcements, such as those posted to the National Communication Association COMMNotes Listserv (and you do not need to be a member to join). Whether through listservs, the sponsoring organization's website, a unique conference page on those websites, or even via social media, conference organizers typically provide an announcement that spells out expectations for potential submissions. Your job is to make sure that your proposed contribution matches those expectations as closely as possible.

Before taking the time to craft a submission, though, it is important to remember that building and protecting your reputation in academic circles potentially begins and ends at the level of submission. Without a doubt, there is an ethical responsibility that comes with sharing your work. The adage is true: "If you submit, you must commit." Thus, you need to consider if you have the time and financial resources to attend if your paper is accepted for presentation. After all, there are a number of investments that go with the review process. It is unfair and unprofessional to ask others to make an investment in you and your work only to have you pull out of the event after acceptance. Plus, if there are a limited number of spots allotted, your work's acceptance potentially means the exclusion of others that may be more committed to attending. Avoid the unethical practice of merely submitting your work just to say you did so or submitting more than you could complete with a degree of excellence.

Once you have made the decision to submit your work, there are still more decisions to make. The following list provides just a few of the questions that should be considered at this point in the submission process.

- Does it make more sense for you to submit a completed paper or an abstract for a future project?

- Would you prefer to put together your own group of presenters for a panel, submitting a collective set of abstracts all fitting under the conference's theme?

- For a completed project, is it ready for submission for a Top Paper Award?

- Will you need A/V equipment if it is available?

- Are you thinking of submitting more work than you could realistically complete?

The Paper/Panel Review Process

Once your work has been submitted to a conference for review, it will be considered by members of the planning committee for the conference or a particular division (or caucus) within the organization's larger structure. It is usually peer reviewed by two or more people who make a recommendation to the planner. There are a number of factors that go into the likelihood of your work being chosen for inclusion, so it is important to remember that submission does not guarantee acceptance. Mitigating factors include the quality of your submission—especially when compared to the submissions of others—in conjunction with the appropriateness of the submission for the conference, the particular theme, and the specific panel for which it is being considered. There are constraints on members of the planning committee related to time and space allotments, interest in particular submission formats, the implied relationship between past attendance and support of particular interest groups/causes/areas of study, and the proportion of membership connected to specific areas of research (as determined through alignment with particular divisions, caucuses, special interest groups, etc.). Thus, the likelihood of acceptance is influenced by a number of factors, not just your decision to share your work in the first place. Conference planners are looking to choose the very best submissions for the limited spaces they have to fill, but if you never take a chance, your efforts can never be rewarded.

Carrying Out Your Obligations

So now you have submitted your work, and let's say it has been accepted. Congratulations! Now what? Well, there are two angles of responsibility that have to be considered: your obligation to the audience as a presenter and your obligation to your respondent (the person who will read your paper and make remarks at the panel), if you have one. As a communication scholar, the expectation for effective delivery should be clear. However, to remove all uncertainty, the following tips are offered.

- Find out the time limit for your paper (you may email the panel chair), and practice to meet your time requirement.

- Avoid reading your work to your audience. Extemporaneous delivery should be the strategy you adopt since it affords the opportunity to look at your audience, convey a sense of familiarity with your subject matter, and keep your audience engaged with your content.

- If you are not a performance scholar, maintain a professional presentation style in line with what might be expected of an established scholar in the field.

- Practice your presentation out loud to an audience, especially faculty members who can give you helpful feedback. Perhaps request a practice section for graduate student presenters.

- Have multiple ways to present in case the unthinkable happens. Remember, the show must go on even if you lose your notes or the digital equipment does not work.

- Practice mindfulness to avoid offending your audience.

- Consider your reputation. While this starts with the submission stage, the delivery of your content is yet another opportunity to establish and protect your reputation. You want to be seen by your audience as a prepared, polished, budding scholar and not as someone who cavalierly threw something together at the last minute without putting in a respectable degree of work or thought. This does not mean you must be perfect; it does mean you want to be professional.

Most of the focus on sharing your work is in the buildup to the big day. However, the responsibility to your respondent should be met before the day of presentation. Plan to send your paper to the respondent two weeks in advance (this expectation should underscore why overcommitting is a bad idea). Submitting a lot of panel proposals means you will ultimately be expected to write and present a lot of papers. Again, these realities point back to the importance of maintaining your reputation.

Earlier we spoke of planning with your goals in mind. A respondent is an invaluable resource that provides feedback on your work. Use the respondent's feedback, in conjunction with helpful feedback from your audience, to further enhance your project. If your ultimate goal is publication, you cannot afford to squander this opportunity. Keep in mind that creating a revolving cycle of conference presentations that are produced and then shelved means that the potential reach of your work is closed immediately after your conference presentation. A high number of conference presentations and low number of publications may also signify to those reading your CV that you must be presenting low-quality work that is incapable of being published. Presenting at conference is a great first step. Publishing is another significant step toward sharing your work within a community of scholars.

Publishing Your Work

Perhaps one of the most daunting tasks in the mind of most beginning researchers is getting their work published. If you have never done it before, then it makes sense you would have lots of questions, including the following: (a) why should I publish my work, (b) how do I know my work is ready for publication review, (c) how should I structure my manuscript, (d) where should I publish, and (e) what's the process for getting published? These are all critical queries of which every novice should have some concern, and these questions will be addressed in this chapter.

Why Should You Publish Your Work?

The purpose of publication is to widely distribute new knowledge. While master's students may publish their work, publication is usually more expected of doctoral students. You may have heard of the word "heurism," or "heuristic." It is used to describe scholarly work that contributes to the advancement of discovery and practice. People publish or showcase their work in a wide variety of platforms, such as documentary film, professional practice magazines, academic journals, edited books, scholarly monographs, performances (e.g., stage plays, spoken word poetry, dance, oral interpretation, and drama). When most communication scholars use the words "publishing my work," they are ordinarily referring to having their work published in the form of journal articles or books.

The primary impetus for publishing one's work is to contribute to extending the understanding of known phenomena. Research has the power to enhance our collective understanding and/or transform practice. Many new pivots in humans' understanding of the world began with asking questions and seeking to address answers through systematic investigation. As our world evolves, so does what we know about it. Consequently, the publication of communication research will always be necessary as a way to document our paradigm shifts.

There are other motivations for publishing as well. Those who choose to establish a career in academe as a professor will likely be on a tenure track or some system of evaluation. For many systems, a major evaluation criteria is publication of one's work. It is proof that one has added value to the profession. Although we will not elaborate on the details here, universities across the globe have their own standards regarding the frequency and placement of one's published research. If you are a graduate student with an interest in joining the professoriate, then there is a bit of added pressure. It will be incumbent upon you to start publishing early in graduate school if you want to land your ideal job after graduation—especially since the job market has become quite competitive. You should ask yourself: "What do I want to be known for?" Next, you need to take time to write an outline of your 3-year research plan. This simply requires that you map out article titles that build on one another so that you ultimately have a program of research with more depth than breadth. Your goal should never be to become a jack-of-all-trades, master of none. We suggest you work with your advisor or other faculty for advice to help you plan.

Beyond a general interest in contributing to new knowledge and attaining tenure, one might also be motivated to publish for no other reason than for the sake of posterity. Consider how long the writings of Cheikh Anta Diop, Aristotle, W. E. B. Du Bois, and others have been with us. They have survived the test of time. We doubt Aristotle imagined that his work would have been studied in classrooms around the world thousands of years after his death. There is something exciting about knowing that your work has the potential to influence people for generations to come.

Now that you have a sense of a few reasons why people choose to share their work through publication, it might be useful to know how to ascertain whether your work is publication-ready.

How Do You Know You Are Ready for Publication?

Every graduate student has been assigned a written research paper, usually a literature review for a class. That is a great place to start. No matter where you are in your matriculation through a graduate program, it is really important that you find mentors you can trust to give you honest and detailed feedback about your work. Let your professors know that you would like to get your work published, and ask them to read your work with an eye toward publication.

So how do you know when your writing is ready for publication? There are at least three ways of discerning whether your work is ready to be submitted for publication review, and by that we mean having your manuscript submitted to a journal. For our purposes here, we have excluded discussion of publishing a book as a first step since that is ordinarily an advanced next step after graduate school and establishing a track record of journal article publications.

First, the easiest way to get started is to thoroughly acquaint yourself with the mainstream and specialty journals of the field. This is where most of us get our initial inkling of what a journal article looks like. As you get to know the journals, you need to look for specific things. You should be trying to ascertain which tone and writing styles are appropriate for which journals. Look at how authors introduce and then develop their main ideas. Consider what literature they use. Before you get started preparing your manuscript for publication, think about the journal outlet where you want to send your work. This will have some bearing on how you write the manuscript.

Years ago, the first author here wrote an article for one of the major journals in our field. He studied the journal, as we are suggesting, before submitting his work for review. He knew his theoretical approach, literature review, and methods were sound, but he had to get the tone and writing style right. He found the writing in this journal a bit obtuse and unnecessarily complicated, but it was considered the top journal in the field, so he felt he had to place his work there. The authors of each of the articles in several issues of this journal seemed to enjoy using highfalutin vocabulary, and apparently, it led to them being successfully published, so the author surmised that he had to emulate that approach. To his surprise the formula not only worked like a charm but he also might have overdone it. One of the reviewers commented that the use of big words to describe ideas was excessive. He took this as a lesson that he needed to not just use grandiloquent word choices, but also had to ensure his ideas were clearly articulated and understood!

Stefanos, an international second-year graduate student from University of Cincinnati, writes:

> When I am beginning the process, my major concerns circle around what I want the paper to be. I wonder how personal versus academic the paper should be, the content, as well as the writing style. Also, I'm drawn to topics that are still considered taboo or progressive (e.g., drag, gender fluidity, sex, etc.). That adds a lot of pressure in terms of discussing what I'm interested in, and what is deemed as acceptable. After I'm done writing, I am more worried about having made my writing more personal and to how I (and my writing) will be perceived.

Stefanos expresses common concerns about writing style, topic selection, and readers' reception of the work. While familiarizing yourself with journal writing styles and aligning one's own writing with those styles is one way of ensuring one's own writing is publication-ready, there are at least two other ways. Consider these approaches:

- Find two people who might even be peers (perhaps a year or two ahead of you in your graduate program) to proofread your work and give you feedback. Ask them to look for tone, style, structure, and approach. The approach may include the extent to which the manuscript demonstrates conceptual consistency and/or methodological rigor.

- Ask well-published professors for guidance on the structure of publishable manuscripts. Take copious notes, then ask them if they would be willing to read your final draft and give you feedback.

You should take your cues on how to structure your manuscript from these three sources—independent read of journals, peer review of your manuscript, and professor/mentor review of your work. Ultimately, you will know you're ready to start thinking about publishing when you are clear that you have something important and unique to add to the extant literature. Once you know you have something heuristic to conceptually contribute, then the next step is figuring out where to publish.

Where Should You Publish?

This is the million dollar question. We learned a long time ago that no matter what you write, there is usually a home for it somewhere. This is precisely why the standards for publication are as rigorous as they are, because at some point the quality of communication inquiry suffers if authors can write anything and have it automatically be accepted. Unfortunately, over the years, there have been independent journal outlets with vastly different degrees of quality content from one issue to the next. Some are online-only journals. Some journals even come with corporate ads inside. In order to cut through the ambiguity, we suggest you decide where to publish based on three basic criteria:

- **relevance:** Align your topic with what your target journal tends to publish. In other words, the journal's audience reflects how relevant a given journal is to your area of inquiry. If you are a relational communication scholar who studies dating and mating behaviors, then *Quarterly Journal of Speech* is probably not going to be your ideal target journal unless you are studying the rhetoric of these behaviors. It is far more likely you will want to go with a specialty journal like *Journal of Social and Personal Relationships* because they tend to publish work aligned with your topic.

- **methodology:** There are some journals that are historically more friendly toward one methodology over another. Keep in mind methodology refers to the philosophical approach that guides inquiry. To put it perhaps overly simplistic, most people think of methodology as quantitative versus qualitative or even triangulated (combined) methods of collecting data. So the point here is that some journals tend to publish mostly or entirely quantitative research. If your study takes a qualitative approach, then you will want to steer away from journals that do not tend to accept the kind of work you do.

- **prestige:** Journal prestige is measured in different ways. The most conventional way that universities measure prestige of a journal is by looking at the quality of the publisher, rigor of the journal, and the reputation of the editor and/or editorial board members. The publishing industry has been consolidated over the years. Many of the small publishing houses have been subsumed under bigger presses, so now the biggest names in journal publishing are a handful of university presses (e.g., Oxford University Press) and then a set of academic presses (e.g., Routledge, Sage, etc.). The most prominent publishers make it their business to show up to the national convention every year and exhibit their latest titles. The rigor of the journals has been a controversial issue. The rate of manuscript acceptance or rejection is one indicator of rigor. If a journal has less than an 80% manuscript acceptance rate, then it is usually frowned upon. The impact factor is another measure of rigor. Impact factors are calculated using a formula that takes into account the number of times a given journal and its articles are cited by an exclusive list of journals deemed prestigious. Finally, the third way of evaluating journal prestige is by looking at the reputation of the journal editor and editorial board. The assumption is that high-quality journals will attract the best of the best to review for them.

One or more of the above-mentioned criteria should in some way inform where you choose to publish your work. Ralph Ellison once stated, "The end is in the beginning, which lies far ahead." That means you should start thinking now about and planning for your future career. Think ahead. If you plan to be at a major research university as a professor, then start publishing with the same frequency and in the same high-quality journals as faculty at that institution. It makes your candidacy that much more attractive when a potential employer sees evidence of your ability to sustain a quality record of publication.

Publishing can be a lot of fun once you get started, but admittedly, it is a little nerve-racking at the beginning. It is also a nail-biting adventure for those whose employment, tenure, or promotion is hanging in the balance. Make every publication count. Do not just throw away or bury your work in an obscure journal because they immediately accept your work. Acceptance is affirming, but in the long run, strategic placement in top-tier journals is critical.

What's the Process for Getting Published?

Okay, so let's say you followed the steps so far, and now you want to know the process for getting published. Given that all journals now exclusively accept manuscripts electronically, the process is relatively straightforward. Once you select the journal to which you want to submit your manuscript, then you will need to go to the journal webpage and click "read the journal" or "submit an article" or something similar to start the submission process. Most electronic submission processes will ask you to create a login profile and upload your manuscript for review.

After submitting your manuscript via the online system, the editor will take a quick look at the manuscript to ensure the journal is the appropriate outlet and the author has uploaded all necessary materials (usually abstract plus manuscript). If the editor does not believe that is the case, they may return your manuscript and suggest options for you. If all checks out, the editor will assign your manuscript to two to three "blind" (impartial) reviewers who never see your name and are not revealed to you. Reviewers focus on the content, tone, quality, clarity, accuracy, conceptual consistency, methodological rigor, and heuristic value of your writing, then provide their written feedback to the editor who ultimately makes the decision based on the reviews. There are four major decision options that are available: (1) accept as is, (2) accept with minor revisions, (3) revise and resubmit, or (4) reject. It is possible to have a 20-year career and never have received an "accept as is" decision. The "accept with minor revisions" is also relatively uncommon.

Most articles that have ultimately been accepted for publication initially receive a "revise and resubmit" decision. In this case, after the author revises the manuscript as recommended by the reviewers, the author will resubmit the manuscript; subsequently, the editor will resend it to the reviewers and ultimately make a decision to accept. Do not be surprised if the feedback is extensive and feels overwhelming at first. Stay calm, and read the feedback multiple times. Ask a mentor to read the feedback with you. Create a plan for revision, and take it one step at a time.

You will resubmit the manuscript with an anonymous and nondefensive letter back to the editor and reviewers detailing how you addressed their feedback. Each will reread your manuscript and letter, and the editor will make a decision on the revision. This does not mean the editor is obligated to accept all revised manuscripts. If the manuscript has not been revised satisfactorily, it can be rejected. Of course, no one wants to receive a letter noting the editor's rejection of a manuscript, but it happens. If it does, life goes on. Don't wallow for long. Be encouraged. Some other journal will publish it. Revise it so it is stronger, and resubmit the manuscript elsewhere. Each rejection is an opportunity for growth.

Incidentally, the editor rarely disagrees with the reviewers' recommendations, so the reviewers play a very important role. They are essentially gatekeepers, so if you get a revise and resubmit, do not get into a back-and-forth exchange with reviewers. It is not wise to do so, since they may not entertain your comments, and it is likely to lead to a negative decision. If you disagree with one or two of the reviewers' recommendations, then explain in your letter why you chose not to make the respective modification to your manuscript, but be prepared for that same reviewer to disagree with your assessment and maintain "recommend rejection" of the manuscript if it is a major concern for the reviewer.

The initial review decision ordinarily takes approximately three months. After that it depends on how long it takes the author to complete the revisions (if you receive a revise and resubmit), but if all things are going smoothly, the entire process, from submission to acceptance, usually takes eight to 12 months. This is why you cannot submit a manuscript and then wait for a decision before starting the next manuscript. You have to submit one, take a very short break lasting no more than a few weeks, then start the next manuscript. Remember you would not have made it this far if several people didn't believe you could be successful. You are more than capable!

Final Reflections

Generally, the process of sharing one's work by presenting at conferences or getting published is relatively easy. The real labor is in deciding what you want to write, why it is important that you write it, and where you want to publish it; and then you can start writing it. The first manuscript is always the most challenging because you have to get used to how to structure your ideas. You have to establish your own voice. Once you have done that and had your work peer-reviewed, you will gradually become more confident with your writing. It is like lifting weights. No one shows up to the gym on day one and starts lifting 500 pounds. They have to work up to that. On day one you might struggle with 50 pounds, but the more you train your muscles, the better you will become. It is the same with writing. You must practice your writing and get used to what it takes to succeed. After that, it is all a matter of where and how often you want to share your work.

For Further Thought and Reflection

1. What fears, insecurities, or anxieties are holding you back from sharing your work?

2. Do you have a mentor? Have you considered getting mentors for multiple purposes (e.g., for navigating your career as a woman or person of color, for publishing, for grant writing, etc.)?

3. What does career success look like for you? What steps must you take to get there? How can you be more intentional in your journey to your dream job?

4. What motivates you to excel? What obstacles commonly get in the way of you achieving your goals?

5. Stop to breathe. Empower yourself to think about a timeline for submitting a manuscript for publication. How soon can you produce a quality piece to be submitted to a journal for publication?

From Sitting in the Classroom to Facing It

Becoming and Growing as a Teacher

9

Kirstie McAllum

Simon Mallette

Tyler S. Rife

Uttaran Dutta

J uggling teaching with your own studies can be an intimidating, disorienting, and liminal experience. On the one hand, you are suddenly tasked with the responsibilities of developing or delivering course material, cultivating a meaningful classroom environment, and learning how to respond to unforeseen scenarios. On the other hand, you are still learning to manage the ever-evolving time, mental, and emotional pressures that come with being a rigorous graduate student also tasked with advancing your own scholarship.

> It does stress me to think about starting to teach. Sometimes I
> don't feel legitimate because I'm young, but being a TA has given
> me some confidence, and I can count on that experience. (Laura,
> master's student, Canada)

Meanwhile, you will likely be negotiating the personal, professional, and political qualities of your selfhood in relation to these roles, encountering commitments on levels both individual and communal. No doubt, taking on the role of a teaching assistant or graduate instructor is a transformative part of the teaching journey because it is at this stage that you first encounter what it means to truly become a teacher.

We write this chapter as faculty members and graduate students living, becoming, and teaching in different corners of the globe: Hamilton, New Zealand; Phoenix, Arizona; and Montréal, Canada. Thus, our chapter is composed as a collective synthesis of our individual voices and perspectives sharing pedagogical experiences and promising practices. In short, our chapter can be read as a conversation threaded through a shared passion for teaching. Across this chapter we discuss the ongoing project of finding meaning and purpose in the craft of teaching, the co-creation of the teaching environment, resiliency, and the advantages and challenges associated with coinstructing.

Navigating the Landscapes of Teaching: Exploring Meanings and Purpose

For all of us, teaching is a continual source of stimulation because it is a moving target; teaching is change focused at multiple levels. Tyler explains that when he first started teaching, he viewed his role as helping students learn concepts and skills that would help them navigate the world more smoothly. Teaching fosters change by providing students with a new set of intellectual or disciplinary tools that enable them to see the world differently and to problematize and even "unlearn" what were previously uninterrogated assumptions about the way things work. This never-ending effort of reflecting, recalibrating, and relearning generates personal and communal growth.

Yet, teaching can also generate change that transcends individuals' intellectual development. As Uttaran points out, when less than 8% of individuals, globally, have an opportunity to obtain a bachelor's degree, teaching is not just a means of helping students in their career progression but also a rare opportunity to make them cognizant of lack of access to education and to co-create networks of compassionate people who can contribute to overcoming such disparities. He concludes that teaching is a way of encouraging students to look beyond the classroom, academia, and corporate spaces and take responsibility to enact meaningful changes by becoming mindfully responsive and socially embedded.

Teaching also changes us, intellectually, emotionally, and ethically. Anyone who has taught unfamiliar subject matter will attest to the fact that there is no better way to master it than teaching it to others. The best teachers teach because they love to learn.

> Being of a rather introverted nature, the pleasure of teaching came as a bit of a surprise to me. I thought that teaching was a task reserved for very extroverted, talkative people. However, I gradually discovered that teaching is a vocation that can be born late in life and is especially accessible to anyone who has the desire to make a difference in others' lives. (Pascale, recent PhD graduate, Canada)

However, we maintain that teaching can never be thought of merely as the transmission of content to students who passively receive information (see Pratt et al., 2016, 2020, for a discussion of teaching perspectives and metaphors). Instead, teaching is a creative and innovative endeavor where our students teach us, push our boundaries, and enlarge our worldview if we embrace their independent, mindful thoughts. Opening up the classroom to a diverse array of worldviews and incorporating students' experiences and perspectives into discussions means that teachers must be ready for the unforeseen and unexpected. In the classroom, this means creating an environment that values listening to and learning from each other and fostering tolerance for opposing/conflicting viewpoints and an appreciation of plural perspectives. Teaching can teach us a great deal about ourselves, our biases, and our worldviews.

Co-creating the Teaching Environment

Teaching will differ depending on context (country, region, university culture), role (teaching assistant or tutor, instructor, or lecturer), size of the group of students (25 versus 350 students), students' level (first years or more advanced undergraduates), and subject being taught (communication theory, research methods, business communication). Our teaching role may range from grading assignments to leading small group discussions, tutorials, workshops, or organizing and teaching an entire course. We may work with someone else's class materials, readings, and activities or have to develop our own from scratch. As teaching involves considerable adaptability to manage these multiple demands, we need to consider how to manage the tension between the planning and organization teaching requires with the creativity that learning necessarily involves.

Certainly, all of us recognize that thinking ahead of time ("at least a week ahead of schedule rather the night before you are going to teach it for the first time," advises Tyler) about what students need or would be interested in creates more satisfying, stimulating classes. Preparation can involve choosing documentaries, examples, video clips, and activities that will work for this particular group and breaking up sessions into lecture, activity, and discussion (see Barkley, 2009; Brookfield & Preskill, 2005, for inspiration). However, as Tyler explains:

> It's vital to let go of that ego defensive shield and embrace the power of
> vulnerability, framing discussion around learning as a process rather than
> an end. Not only has this approach generated more thoughtful, unexpected
> conversations in the class, it has communicated to my students that it's okay to
> be confused about something or not know an answer.

For a new teacher, learning to conquer overreliance on teaching technologies, such as PowerPoint, and leave space for the unforeseen may seem a terrifying prospect. Tyler initially dealt with uncertainty by focusing on expertise. He describes his initial experience of teaching:

> I was informed by my misguided impression that all my teachers knew
> absolutely everything about the course material. To me, they had achieved
> some transcendent level of knowledge. When I started teaching, I felt I needed
> to prove myself as the carrier of this knowledge. In reality, I was just two days
> behind my class in learning the material.

Consequently, when students asked Tyler challenging questions, he would "stumble through a response with the hopes that it would be good enough" for that moment, later do the research necessary to construct a more reasonable response, and then provide a follow-up response the next time the class met.

Similarly, Kirstie's first university teaching experience during her master's program generated a perception that she needed to "manage" problematic classroom situations:

> As a tutor (in the United States, a teaching assistant) for a second-year undergraduate class, I was expected to facilitate discussion around course readings and answer students' questions. Five minutes into the first tutorial, I realized with horror that the students hadn't read the assigned texts and that the conversation was not going to flow well, if at all, especially as the course convenor had decided to sit in the back of the room to see how I got on.

This experience transformed Kirstie into a "planning freak" because it inculcated the belief that "failing to plan is planning to fail." It took her a long time to let go in class because the list of potential disasters was endless—technological failures, students being underprepared or overprepared, missing equipment—so she developed resources and activities that would enable her to continue the class with a semblance of calm, if not flair, if the worst did indeed happen.

Simon found that although his first teaching experience went well due to preparation, a sense of humor, and a good relationship with students, the second class he taught was less successful because he relied on what he had done the previous semester. Simon recalls, "I said to myself that if I go in with the same attitude and openness, I'll be all right, but I hadn't understood that every course, every semester will be unique because the students change, and the subject matter is different." We've all had the experience of teaching exactly the "same" subject with wildly different results and levels of student engagement, which has made us realize that teaching is an inherently collaborative endeavor. What we bring to the classroom is only part of the equation because students are co-creators of the learning experience (Bovill et al., 2016).

This interactive co-construction means that teaching involves continual adaptability on our part. When Kirstie moved to Montréal, she thought that learning to teach in French would be her biggest challenge, but she later realized that learning to teach interculturally would take even more time and effort because case studies, video clips, and examples that "worked" for English-speaking students in Aotearoa New Zealand, were meaningless for French-speaking students in Quebec. Uttaran also found that as a person from the Global South, he had little knowledge and experience about the dynamics, functioning, and expectations of U.S. universities and students. Academic norms are strikingly different. U.S. academic culture is more individualistic and encourages interactions among classroom stakeholders more frequently. As in Kirstie's case, cultural differences made teaching more difficult:

One challenge was my limited knowledge about U.S. politics, everyday affairs, and unspoken cultural expectations. Consequently, I struggled to provide relevant examples and be part of engaging interactions. Linguistically, too, I experienced challenges because English is my third language, and Indian English is different from American English. During my doctoral education, I tried hard to overcome some of these challenges; gradually, over the years, my efforts started paying off.

Yet obstacles are not unique to graduate teachers from different cultural contexts. Simon notes, "I've learned to adapt to rowdy groups by asking them more questions and encouraging them to debate with one another. I adapt to gloomy classrooms with no windows by adding more colors and images to my PowerPoints."

There are also contexts where clarity and consistency take priority over adaptability and change. For instance, we recommend negotiating a "class contract" with students at the beginning of the semester. Simon asks students about their learning goals, their career aspirations, and their class expectations; "In return, I tell them how and why I teach, and I make sure to let them know about my office hours, how long I take to reply to email, who the class TA is, etc. This creates a transparency which I find to be very beneficial in the long term." Keeping up contact with students is even more important when teaching online courses (see Boettcher & Conrad, 2016, for a helpful survival guide).

Assignment instructions and grading expectations need to be especially clear (Race, 2019). Although overly specific descriptions and rubrics can suffocate creativity, vague, sketchy instructions can incite panic. Kirstie found this out the hard way. When the instructions she gave were too open to individual interpretation, she received more than 3,000 emails from her 300 students over the course of the semester! Another context where variability is problematic is grading. Simon notes:

> As a graduate instructor, students appreciate you making yourself a bit vulnerable, because that's how they get to know you. But when you're a TA, if you're not rock solid, the students will complain to the professor that you didn't grade properly or that you have no idea of what's happening in class. So you have to present yourself as solid. This Goffman-esque performance is more difficult for a TA than for an instructor where a relationship develops.

One strategy that improves grading consistency involves two simple steps. When working with a teaching supervisor or other graduate teaching assistants, first grade several assignments together (using a rubric if appropriate), with each person grading two to three assignments individually. Then come together and compare grades, adjusting as necessary before attacking the whole stack. This process also enables you to proceed with a much greater level of confidence that you are grading in a way that is consistent with your course and department. Of course, seek training and feedback if you are not confident about grading. Most universities' teaching units offer seminars, webinars, and written resources on how to write clear assessments, grade assignments effectively and efficiently, and develop grading rubrics. If your institution does not provide this service, hundreds of helpful websites provide advice and templates (see, for instance, GSI Teaching & Resource Center, 2020).

Our conversations about teaching as we worked on this chapter showed that all of us manage the adaptability-consistency tension quite differently, which highlights the importance of finding one's own voice in teaching. It's good to be a sponge that absorbs perspectives and strategies from others but also to realize that these will need to be adapted to our own teaching style.

Becoming a Resilient Teacher

Because teaching involves embracing the unexpected, taking risks, and maximizing creativity, it means that things can go pear-shaped. Although we all began by describing teaching as "stimulating," "engaging," and "liberatory," that didn't stop us from identifying issues that can make teaching heavy or difficult. Here we discuss strategies to address four of them: perceived failures in the classroom, emotional stress, negative teaching evaluations, and excessive time spent preparing classes.

Facing Up to "Failures" in Teaching

When abstract concepts elude students, material seems too complicated, or students leave bored and frustrated after spending more time updating their social media profiles than listening during class, Kirstie ponders if she is in the right profession. Simon also experienced a group of three or four students who always arrived late to class; while he was talking, they would roll their eyes and whisper amongst themselves. He relates, "I really started to take it personally. Each class, I only looked at them, wondering, 'What did I just say that made them react like that?' I started thinking, 'I'm not cool, I'm past it, I'm missing the point completely.'" At other times, it's not just one class period that goes wrong but the entire course that seems a little off track. Tyler remembers that, as a master's student, during his first semester teaching a speech class,

> I started to get the inkling that lots of students weren't taking it seriously because I was so close in age to many of them. I sensed that people felt comfortable joking around with me, making the class kind of a joke, making their speeches a joke, and I started to take offence to this, but I had no idea really how to confront it. I was just floundering.

Tyler resolved the issue by discussing what was happening and how the class might collectively proceed from there to make it a positive experience for everyone, and the class climate improved.

If we don't find fault with our classroom performance, it is tempting to point the finger at our students. Tyler and Kirstie talked about how some graduate instructors have the tendency to "trash talk about their 'difficult' students to each other to make themselves feel better." They recognized the need to find a healthier alternative to this toxic habit:

> KIRSTIE: Talking about students in an objectifying way is very limiting because teaching is what we do together with our students, not something we do to them. I deal with moments where I've face-planted by describing the situation to friends. When they kill themselves laughing, it de-dramatizes the situation significantly.

> TYLER: I see. Let's see how we can take this experience and the story and translate it into something that's more digestible than how it felt in that moment.

> KIRSTIE: I deal with it by laughing. That's how I get it out, because otherwise I'd be crying.

> TYLER: What you're doing in making sense of the situation is objectifying the experience so that you are not carrying it in your body, but without objectifying the student.

We also decided that it's important to realize from the get-go that you're not going to be perfect. Simon reiterates the importance of not setting up an expectation that you're going to be amazing the first time around: "Even with more experience, the classes where you're on fire, 100%, you can count on the fingers of one hand." It's also helpful to engage in some sort of debriefing activity after each class. Simon undertakes this debriefing by writing comments in two columns: "What went well?" and "What could go better?" Simon reflects that sometimes the first column isn't very substantial when you first start out, but it gets longer as you gain confidence.

> I ask for feedback throughout the semester through discussions and anonymous online surveys. … Though this is a vulnerable and humbling process, especially the first time, it helps me to better respond to the students before me. (Simon, PhD student, United States)

All of us recommend avoiding the tendency to focus exclusively on the negative, by identifying what went well and what we can improve in the future. Kirstie writes entries in a teaching diary when she perceives her class has collapsed or "turned to custard" because writing about what actually happened helps to see that there was some good mixed in with the bad. Of course, sometimes classes really do not go well:

When I first started teaching in French, I mixed up words quite often. Once I enthusiastically told my students that I wanted them to flourish (s'épanouir) over the course of the semester, but I unintentionally told them I wanted them all to faint (s'évanouir). After a minute of horrified silence, the students cracked up. After embarrassing moments like these, I reread words usually attributed to Winston Churchill: "Success is never final, and failure is never fatal. What counts is the courage to continue."

To remember that she has some constructive qualities in the classroom, Kirstie also periodically reads her *FIGJAM* ("Far out I'm good, Just ask me") folder, which contains positive feedback from students and colleagues.

Maintaining Emotional Equilibrium

Teaching can be an emotionally taxing occupation, especially if you lead with empathy. Elegantly communicating concepts, facilitating discussion, and creating a healthy learning environment is challenging. Add in giving feedback and grades that don't align with students' expectations, and you have a recipe for major emotional stress. Simon recalls:

One unhappy student who'd turned red as a tomato took me aside to complain: "I've never had such a bad grade. I'm an A+ student, and you've given me 60%." I tried to reason with her: "Second-year courses are a bit more demanding. I know it's not always easy to split up tasks in group projects, but I'm available to help the group, and if you want to improve your grade, we'll work on it together." Diffusing tension requires a lot of personal investment. To be honest, I think that my problem—and also my strong point—is that I'm very emotionally engaged.

Teaching students who seem disinterested, critical, or even hostile is also an emotional challenge. Simon sought advice from an experienced teacher he respects:

I asked a professor whom I admire what to do with students who seem unhappy during my class. Straight away, she smiled and said that even after more than 20 years of teaching she regularly has students like that. The trick was to not look at them: "Force yourself to look for the kind eyes in your class. Focus on the students who are engaged with what you're saying and stick with them." This was a game changer for me because I think it's something we struggle with when we start to teach; you cannot and will not please everyone. Thinking that you will is too emotionally draining and simply counterproductive.

Another challenge involves being the "voice of authority" in a classroom setting and taking our responsibility to care about our students seriously. This care extends beyond our intellectual expertise to encompass the well-being of our students.

> Before I started teaching, I had given a lot of thought to different ways of engaging with the group and teaching in a passionate, dynamic way. What I hadn't foreseen was how to approach individual interactions. Contrary to my expectations, many students open up about stressful experiences at university or their workplaces. I worked on my role as a coach by offering friendly advice and referring some students to university resource people for help. (Emanuelle, PhD student, Canada)

Our students may be fearful and distressed by current events, anxious and stressed about their ability to manage university-level study amid widespread pressure to succeed (Mazer & Hess, 2016), depressed by relationship woes, or victims of campus violence and injustice. We do not always have the tools to help them, and nor is it our role to do so, but our knowledge of how the university system works means we play a vital intermediary role. Tyler explains:

> Confronting the trials and tribulations of teaching takes effort, but when we notice that students are spiralling in some way, teaching requires bravery. The easy way out is to ignore your observation of a student who seems depressed, but passing the buck to other figures in their life is to fail as a teacher. If you sense something's wrong but you haven't had this experience before, you need to find somebody you trust and relay this information. Ask them: "Do you think this concern is valid?" If so, you may need to send an email to your student, expressing: "I noticed X about your presence in class today. I just want you to know that I hope everything's okay. I'd be happy to meet with you and talk at some point, if you're struggling."

Uttaran reinforces that in most universities, students come from different parts of the country and all over the world. The culture shock and mental health issues many confront as they learn to cope with the academic environment can become critical for students who experience stigma and discrimination because of their identity markers. Therefore, we need to become intercultural allies who help them negotiate their everyday struggles and sense of uncertainty.

Confronting Teaching Appraisals and Improving One's Practice

Most of us take a deep breath before opening our course evaluations that are distributed to students in most universities after the end of the semester. Yet anonymous feedback can be useful.

Majority of the students would say they loved and learned a lot from my course, but there was always a sprinkle or two who would say that there is a language barrier. Of course, it always stings when I read that, but what am I going to learn from that comment? So I appreciate my wins, take note of what works, and focus on the feedback that actually helps my pedagogy. (Ligaya, PhD student, United States)

Uttaran reflects: "Over the years I learned how to make eye contact with students and coinstructors in the classroom, overcome overreliance on PowerPoint, and make the class interactions dialogic." But feedback can also be disheartening. Most of us tend to remember the critical comments more than positive ones. At times, the quantitative assessments seem far removed from our experience of the course, such as receiving poorer evaluations for a class that we know was significantly better than the last time we taught it. The appraisal system itself also has flaws. For example, students' participation rates drop significantly when appraisals are done online, and only students who loved or hated the course complete them. There is also evidence that student evaluations can be skewed by gender and culture of the instructor. Tyler confirms:

I'm afforded certain privileges as a White, male-identifying teacher, whereas other grad students receive reviews that target, aggress, and microaggress their gender and race. I know one grad student who receives feedback about how her voice sounds shrill or the way that she dresses. I don't experience this, so when I read through course evaluations, I don't feel the same sorts of traumas that others do where they receive a review that is emotionally cutting and that has nothing to do with course material. Our bodies are not apolitical— your students' evaluation may be predicated simply on the way that you look or sound, things over which you have no control.

It is important to discuss teaching evaluations that are worrisome or that you don't understand with trusted mentors, obtain the support you need, and develop best practices in response to feedback. An alternative way of gaining insight into teaching in a way that can benefit students during the semester is to organize a class debrief strategy four to five weeks into the semester, either seeking written feedback or in discussion with the students. Simon tells his students, "I'd like to see what's going well, and what you'd like to change. Tell me what you think, and I'll also let you know about things I'd like to see change." At the end of the semester, Kirstie asks her teaching assistants what she should keep doing, stop doing, or change. Mentors and fellow graduate students can also form an invaluable resource in reading and reacting to feedback (see Moon's 1999 text on reflective practice). If not a practice in your department, you might invite a course director or a mentor to observe your teaching and give you feedback.

Taking Stock of Time Spent on Teaching

Demands of teaching, especially when you have to prepare new courses, can seem to suck up all available time, to the detriment of your own classes, research, and personal life. It's important to realize that this is, to some extent, normal and to accept that it will get better the next time you teach the course. If you have a choice, we recommend reteaching the same class multiple times. Because you've already prepared the material, you just need to refine and refresh it for each new group, taking into consideration changes in context and students' needs. If, after graduation, you want to work in industry, for the government, the nonprofit sector, or start your own business, repeating classes leaves you more time to prepare for your career.

If you are after an academic career, however, it can be useful to have taught multiple courses at different levels and perhaps courses of different sizes or structures. In this case, time devoted to teaching can be an ongoing concern, and it is always important to balance time spent on teaching against your own coursework and other life demands. Kearns and Gardiner's (2013) short book aimed at graduate students and researchers is jam-packed with tips for managing time and energy. One rule of thumb is to evaluate whether what you're doing right now will make a significant difference to your teaching and/or your students' learning. If not, stop doing it, shut your laptop, close your office door, and go home. To keep her teaching workload manageable, one of Kirstie's mentors recommended that she change 10% of a course each time she taught it. Setting these kinds of limits has often been possible because others in our network (faculty and/or other graduate students) have generously shared resources, activities, and even PowerPoint slides that we could adapt or integrate into our own practice.

Whenever you need to prepare a course alone, make sure you have clear learning objectives. "SMART" learning objectives that are specific, measurable, attainable, realistic, and timebound state precisely and concisely what you want students to learn during a class session or over the course of several weeks (see Svinicki & McKeachie, 2010, for teaching tips with explanations and examples). Developing specific learning objectives avoids trying to cover too much and helps you to prepare, present, and engage with a reasonable amount of material in the time available. Well-written objectives also enable us to align classroom activities and assessment tasks. Obviously, learning outcomes don't usually capture the most important learning that students do in our classes, such as obtaining a genuine appreciation of difference (a value for different sorts of people and perspectives and learning different ways of relating to the world). However, learning objectives do enable us to think critically about the unwritten and perhaps unintended "invisible curriculum" that privileges certain types of knowing, values, and perspectives. We can remedy this situation by asking those in our teaching support network to help us diversify the types of readings and examples that we use, so that a course syllabus reflects in some way the diversity of the classroom, and students are able to see themselves presented in the literature that they are reading.

Making the Teaching Team Work

Graduate students often form part of a teaching team working alongside a faculty or staff member, or they may end up coordinating teaching assistants themselves. We first want to highlight the indispensable contribution that teaching assistants make to learning. As Uttaran explains,

> I learned a great deal from my teaching assistants. In several instances, they shared brilliant assignment and activity ideas and provided constructive criticism that improved students' classroom experiences. Teaching assistants also opened up communication avenues where they represented students' voices and perspectives and cleared up students' doubts.

In short, graduate students play an important role as pedagogical leaders.

However, for the teaching team to work, ongoing communication is essential. Simon recommends meeting before the semester begins to clarify expectations and ways of working on both sides. Tyler remembers that when he co-facilitated a seminar with other graduate students, he and the other seminar assistants relaxed into a weekly rhythm as the semester progressed:

> We stopped regularly asking clarifying questions, stopped tracking our individual expectations, and stopped diligently attending to out-of-class duties. Late in the semester, both myself and the other seminar assistant forgot that one of us needed to unlock the week's readings for the upcoming class session on our course website. Because neither of us remembered, no one read the texts. Part of making the teaching team work is maintaining that effort to check in with coinstructors and ask clarifying questions. What might have seemed concrete at first may need to be returned to later.

Kirstie advises making sure that hours worked and tasks to be done are clearly understood by all parties, and set down in writing, to avoid misunderstandings or an abusive situation where a teaching assistant with less power ends up working far longer and harder than they have been paid for.

Keeping the communication up among the instructional team is vital when it comes to grading. Kirstie expects graduate assistants to let her know if they are struggling with their work or if they can't get it done in the time frame they agreed to, whether for personal or professional reasons, so that she can step up and support them. She remembers when a teaching assistant called her panicking because he thought that his backpack containing graded student work had been thrown into the university's recycling system: "I proceeded to search through the six-foot-high recycling bins in the basement. We're still friends—and not just because he found the backpack at a friend's house an hour later." In contrast, she struggled to help a teaching assistant who had been withdrawn and disengaged throughout the semester. The problem came to a head when the TA skipped a team grading meeting:

> The evening before we handed graded assignments back, she told me she hadn't written any comments on them because it took her too long. I wished she'd mentioned this issue several weeks earlier—I could have shared tips for grading more efficiently or helped her manage the process. I finished grading her entire pile at 3 a.m. Two months later, I said little when two colleagues wanting to hire a TA asked me if I'd recommend her, but my silence was probably eloquent.

For graduate teaching assistants, it can be hard to decide what we should do, or refuse to do, when what we do in one context is potentially going to have an impact down the line, in terms of future employment opportunities, recommendation letters, and professional reputation. If you have concerns about expectations or evaluations of your work ethic, talk with your course director, department chair, advisor, or other mentors who can help you navigate your concerns.

Conclusion

As we've seen, teaching while being a student yourself requires a great deal of agility and flexibility. Not only is teaching an opportunity to discover your voice as an educator, but it is also an enriching and rewarding experience. We hope that our testimonies have shown you that being patient with yourself and adopting a certain reflexivity are key to managing the stress of teaching your first classes and growing as a teacher. Feeling confident in your pedagogy takes time, so it's important to recognize and embrace the learning curve, even when you're the teacher!

The accelerated implementation of information and communication technologies in the classroom and the push toward online teaching will certainly bring new challenges. This is why we believe it's important for us, as teachers and teaching assistants, to keep connecting with students and with each other so that we can teach in an engaging and person-centered way.

For Further Thought and Reflection

1. How has your experience teaching in the classroom differed from your impressions of teaching (and teachers) as a student? How might knowledge of that difference inform your teaching practice?

2. In an increasingly technologically mediated world, how should teachers respond to the role and use of technology in the classroom?

3. How can graduate instructors and teaching assistants prevent/mitigate the hazards of group projects in both face-to-face and online classes?

4. What kind of strategies and tools could you use to reflect on your teaching experiences in ways that help you maintain resilience?

5. How can you maintain resilience as a teacher when you need to make major changes to the way you've always done things (e.g., by moving a class completely online or developing hybrid online/in-person classes)?

"Without People in My Corner, I Will Fail"

Personal Resources for Graduate Students

Vincent R. Waldron

Brianna Avalos

Dayna N. Kloeber

Jameien R. Taylor

Resilience is often conceptualized as a quality of individuals. "Resilient people" are assumed to possess certain personality traits, attitudes, or strategies that give them an advantage in responding to adversity. But this approach downplays the important role of social environments in inhibiting or facilitating resilience. Graduate school is, in some ways, a harsh social environment, one that evolves as the student progresses, with each academic year marked by waypoints of accomplishment and, sometimes, punctuated by disorienting experiences of adversity. But, as we have come to learn from our students, resilience in graduate school often comes down to resources. Universities that are generous in making resources available and students who are mindful, assertive, and creative in accessing those resources—these are keys to surviving and thriving in graduate school.

Although one of the guiding metaphors for this volume is resilience, our chapter is grounded in the metaphor of *resource*. Indeed, the capacity to locate, cultivate, and use resources is a component of most resilience frameworks. Having studied victims of abuse, combat veterans, and trauma survivors for several decades, Charney and his associates identified 10 key elements of resilience (Southwick & Charney, 2013). These include utilization of such resources as social support, spiritual sustenance, role models, and sources of personal wellness. Recent communicative approaches emphasize the utilization of social networks (Buzzanell, 2018) and the role of relational resources in managing stressors (Afifi & Harrison, 2018). Against this backdrop, we identify the kinds of resources that facilitate graduate student success and the strategies students use in developing those resources.

We draw on the experiences of a diverse group of 15 graduate students who agreed to participate in interviews. Of these, 12 were female and three were male. Nine students identified as racial/ethnic minorities. Three identified as international students—one each from China, India, and Pakistan. Ages ranged from 23 years to

"65-ish" years. Seven students were enrolled in master's programs or had recently graduated, and the remainder were studying for the PhD or had recently finished. All were enrolled in programs located in the United States.

Before delving into the types of resources graduate students found helpful, we share the sometimes jarring adversities experienced by our participants. Second, using the informants' own words, we present the characteristics of successful students. Next, we transition to discussing how graduate students harness their network of professional support by developing quality faculty relationships and the comfort of colleagues. Finally, we provide a synthesis of resilience strategies, or what we refer to as the "5 Bs," and provide some closing thoughts about graduate student resources.

The Faces of Adversity

Why the emphasis on resources? Well, as you will hear in their voices, graduate school is an experience that stretches students, often in helpful, growth-promoting ways. But every one of our interviewees described moments when they felt tapped out, worn down, or "at a loss"—in other words, their personal resources were exhausted, and the capacity to survive, much less thrive, depended on finding and using sources of support.

Sources of adversity ranged greatly. Students described moments of profound isolation and loneliness while others were daunted by hypercompetitive peers. Some described staggering workloads, with reading and writing requirements that far exceeded their undergraduate experience. Still others focused on faculty expectations that were unrealistic and faculty mentors who were distant or unhelpful. Reflective of the growing diversity of the graduate student population, students noted the exhausting role stresses that come with being a parent and student, a working student, or a cultural or racial minority in a homogeneous academic culture.

Indeed, adversity was compounded for students of color, who sometimes felt uncomfortable in departments dominated by White students and faculty. Angelee, who recently received her PhD, observed that "being a woman of color can be difficult in the academy." She described her experience with a White faculty member: "I mean she was very pleasant to a lot of White students, specifically White female students, and really just didn't know how to treat students of color." Some students experienced overt prejudice in the local community. Xian Lin is a Chinese PhD student working on her dissertation in health communication. She described an appalling visit to a doctor's office where the medical assistant, faced with an unfamiliar name, insisted on calling her "Ching Ching."

And money was a big stressor. Students struggled to pay for housing, health care, transportation, and/or research expenses on meager stipends. "The biggest obstacle that I have experienced is financing my education," said Beulah, a student who described her race as Asian Indian. She is finishing the first year of a master's degree and noted that "as an international student, you are not eligible for many of the scholarships."

The stresses of graduate school were magnified for students with disabilities. Corey is a doctoral candidate who identifies as a D/deaf/hard of hearing person. "That has created some challenges within the classroom where sometimes I can't always hear the instructions or have to ask for accommodations." Faculty and peers assume he is going to fail, Corey says, so "I have to constantly battle to succeed … to show my success. I have to prove myself, and that shouldn't be the case." Health adversities drain student energy, including grinding "invisible illnesses," such as rheumatoid arthritis, and mental health conditions, such as depression and extreme anxiety.

In this chapter, while we focus less on the nature of adversity and more on the resources that help students manage it, we also understand the importance of normalizing adversity and pushing against narratives that stigmatize or pathologize adversity. We hope that by sharing a few students' testimonials, our readers will not only find solace but will also feel emboldened to air their own struggles to safe individuals so that they can garner adequate support while in graduate school. Having heard some sobering stories of adversity during this project, we offer this editorial comment: *Faculty, staff, and administrators must all do better in supporting our students.* Graduate study can be humane as well as rigorous, selective without being dismissive of students who vary from traditional notions of graduate student identity. We should not expect students to be resilient unless we create communities that provide ample personal and professional support. The alternatives are often grimmer than what we might realize.

> The first year in the PhD program was very challenging. It was very tough for me … really lonely and I felt no support. I thought about suicide. I went to talk to the therapist. And I remember like, they gave me this form, asked me to fill out emergency contact information. And I could not think of a single person [to be] that emergency contact. (Xian Lin, PhD student)

Characteristics of Successful Students

The students we interviewed viewed themselves as resources. They described personal qualities that helped them succeed and some that got in the way.

Resilience-promoting Qualities

Our informants recognized in themselves numerous helpful qualities, including a passion for the work, a strong work ethic, inherent optimism, maturity and life experience, willingness to seek help or feedback, the ability to create and maintain strong relationships, tenacity, assertiveness, flexibility, and open-mindedness. Two years of graduate school changed Leroy, a potential PhD student.

> My ability to listen to those around me. … My mentality my first year in grad school was that I was on my own, and no one would help me. Because of this I had to step away from the program for a semester. When I returned, I started to ask for help and listen to what others had to say. The difference in my success was night and day.

Kathryn is working on her dissertation. Her extensive work experience taught her that "you don't win everything all the time." She also noted, "I'm pretty tenacious. I'm kind of like that weed in the yard that won't die."

Resilience-inhibiting Qualities

Students described qualities that sometimes got in their way. These included a tendency to overcommit and engage in social comparison, perfectionism, self-criticism, and excessive independence. The most pervasive of these was perfectionism. As a group of high achievers, our participants learned to accept such "failures" as the occasional A- or B+ grade, flubbed assignment, or rejected conference submission. Several students described their relief at finally accepting that it "really was okay" to take another year to graduate. Megan, who is finishing her first year in a PhD program, has this to say: "In graduate school, perfectionism will be the death of anyone. It is simply not possible to be a perfect teaching assistant while completing perfect coursework and publishing perfect manuscripts." Of course, many personal qualities both enhanced and inhibited success.

> My combative nature has been a contributing factor in my success… but it has put me in awkward and unsavory situations as well. I refuse to be unheard because of my age or gender, and this has served me well. … At the same time, this combative nature I embody has resulted in the dissolvement of relationships with former colleagues. (Alice, PhD student)

One of the patterns we observed among our graduate student interviewees was them coming to terms with the adversity they faced, taking a personal inventory of their resources (individual and social), and then reaching into their networks for support. Next, we transition to what graduate students shared about how they created quality relatonships with faculty and peers.

Developing Faculty Mentorships

Students found their faculty mentors to be valuable sources of support, and they had much advice to share about forming this important bond. Juliana, a first-year PhD student, shares, "I know that without people in my corner, I will fail. I need the support of those that have 'been there, done that' to say my emotions and experiences are valid, and I, too, can make it through." Faculty mentor relationships are crucial for graduate students because they involve building social support networks, professional relationships, and committees. Graduate students interact and experience self-disclosure, support-seeking, and social connectedness differently—no mentor–mentee relationship is the same. Megan, a first-year doctoral student, shares, "Not every faculty member is willing to have this relationship, so pay attention to who is and who is not."

Assigned Versus Chosen Mentors

Incoming graduate students are often assigned a faculty advisor their first year and, throughout their time in the department, gain understanding and awareness of faculty interests and work styles. Leroy became familiar with faculty within the department and states: "Many times you hear that you need to find one faculty member and stick to them. I would disagree with this as it limits your options. The research and path you want to take is your own." This includes building mentor-style relationships with faculty members whose interests align best with yours.

How (Not) to Choose a Mentor

There are many resources that a graduate student can use while searching for a mentor. Cold emails are often the first step, and as Beulah shares, "Introduce yourself to the faculty, write an email, and fix a time where you can share about yourself and your goals." Rizalino, who just finished his master's degree, took a similar route and offers, "Do not be afraid to get in contact with faculty you do not know. It can be nerve-racking, but take the leap, and make those connections." By being open and honest, graduate students are able to build authentic and respectful relationships with faculty members. However, Carpenter and colleagues (2015) state that faculty mentors often do not discuss philosophies or strategies of mentoring when establishing an interpersonal mentor-mentee relationship. Pam, a recent master's graduate in interpersonal communication, noticed that each professor has their own "vibe," and graduate students should try to "adapt to it" by understanding their respective faculty member's idiosyncrasies and teaching styles. It's an important step towards recognizing the faculty member's preferences as well as identifying the student's wants and needs in this mentorship.

Professional Mentor–Mentee Relationships

Alice shares her primary concern regarding mentor relationships: "I think the best thing a graduate student can do to ensure the development, consistent growth, and longevity of relationships with faculty is setting boundaries immediately." By setting boundaries immediately, both parties have an opportunity to express respect toward one another. For example, what will be the norm for returning emails, hours worked per week, working during evenings or on weekends? Avery, a recent master's graduate, reflects that it's a "balancing act" between building new relationships with faculty members while also not "overextending" these professional invitations. By being vulnerable and sharing their own experiences, mentors open new doors toward a trusted and professional relationship with their mentees. For example, Kelly, a recent master's graduate, states that "being open with professors" helped her "create a bond" due to their interests aligning both professionally and personally. During this balancing act, it's recommended to have these vulnerable and authentic conversations with potential mentors in order to find a relationship that is most fulfilling on both ends. While quality relationships with faculty are an essential part of the graduate school experience, all of the students we spoke with explained that there was often no substitute for the camaraderie they found with their peers.

The Comfort of Good Colleagues

The graduate school colleague relationship can be one of the most rewarding, albeit complex, relationships. Our interviewees were insightful about what they consider essential qualities of supportive relationships. They also offered warnings about how to avoid creating toxic patterns with peers.

BUILDING RELATIONSHIPS WITH COLLEAGUES

- Take an interest in others' work.

- Create mutually trustworthy relationships.

- Be collaborators, not competitors.

- Avoid cliquing.

- Colleagues are not therapists.

- Ask colleagues for help.

- Leave your judgments at the door.

Take an Interest in Others

Take an interest in others' work. Getting into graduate school takes years of dedication and focus on your own learning, setting and sticking to your own goals, and highlighting your accomplishments in the graduate school application. During welcome week, orientations, and class introductions, you are again asked to share your interests. However, doctoral candidate Corey says he would advise graduate students to widen their perspective and consider others' research interests early in the graduate program.

> I think the biggest thing is taking an interest in others. It seems simple, but your research is not the biggest thing in the world. Your research is a tiny, little niche. Um, and it's great and all, but at some point, you're going to get bored with it, because you're constantly doing it. I find it more fascinating to learn about what other people are doing.

Corey says a "curious eye" about others' work helps make graduate school more interesting, rewarding, and certainly helps build and maintain strong relationships.

Create Mutually Trustworthy Relationships

The group we interviewed strongly recommended investing the time in finding and keeping trustworthy friends. This also means that you should be a trustworthy colleague. Not everyone is trustworthy all of the time (shocker, we know). Graduate students need to have a safe place to vent stress as they acculturate to higher education. Learning whom to trust is often a bumpy ride in environments that breed competition. Kathryn, a doctoral candidate, offered, "A word of caution: Carefully choose your friends, and make sure you can trust them." She warned, "If you're going to complain about faculty or things, some people will take it and turn it around [nefariously]."

Be Collaborators, Not Competitors

First-year doctoral student Megan was adamant about this: "Don't participate in any of the hypercompetitive bull*&%#! (sorry for my language!). In such a competitive space, a lot of people are tempted to engage in undercutting behaviors toward their colleagues or just petty drama. Don't let them drag you into it." Megan's quotation drives home an important point: We all choose whether or not, or how, we will engage in competition. Megan admits that graduate school is, by its very nature, a "competitive space" due to competitive paper awards, department awards, internal and external funding, and so few tenure-track faculty positions at the end of the rainbow. Megan doesn't dispute this, but she advises, "First, that mindset is just too draining, and you need your energy for your work. So, when people are *%##!, and they will be, don't engage. Focus on your behavior, work, and relationships, and you'll be fine."

> It's a myth that stepping on other people will make you taller in the field. You'll get more recognition for being well-liked and having a breadth of work that comes from collaboration. (Megan, PhD student)

Avoid In-Groups

As Pam noted, "In large working groups, there are small groups that can form and make others feel left out. Try hard not to let that happen, and welcome an inclusive cohort." Cliques are a painful and baffling reality for which many believe there are no clear solutions, especially given the unrelenting institutional culture that often perpetuates the problem. Even in our small sample of graduate students, marginalized people spoke loudly about how institutional policy and culture propagates socially exclusive behavior, particularly when it comes to funding inequity.

> Part of our cohort's problem when we came in was that we were a very large group. There were 12 or 13 of us, but only about eight people were funded. They were younger people. There were about four or five of us that were not funded—myself, and another student who was in the same age group, and a couple of international students. And so (socializing) did not gel very well in a lot of ways. (Kathryn, PhD student)

Angelee noted that methodological diversity also created some "weirdly cliquey behavior" that she actively worked to resist, as noted in this chapter's introduction. "I would not be clique-like," advised Pam.

Colleagues Are Not Therapists

Alice shared that she was grateful for the reciprocity of healthy graduate school relationships. She also shared that when reaching out to others for support, it is important to remember that "each person endures their own struggles, even if they don't make it known!" Alice suggested inquiring about their current bandwidth or "headspace before you ask if you can rant/vent/complain/etc." And she cautioned, "Colleagues are our support networks and our friends. But they are not our therapists." We also heard from our interviewees that having study buddies and meeting in coffee shops or local restaurants was a productive way to be with each other. Angelee said, "I've also used (colleagues) as study buddies. So even if we're not necessarily doing anything related to each other's work, just having someone that'll say, 'Yes, I will meet you from 12:00 to 3:00,' and we'll just sit and work."

Ask Colleagues for Help

Leroy thinks the "biggest 'do'" in graduate school is to "ask for help when you need it." He noted, "I am not nearly as smart as anyone who I have met in the program, and I'm pretty smart." Asking for help is important because "no one can help you if they don't know you are struggling." He warns that "you will be weeded out if you can't keep up, so ask your friends if you do not understand a concept or need help finding that perfect source." Angelee shared she'll ask, "Could you send me that article that you used?"

> Do not assume you are the smartest in the room. Every time you walk into
> your seminar/class, you are not the smartest, and that is okay. It's why we
> are in grad school. To learn! If you walk in thinking you are the smartest, and
> you already know the material, you are doing yourself a disservice. (Leroy,
> PhD Student)

While Leroy strongly recommends asking colleagues for help, he also warns against unrealistic expectations. "Now if you expect them to get back to you at 2:00 a.m., you are a little misguided. But I assure you that your colleagues want to see you succeed as much as you do."

Leave Your Judgments at the Door

Angelee said she thought future graduate students should understand from the beginning that they and their graduate school colleagues are going to say and do stupid things.

> I think when people start in their first year to where they end up in their fourth
> year, people grow so much; they will say horribly stupid things. At some point
> they will be ignorant, they will be offensive. You will be ignorant; you will be
> offensive. We will all do something wrong. Yeah.

She adds, "It's leaving space for people to grow, and I feel like not everyone does a good job of letting other people grow."

We wish we could report everything our interviewees shared about having fun and sharing community. Here are some highlights: Leroy states, "Get to know your colleagues ASAP." Beulah shared, "I'd recommend taking the first step and initiating the conversation." Finally, most of them recommended finding time to laugh with your peers. Never underestimate the power of eating and drinking together. Celebrate your colleagues' triumphs and accomplishments.

Addressing Personal Needs

Having inventoried their personal qualities, located mentors, and navigated peer bonds, students talked about the importance of tailoring the graduate experience to their unique personal needs. Student responses were assorted, and this seems to reflect the uniqueness of personal needs that researchers have found across graduate student populations relating to aspects such as where students are within their respective programs (Gardner, 2013) and the needs of master's versus PhD students (Kinsley et al., 2015). Though varied in their responses, two main themes emerged as fundamental to the overall well-being and satisfaction of graduate students.

Personal Connection

Participants highlighted some complexities of needing a connection with others.

> Being in a romantic relationship in school can be a blessing or a detriment, and mine was both at times. Having someone there to support me was great, but having a partner that did not understand all I was doing was challenging. I wasn't having fun on the computer all day; I wanted to spend more time with her, and I wanted to be more engaged at times, but I was mentally drained from reading and writing all the time and wanted nothing more than to do nothing. (Rizzalino, master's graduate)

Juliana, a first-year doctoral student, said it succinctly, "I am a people person. I need others to survive," while Megan discussed a sense of this need more subtly: "It's really easy to withdraw from people when you're feeling overwhelmed in graduate school. I've done it several times. ... Getting through graduate school is and should be a team effort." Though one can withdraw out of being overwhelmed with work, as Megan mentioned, some graduate students self-isolate from feeling out of place as underrepresented minorities (Smith & Virtue, 2019). This demonstrates that fulfilling a need for connection is not always in students' control.

Balancing the Personal and Professional

Our interviewees expressed a need for work-life balance in a variety of ways. For example, Ananya, who recently completed her master's degree, conveys her sense of needing balance by recognizing that caring for others too much does not leave room for herself:

> I always want others to be happy. ... I will focus on helping others and forget to do my own work in the process. Especially with working in the lab, and knowing so many students look up to me, there were times where I started to put all my energy on them rather than in my studies. It took me a while before I was able to really get a balance on that and know when to say "no."

Interestingly, Ananya demonstrates how too much connection may also lead graduate students to become drained. Beulah described her approach to balance in this way: "I try and take a day off each week where I don't have too much technology around me so that I can recover mentally and physically. ... Breaks are important as they renew perspective and reduce stress." Juliana expressed both her work-life balance challenges and her methods for trying to manage a balance:

> I am pulled in many different directions since I have a family, and at times
> I struggle to determine where to spend my time/energy. This first year has
> taught me that it is okay to ask for help [and] request extra time. ... I am a
> single mother of a 7-year-old son. ... What I have found are more effective ways
> to use my time, to care for myself when I need it, and to learn to hold tight to
> boundaries.

She went further to distinguish a more subtle need to balance the now with the future:

> In the first year, I have learned that some mentors want students to think
> about their fourth/fifth year of graduate school, submitting for conferences,
> and the dissertation process. I have decided that looking that far in advance
> is not healthy for me as a student, a mom, or a human in this world. So I have
> decided that small steps are best. I am focusing on one semester at a time.

What we find in this section is a recognition that adversity is an expected, even normal, part of graduate school. At the same time, our student informants learned to let their vulnerabilities show, at least occasionally, especially in relationships with trusted faculty and colleagues.

The "5 Bs": Synthesizing Strategies for Resilience

Having reviewed the adversities students face and the resources they find valuable, we wanted to synthesize the resilience-enhancing strategies they shared. To help readers make practical use of the material, we offer five resilience strategies, the "5 Bs."

THE "5 Bs": SYNTHESIZING STRATEGIES FOR RESILIENCE

- Build in self-care.

- Be realistic and flexible.

- Be you.

- Be clear about boundaries.

- Be connected diversely.

---

1. Build in Self-Care

Students told us that the rigor and rapid pace of graduate school leads to burnout and waning enthusiasm. To ward off exhaustion and renew the spirit, they offered specific advice, such as tending to hobbies and interests. Xian Lin renewed her interest in calligraphy. Lily, who recently received her PhD, maintained her passion for reading fiction and cooking throughout the program. Others recommended hiking, bike riding, attending community events, and other forms of play. The key was to schedule self-care. For Megan, that meant one day a week; others required more downtime.

2. Be Realistic and Flexible

Time and again our interviewees admitted that their own goals, or those imposed on them by peers or faculty, needed to be adjusted if life in graduate school was to be sustainable. Lily noted that during comprehensive exams, she asked for an incomplete in a seminar and was relieved that the faculty member did not hesitate to make this accommodation. Unrealistic goals only amplified the workload, drained energy, and fed self-critical tendencies. Adjustments included more attainable graduation timelines, willingness to turn in a paper that wasn't perfect, changing the focus of research, dropping a class, or letting a submission deadline pass. Kathryn spoke for several of her peers when she described her goal as:

> Finishing. You know, I uh, I just want to finish. ... I'm just sitting here thinking, "Well, you know, everybody wants to finish in four years. Right?" And you feel like such a failure if you're not going to. [But] if you've got a study that's taking longer than necessary for whatever reason ... it's just some things take longer than others, and you can't just, you know, fast-track.

3. Be You

Our informants learned to avoid social comparison because it unnecessarily drained energy and self-confidence. Pam noted, "There were times that I felt inferior to others based on their behavior or attitude. I noticed that my self-talk was damaging." Xian Lin's confidence in herself was shaken when she was unhelpfully compared to another student who had accumulated many publications. Then, in her third year, the PhD student decided to review the letters of recommendation written by her previous mentors. "Borrow their confidence," she advised, and "embrace the qualities that brought you this far in life." Other students channeled their past accomplishments when present adversities left them shaken. Having succeeded in the past as parents, employees, or students, these memories bolstered their courage and reinforced their sense of identity. The importance of speaking your truth was emphasized by several students, guided by the idea that you won't get what you want (resources, respect, acceptance) if you choose to deemphasize your needs and mute your voice.

Never be afraid to speak truth regardless [if] anybody wants to hear it. But speak the truth in a way that is not blunt and going to be offensive or inappropriate. (Corey, PhD student)

4. Be Clear About Boundaries

Many students described a desire (sometimes a pressure) to be involved in everything, to say "yes" to every faculty project, to accept ever more responsibility. Some described a "fear of missing out" (FOMO), a sense that they might lose an opportunity to publish their work, gain a new experience in the classroom, or form an important peer or faculty relationship. As a result, some felt "spread too thin," with too many projects, none of which were done well. Ananya wants students in this situation to know that "you are allowed to have a break. … If I truly cannot do something, I will be honest about it."

5. Be Connected (Diversely)

As the resilience literature makes clear, meaningful social connection is a source of strength during times of adversity. But as our informants made clear, the weight of graduate work can bend, and even break, bonds of support. We heard how important it is to stay connected to the "outside"—that is, to family, friends, and members of the larger community. Beulah found outside connections at a local church, one that reminded her of a faith community in India. Other students made time for weekly phone calls, Facetime, or Zoom sessions with parents, siblings, or old friends. As Corey attested regarding relationships on the inside, the intensity of the graduate experience often forges close bonds.

But even within your graduate program, the diversity of social connections is important. When it comes to making social connections, look beyond your area of specialty, suggested Angelee. "Some of my closest friends do not share the same methodology," she noted. "But also, they're going to always offer some unique perspective because they haven't read your same 10 books. They're going to offer you something valuable."

Conclusion

As we reflect on what graduate students shared with us about the adversities they faced, the characteristics they associated with success or struggle, and what they considered optimal strategies for creating enduring relationships with faculty and peers, each of us has a final thought to share. Vince was struck by the fact that the students we interviewed rarely talked with faculty about the need for help in the classroom. Perhaps the culture of graduate school has convinced students that asking for help is a sign of weakness rather than a sign of maturity and willingess to learn. Vince realized that as a faculty member, he needs "to watch more closely for students who need emotional support and help connecting with faculty and peers." Toward that end, Brianna noticed the importance of vulnerable conversations with both graduate students and faculty members. She said, "Don't be afraid to engage in authentic conversations with peers and mentors. I have been able to connect with those around me and realized I'm not alone when I finally put my guard down." Reflecting on participant responses and his experience, Jay observed: "Fulfilling a need for personal connection can ease the many stresses of graduate school. Additionally, regularly working toward balancing the many obligations and tasks of graduate school with similar obligations of one's personal life can be tremendously valuable." Finally, for Dayna, our interviews "reiterated that the structural and procedural status quo in academia continues to privilege those with power. If you are going to succeed in higher education, you had better polish your personal fortitude as much as you are able, because you're going to need it." Dayna leaves this project "more resolved and determined than ever to stay focused on making the acquisition of financial and social resources a more just affair." She hopes that the next generation of scholars is up to changing the status quo so that not quite so much rests on personal fortitude. We all agree.

For Further Thought and Discussion

1. What are some practical activities during graduate studies that can help foster personal connections while also maintaining coursework?

2. What is an important factor to consider when searching for a mentor-style relationship with faculty members?

3. Which of your personal qualities or life experiences will most help you remain resilient through graduate school, and which will hinder you?

4. What traditions can you begin with your cohort to celebrate milestones (e.g., finishing coursework, defending comprehensive exams and prospectus, defending dissertations, etc.)? What steps will you take to ensure all members of your cohort are included?

5. How can you and your cohort actively include colleagues who have life circumstances that socially separate them from you or others in the group (e.g., age, work outside academia, international student, disability, etc.)?

One Mountain, Many Paths

Navigating Roadblocks and Succeeding in Graduate School

11

Jordan Soliz

Megan E. Cardwell

O ne mountain, many paths"—this phrase was often introduced in the graduate orientation sessions in our department to emphasize to students that there are many routes to successfully completing a graduate program, however one defines "success." Where some are steady ascents to completion, others follow more winding trails to success. Where some students encounter initial setbacks, achieving recognition and reaching important milestones later in their academic tenure, others may have very positive experiences early on, only to encounter barriers later. What is stressed by introducing this phrase is that no path is better, no path is a reflection of whether one succeeds or not, and graduate students should focus on reaching the peak based on whatever path they choose.

In their 1999 essay, "The Complexity of our Tears: Dis/enchantment and (In) Difference in the Academy," Brenda Allen et al. invited readers into their lived experiences to engage their personal accounts in order to gain insight and understanding into what can lead to feelings of disillusionment and marginalization as one navigates the academic space. This is an essay all emerging and established scholars should read given that it speaks to challenges individuals often face in academia that not everyone recognizes. As academic advisors, peer mentors, and/or friends, what we can do in supporting our colleagues is limited because we can only support and advise based on our own experience—our own paths. Thus, it is their essay that, in some ways, inspires our approach to the current chapter, as we believe it is most beneficial to learn from the journey of others because you can find both similarities and connections with experiences while also identifying challenges for which you are not currently aware. Our goal in this chapter, therefore, is to provide insight into the roadblocks graduate students experience on their path to successfully completing a graduate program. More importantly, we hope to provide insight into strategies to overcome these roadblocks to better position all of us for successful and lifelong journeys in the academy as both individuals and mentors.

Who Are the Voices Included in This Chapter?

We will not pretend the experiences put forth in this chapter are 100% comprehensive and exhaustive. Yet we have done our best to provide a multiplicity of voices in our discussion. We rely on our own individual experiences, what we have witnessed in our respective paths, what we have discussed with others in our academic careers, and perspectives from colleagues in and outside of the communication studies discipline.

Jordan's Story

I am a first-generation student who grew up in multiethnic and multifaith households. My college career began at a community college as a full-time and part-time student prior to transferring to a 4-year university. After completing my master's degree, I worked as a research analyst for a publishing company before returning to earn my PhD. After completing my doctoral program, I started at my current institution where I have advised 14 PhD/MA students. I served as the Director of Graduate Studies from 2011–2019.

Megan's Story

I am a multiracial Black woman, the first of my family to attend graduate school, and a current PhD student in communication studies. Although I did not expect to attend graduate school, I started my undergraduate career at a 4-year university directly after graduating from high school, started my master's program immediately after graduating from college, and started my PhD program directly after earning my master's degree.

Other Voices

Quotes and exemplars in this chapter also come from formal solicitation of current and previous graduate students from a variety of programs, discussions with individuals in our social and professional networks, and reflections on conversations we have had in our academic careers.

Roadblocks to Success

In the following section, we provide a description of various personal and social barriers graduate students have faced in completing a program. As you read these, we imagine you will feel simultaneous emotions of connection ("Someone has experienced what I am going through!") and trepidation ("This is too challenging!"). We encourage you to embrace both emotions if they arise. But we also encourage you to remember the overall goal of this chapter: to highlight strategies that students have used to succeed. These strategies are offered in the next section.

Life Is Still Happening!

When you start on an academic path, you may fixate on the parts of your journey that feed your academic success ("How many credits will I need? How much time should I spend studying? Will this publication be accepted?"). However, many of us know that the choice to pursue a graduate degree, as with the choice of working toward most professions, affects more than just our time "at work." Rather, the commitment that it takes to pursue a graduate degree and the unique nature of academia (i.e., not a typical 9–5 "time in, time out" job) means that our personal lives often deeply affect our academic lives as well. For example, a student who has medical concerns may find very little space to devote to education when they are suffering through agonizing pain. Individuals with chronic health conditions, both visible and invisible, may find it hard to communicate their needs to tailor their program to accommodate their health concerns.

Taking care of medical concerns can lead to financial concerns that weigh heavy on the wallet and the mind. Simply put by a student who is chronically ill, "Health issues lead to more issues." In this student's case, "The bills from the ER and hospital visits started adding up quickly, and as a PhD student, I have a limited stipend. It was a struggle to pay those bills on top of every other bill I have." This student's and so many others' financial concerns during graduate school can cause an unbelievable amount of stress. Focusing on assignments, teaching, or research while wondering if your basic needs will be met this month can be overwhelming. In addition to bills that pile up over time, sometimes we go through sudden and unexpected life events that turn our worlds upside down.

> During the fall, I dealt with some major reproductive health issues that left me in crippling pain. I would have to cancel some of the interviews I needed to conduct for my thesis, cancel classes I was teaching, and if I couldn't cancel or miss class, I had to suffer through agonizing physical pain. It was a huge barrier since my health issues were invisible, so it made it difficult for me to let myself heal, and it was difficult to complete the work I needed to on a daily basis.

Students may also experience traumatic events such as loss of loved ones. When talking about the grief of losing her father amidst starting her graduate program, a student told us that "learning to grieve was hard enough on its own, but moving to a new town, trying to make new friends, and the intensity of coursework make grieving all the harder. I would actually feel bad for taking time off of school whenever grief came crashing down, even on the 1-year anniversary of his death. It was a very tough first year for me."

The loss of a family member or friend, dissolution of a relationship, and maintaining long-distance relationships with partners and friends are all common roadblocks faced by graduate students, especially those who travel far and wide away from their home base to attend programs that fit their areas of interest. Our personal relationships can affect our professional lives not only in terms of our professional relationships but also as social creatures because we tend to prioritize relationships with others, which can leave little room for channeling all of our energy toward professional goals.

> At one point, my sister was suicidal, and I felt like my family was reacting very harmfully. I was hundreds of miles away but felt like I had to keep intervening on behalf of my sister. The situation also included a period of time where my mom told me she did not want to talk to me (that lasted for about five months). I remember thinking over and over again, "I just want to be stressed out by regular grad school things!"

Where Is My Community?

In any endeavor, the people we meet along the way are important. Sometimes, they carry us when we cannot carry ourselves. Whereas many are fortunate to find support and community in graduate programs, this is not always the case, and it is difficult to find that connection to others. As such, while there can be great camaraderie among graduate student cohorts, one can feel isolated simply for not being part of that community:

> I really respect the students in my program, and for the most part, they are good people. I just am not one to live my life 24/7 thinking and talking about graduate school. Because I did not spend the whole time on campus or going out with fellow students, I felt I was viewed as an outsider and not really able to talk to them. At the same time, my friends outside of the program do not really understand what goes into all of this to be supportive. It can be kinda lonely even though I have good friends and a great partner.

Similarly, a first-generation student, for instance, often experienced a disconnect between graduate school and their friends and family. They noted:

> Even in times of success, you can still feel somewhat alone because your friends and family simply do not understand what this is all about and what goes into it. They can only be proud in the abstract. You end up relying on your graduate student friends or peers to share more details about accomplishments, and that's fine. But these aren't necessarily the closest friends or family. And sometimes the success amplifies that difference.

Of course, the struggle to find community and connection can be particularly amplified for those of us who come from standpoints in life that are underrepresented in the academy. For many Black, Indigenous, and People of Color (BIPOC) in academia as well as international students, especially those from non-Western countries, experiences are too often characterized by isolation, (in)direct prejudice and discrimination, misunderstanding, and lack of attention to histories and standpoints:

> When I proposed a study on race and identity, I was asked by a faculty member, "Why is this is important, and how is this communication?" Others don't understand that this feels like being asked to justify why my experiences are important. And I know this is a common experience, especially for Black scholars.

Likewise, a first-generation BIPOC student told us, "I was actually told by my advisor that due to my parents' uneducated background, I did not know how to be 'professional' unlike my White lab mates. I did not take this well, and it has continued to make me uneasy and feel unsafe with my advisor. It was a barrier because my advisor telling me that made me question one of my biggest insecurities." This lack of kinship and inability to connect with others that understand what it is like to be a first-generation student left this student fending for herself without advice and support from individuals that truly understood the roadblocks she was facing, especially with her toxic advisor.

> I look around at my cohort, and I am the only brown body. I look around in the classroom, and I am the only brown body. I look at the faculty and I am the only brown body. I want to think, "I will be the one who changes things!" But, too often, I think, "I don't belong."

Mentors Are Supposed to Support You, Right?

As referenced in the previous example, one of the more common roadblocks individuals experience is with mentors that are not supportive or active in mentorship. As one student noted, "I expected him to guide me and assist me in progressing to my degree. But it really seemed like he was focused on his own work. Other students had great mentorship experiences. I was envious of that."

> I distinctly remember a phone call in August (at the beginning of my second year, nine months before my thesis had to be defended). This advisor berated me like a child in a way that not even my parents had done. She accused me of "hustling" her, noting that I made her believe that I was capable of much more than I am. She was angry, enraged even, that my project was not publication-ready, given her entrance into a new institution where her publications matter for her tenure and promotion.

In some cases, the advisors and mentors are actually detrimental to our journeys. One student shared experiences with her advisor: "I felt like I was there to serve her rather than the other way around." As in many fields, those in positions of power in the academy sometimes abuse their positions for the sake of prestige, promotion, or "paying forward" the poor treatment they received in their own programs. In fact, graduate student (and fellow faculty) abuse is a major issue that deserves more attention in higher education (see Amienne, 2017). Whether individuals experience more subtle nonsupportive behaviors or more explicit negative behavior leading to emotional trauma, the behavior of mentors and advisors can inhibit growth and success for students (see Chapter 7 for more information on mentor–advisee relationships).

In many programs, students look to advanced graduate students to offer guidance and mentorship. But these upper-level students may have attitudes that range from uninterested or downright toxic. A former student spoke about this, saying, "From day one, I was treated as if every idea or thought I had was rudimentary and almost childlike. Rather than helping me find places for growth, it was implied that I did not belong."

It's Really About Me!

In our own reflections, discussions with colleagues and peers, and in stories shared with us, it was clear that many current and former students believe that "sometimes, we can be our own worst enemies." In this, it is not inferring that we self-sabotage. Rather, we often create standards and expectations for our success that can be the toughest to achieve. We look to other students' journeys and think that ours should be modeled after theirs, and thus we unnecessarily place more pressure on ourselves. A student shared with us a related experience, saying that "I would constantly look to my fellow students and think that because of their successes I was not doing enough." Comparison with your fellow students is often actually a competition with yourself, as everyone's academic path looks different. She went on to say that:

> I took on so many responsibilities to try to prove to everyone around
> me that I was impressive that, after a while, great opportunities felt like
> strenuous burdens. This hit particularly hard during the pandemic, as I was so
> preoccupied by fear and uncertainty, navigating shifts to online, and engaging
> in activism after the murder of George Floyd that I felt like I was falling behind
> on my research. I realized that I only valued myself for my productivity, and I
> had to reevaluate my goals and priorities.

Clearly, our self-standards can get in the way of taking care of ourselves and ensuring our success. This fallacy of self-standards often takes the form of imposter syndrome, or the idea that you are the only one in the room who is not qualified to be in graduate school. One student told us that "imposter syndrome is pervasive and very real. And as much success as I've had in publishing, teaching, and my coursework, I still feel this need to compete and prove my worth because others around me may think I'm not where I'm supposed to be." Engaging in comparison is natural in academic fields that are often competitive. However, a lack of faith in oneself can make self-standards insurmountable (see Chapter 10 for more on this issue).

In the preceding discussion, we provided some of the more common barriers to success based on the voices included in this chapter. However, we want to again stress that the goal in including these barriers is so we can recognize many of our experiences are shared, in that others likely can speak to the same experiences. We do believe there is some sense in comfort in knowing that you are not alone in figuring out how to navigate these personal, social, and structural impediments to your graduate journey. We now turn to common strategies employed by current and former students to address various barriers, and we hope this serves as a reminder that, more often than not, scholars are still successful in achieving goals even when encountering the aforementioned roadblocks ... or others.

Strategies for Overcoming Roadblocks

As with any journey, it is not always about the trials and tribulations insomuch as it is about figuring out how to overcome these to reach your goals. The following section outlines various strategies that have been successfully employed by current and previous graduate students. We recognize and appreciate that all journeys are unique, and these may or may not resonate with you. In other words, we are not putting these forth as completely prescriptive. Rather, our hope is that you can identify strategies that may work for you and/or some of these experiences may serve as a catalyst for identifying your own strategies.

My Health and Well-Being Come First!

Whether physically climbing a mountain or running a marathon, the athlete must take care of their body, or there will be no ability to climb in the first place. While being able to overcome tremendous feats and achieve lofty goals takes training and hard work, it also takes attunement to the body's needs. This is no different in the grad school climb. Your physical and mental health are paramount to graduate school success. For some, this means engaging in important practices related to your body physically. As a student told us, "I have to feel good physically. I have always been an active person, and I realized that when graduate school got in the way of running and working out, I could tell that my struggles in graduate school would increase." Many students spoke to the importance of proper balance like gifting your body with movement and feeding it what it needs as a basic and important step to success. As a former student shared:

People always talk about the "freshman 15." But that was nothing like the first year of graduate school. I was lucky because we had a great group of students come into together, and we became good friends. Oh boy, that didn't lead to a lot of healthy habits! It wasn't about how I looked; it was how I felt! Eating better and getting more exercise really paid off in terms of centering me again.

For others, nurturing the mental side of well-being is crucial to success. This may be achieved through effective therapeutic practices, such as finding the right therapist to help you talk through your feelings, gain perspective on graduate school and personal experiences, and prescribe the right medications when necessary. A student told us, "Finding the right therapist and anxiety medications took me years, and I'm glad I took the plunge. It can be scary, but it's so worth it." Others find mental grounding in more spiritual practices, like doing yoga or meditation, to relax themselves or ground themselves in their spirituality. As a student expressed to us, "Listen—like most things we want in life, this is hard. You have to make sure you ground yourself spiritually. For me, that's about my faith. For others, it can be meditation or other practices. But do not lose sight of that in this whole thing." However you take care of your mental health, graduate school is a mental marathon, and equipping your mind with the tools to stay healthy is important before you can produce and consume knowledge.

Seriously, you want to make things easier? Just get sleep! More than anything, get those zzzzz's.

You Gotta Set Your Boundaries!

While graduate school is a lifestyle that brings with it long hours and seemingly round-the-clock thought and dedication, it doesn't have to overshadow our other life goals and responsibilities. In fact, many students rely on planners and lists to stay organized, which helps them set out dedicated time to rest and perform other life tasks and goals. Setting boundaries that allow us to turn off helps to prevent burnout and develop healthy habits that we can take with us into our future careers. The only way to grieve, gain back strength, or get over the bumps in the road is to make sure that we have enough fuel to keep going, which means recharging when it is necessary. For example, one student told us:

I need my other hobbies and activities. Graduate school is different because many of us come from different places, and this isn't our home. We can get caught up in this being everything including our work and social lives. But then we can never escape! We do more and more and more. We go out with friends and only talk about our program. Once I found a social life outside of graduate school, I was able to separate my graduate school life from other parts of me.

> I have always been organized, but these struggles made me become even more organized. I have special stickers and tabs in my planner for paydays, bills, assignments, etc. I have also begun to color-coordinate all of my bills and due dates. This has helped me focus on what is due and when, as well as give me a sense of relief because everything does not fall on one day. Seeing how the dates are spread across each month, I panic a bit less.

Striking this balance between turning off and staying engaged in your program is difficult but rewarding and freeing for many students.

Another part of setting boundaries is clearly communicating your boundaries when you have the space to. A student told us:

> One of the most important strategies I have learned and used is being able to set professional boundaries. I had to set boundaries on other tasks to get my thesis done. However, now I have that skill to use in a more healthy way, such as setting boundaries on fruitless opportunities in the first place. I think if I had this skill before this roadblock, I would have been able to say no to some of the responsibilities placed on me, which would have eased the process.

So lean on your mentors, colleagues, and fellow students when you need to pull back or get help. There is no shame in communicating your boundaries and setting clear expectations with your collaborators. Asking for help is crucial in graduate school, which means finding those that you can trust will help carry you when you need a break from climbing.

Can You Connect With Others?

To put it simply, this experience is impossible to do alone. The academy offers benefits in terms of the niche community that you are exposed to, and leaning on that community often makes graduate school more meaningful. Many current and former students emphasize that connecting with others who understand your career path, what it is like to matriculate an advisee, the pride of getting accepted to a conference, or the disappointment of not earning the grade you thought you would make the experience all the more joyous and bearable.

> I found friends that could support me through my thesis as well as through my graduate career. I relied on friends to have work dates with so that I wouldn't have to read edits and address them alone. I also found friends who knew what I had gone through, specifically those who had also been advised by this person. We share strategies, such as not reading her emails at the beginning of the day in order to avoid panic or how to ask questions in a way that wouldn't incite wrath.

We also recognize that this is easier said than done because it still requires finding others that shared similar experiences and can understand the specific barriers you may be facing:

> I had to join a Black student union to find other Black students on my campus. I remember one of the first meetings I had ever attended, I felt shocked to be around so many Black students at once. It does take up more time that I could be dedicating to my doctoral responsibilities, but it is worth it because of the acceptance I felt.

Sometimes, this may also mean looking beyond your specific discipline:

> I took risks in my classes that were outside of my department. In those classes if I found people that I seemed to relate to, I would gain the courage to ask them to go get coffee to work on a project for the class or go grab a glass of wine after class. While it was terrifying, I knew it was my only way to garner these connections.

Joining groups that speak to specific experiences underrepresented in academia or finding individuals in our niche content areas or just finding people you connect with and seeking advice from colleagues and mentors with similar experiences, or even different perspectives, can offer us clarity and lead us to helpful realizations on our own journeys.

Remember Your Friends and Family!

Although connection in the academy is important for some graduate students, our families and friends can also offer us support and perspectives beyond those of academic confidants. In fact, nonacademic friends have a profound way of pulling us out of siloed thinking and reorienting us to other social bubbles. A student told us:

> I made sure I reconnected with friends outside of graduate programs. Talking with them, sharing stories—a mechanic, a roofer, a salesman, a real estate agent, an IT guy, a bartender. Being around people outside of the academic bubble is important. I thought they would not understand my stress and concerns. At the end of the day, no matter what job you are in, there are going to be things all friends can relate to and help with.

> I eventually came to terms with the fact that these people weren't as similar to me as the people who had been in my last program, and in doing so I discovered that I may have to find people outside of my program to connect with. I ended up joining workout classes at a local studio and from there found

a friend that in turn introduced me to her friends. Through this connection I begin to feel like the new place was becoming a home and that I had finally developed a support system that I so desperately needed.

Additionally, some of us have immense support built right into our homes. To take advantage of this, though, current and former graduate students recommended clearly communicating your needs and boundaries to your loved ones as you would with colleagues: "I asked my partner to be more involved in some of my basic household needs (cooking, laundry). Sometimes people are not great about offering these specific types of help, but they all enthusiastically were there for me when I asked them to do something." Finally, we would be remiss if we did not point out the calls and recommendations for finding support in "furry" friends!

Sometimes, Avoidance Is Best!

While the previous two strategies address connecting with others, it would not be realistic to say that we can always have open conversations with people to solve all problems. Although avoidance seems like a negative word, many of us have faced situations and people who have inhibited our ability to be successful, and sometimes, we are unable to remove these toxic roadblocks from our paths. Sometimes, we engage in all the positive strategies we possibly can and still are faced with situations we cannot control. Not surprisingly, our experiences, as well as those that were shared with us, emphasize that "we must remove *ourselves* from toxicity as much as possible."

At times, this may require avoiding fellow students in a graduate program: A student who was experiencing conflict with another student in her corhort explained, "You know, I just felt like I had to ignore him and not really pay attention to what he said to me or about me. While it was awkward, it made a world of difference." Likewise, as in many relationships, it is important to balance positive and supportive conversation with conversations that create more stress and negativity.

> You are working with the same people day in and day out. In my office, we have five to six graduate students, and we always hang out in each other's office. It is great to let ourselves talk, express our emotions, and support each other. But you have to be careful! There's a fine line between support and toxic rumination. Support and rumination can turn into a lot of negative talk, which can change you and how you approach graduate school.

Unfortunately, in some cases, avoidance is the strategy adopted in working with advisors or mentors. After switching to a different advisor after suffering abuse from a previous advisor, a student told us, "I was able to have more control over my dissertation and have found the whole process more enjoyable because of it. Although not the best, I have avoided frequent contact with my advisor unless they are necessary." While it is important to work through small disagreements, growing pains, and personality differences with the people you work with, removing yourself from a toxic lab environment, mentor, or student circle may just change your entire perspective on graduate school according to experiences shared with us. We also stress that no one should feel powerless in these situations, especially with the power hierarchy in departments. As one student noted, "While it may feel uncomfortable, talk to your chair or graduate advisor or another faculty member when issues arise with your advisor. Do not feel like you have to handle this on your own."

Trust Yourself

Self-doubt is as common in the academy as it is with many aspects of life. For many, it is a whole new terrain to navigate. The idea of walking into an unknown world can be daunting, especially in understanding the new professional landscape. As a current student jokingly mentioned in understanding academic publishing: "I thought a journal was something you wrote in about your emotions and feelings!" In the end, though, it is important to trust our competencies and remember what each of us achieved to get accepted into these programs. One student proclaimed that "I always call myself lucky or only credit the people around me for getting me here, but I always forget that I have been here the whole time, and I deserve to be proud." Finally, as one of us is fond of saying:

> It is helpful to remember that when you tell yourself you cannot complete your goals, that you are not good enough, or that you are not cut out for graduate school, you are simultaneously saying your mentors, advisors, recommendation-letter writers, and all of the others that advocated for you are wrong. Trust that these people believe in you, and just as you respect and look up to many of them, you should also trust their judgment.

Conclusion

When we originally accepted the invitation to write this chapter, we were excited to provide a resource that ideally assists current and future graduate students as well as mentors in navigating the exciting, engaging, and, at times, nerve-racking journey of completing a graduate program. During the process of writing this, all of us experienced a global pandemic and social reckoning with the racial injustice that continues to plague societies—including academic institutions— and affected each of us in significant but different ways. Initially, we had difficulty completing the chapter for two reasons. First, as we discussed above, one of the barriers to productivity in the academy is that "life happens." Even in drafting this chapter, we had to rely on some of the strategies we listed above, and our mutual support, to complete this work. In other words, what you are reading is actually an example of scholars encountering roadblocks and enacting strategies to achieve a goal.

Second, with current events in our society, we were wondering if these roadblocks and strategies we originally identified were no longer sufficient or applicable to the times we are living in. However, based on our own reflection, observations, and conversations, we see our colleagues and students enacting many of the same strategies and approaches to addressing barriers that perhaps are amplified in the current climate. As such, we hope we achieved our goal to provide resources for all of us to use when necessary or beneficial. We again emphasize that the content of this chapter is not to be considered comprehensive, nor is it a panacea to all issues. Rather, our hope is that readers find connection, shared experience, and potential solutions to what they or others may be experiencing at any point in the graduate school journey. Being a scholar-teacher can be an incredible experience. As a faculty member early on told one of us, "Academics is an incredible life. You get to make a living reading, researching, writing, and teaching!" We agree! We hope this chapter and this edited volume allows everyone to achieve this life.

For Further Thought and Reflection

1. What roadblocks have you experienced in your graduate career?

2. What strategies were most effective for you in overcoming barriers you have experienced?

3. What changes do you believe are necessary in your department, college, university, or higher education, in general, to better facilitate success in graduate programs?

4. What can you do now and in the future to assist and/or mentor others as they navigate graduate education?

12

Graduate School Is a Human Experience of Struggling, Celebrating, and Striving Together

Graduate Life as a Collective Endeavor

Jenna N. Hanchey

Samantha Gillespie

Ana-Luisa Ortiz-Martinez

I n this chapter, we focus on collectivity. Each section first comes from an individual voice whose name is referenced in the section heading. Each "I" then shifts depending on the section author, before we come together to write in the conclusion as "we," addressing the collective "us."

Thoughts from Jenna on Collectivity

As I write this, I am sitting on a couch in my living room. Although Sam, Annie, and I have been working on this chapter together, we have not seen each other since last November. It's now June. Since they graduated from the MA program where I teach and headed off to PhD programs in other states, it's much harder to see each other in person. And yet we are still working together, still texting to let each other know when we'll have drafts and revisions finished. This is still a collective endeavor. Unfortunately, our graduate school experiences create conditions that sometimes obscure collectivity by making us feel vulnerable and isolated. There are two different ways to react to these sorts of feelings: Either you may respond individually, looking for ways to secure your own seemingly precarious resources and health, or you may respond collectively, understanding that your security, health, and well-being depend on that of others.

> So much of the graduate school experience, when framed as an individualized endeavor, promotes a notion of scarcity. A scarcity mindset—based in a deep fear that there's not enough to go around,

and any "win" or success for one of my peers is a loss for me—thrives in the myth of isolation and in the interiority of my imagined aloneness. The best way I've found to stave off a scarcity mindset is to stay in relationships with the very peers that scarcity would have me disdain or fear. Reaching out for coffee, sending a quick text, picking up the phone: Being in community always reminds me that graduate school is a human experience of struggling, celebrating, and striving together, not merely the doling out of finite resources and accolades. (Sean Kenney, University of Colorado Boulder)

We'll be thinking about this through Aimee Carrillo Rowe's (2008) lens of *politics of relation*. Carrillo Rowe argues that who we are as subjects arises in and through our relations with others. Specifically, she advocates for forming relationships across difference:

> The sites of our belonging constitute how we see the world, what we value, who we are (becoming). The meaning of self is never individual, but a shifting set of relations that we move in and out of, often without reflection. (Carrillo Rowe, 2008, p. 25)

If who we are is collective rather than individual, how do we create a graduate student atmosphere that allows us to support each other and grow together? One of the things Carrillo Rowe (2008) teaches is to think of allyship as building relations across difference with those who are on a similar level of institutional power in the academy in order to advocate on each other's behalf, and particularly for those who hold the least power. More recent scholarly and activist work has taken this a step further, advocating that we should seek to be more than simply allies, moving to the level of co-conspirator (Hackman, 2015), as allyship can be a means of avoiding responsibility or sometimes even reinforcing dominant power dynamics (Nautiyal, 2020). Co-conspirators work collectively for the benefit of the most marginalized, taking their lead but shouldering responsibility together.

Odds are that, during your graduate school experience, you will face something that throws you off-balance, makes you feel insecure, or leaves you frightened for your own future prospects. Some respond to these sorts of problems by attempting to schmooze people with institutional power in order to get individualized favors. That approach may assist one person in getting by, but it doesn't change the structures within the institution to make sure that others will not have to face the same problems in the future. Instead, for example, consider how graduate students at the University of Texas at Austin responded to the insecurity brought on by the pandemic: They stood together, writing an open letter to the administration "call[ing] upon the university to take immediate and decisive action to support and protect graduate student workers, as well as other vulnerable university employees" (UT Austin, 2020). They worked together as co-conspirators.

In this chapter, we consider what it can look like to think of graduate school as a collective co-conspiratorial endeavor and, specifically, how it can change the way we think about ethics and professionalism, how we handle time management, and our embodied relations with each other—and ourselves. Being a co-conspirator is not easy, and I am continually messing it up. But knowing that you will fail is not a good reason not to try; rather, it's a good reason to figure out how to pick yourself up from that failure, learn from it, and try again. We hope this chapter will help you learn how to do just that.

Rethinking Ethics and Professionalism with Jenna

When someone tells you to "be professional," as a graduate student, they often mean something like don't have too much alcohol, that your manner of dress is somehow missing the mark, or that the emotionality of your writing makes them uncomfortable. What is often left unsaid is how this idea of professionalism as an individualistic achievement of "objectivity" is based on white, Western, masculine, fatphobic norms that render many graduate students "unprofessional" from the start.[1] In this section, I'd like us to rethink professional ethics in graduate school through our lens of co-conspiratorial community support in order to find a version of professionalism that can be accessed by all.

The focus on number of drinks, style of clothes, or objectivity of writing are solutions that answer the wrong problems. Rather than modifying individual behavior, we should work to create graduate cultures of collective support where we take a relational ethical perspective. That is, we need to be thinking about how the collectives to which we belong either support professional relations or make them more difficult.

> Ethics and professionalism, at least in my experience, tend to be words thrown around by white men who are uncomfortable engaging in more critical discussion about race, gender, and identity. Instilled in the idea of "professionalism" seems to be this misguided removal of emotion and personality from research. Critical research, in many cases, requires us to break down common ideals such as professionalism and examine them, understanding why nonnormative individuals might rightfully resist the cultural requirements they have underpinned. Why should the Western notion of professional dress, for example, be upheld when it predominately boxes people into specific types of expression that might not fit their personal/cultural values? (Michael Klajbor, University of Illinois Urbana–Champaign)

---

1   Following calls from Black activists and scholars, we capitalize Black and other marginalized racial identities, while leaving white lowercase in order to support Black struggles for liberation against white supremacist structures (Kapitan, 2016).

From this perspective, the well-behaved, suit-and-tie-wearing detached professional does not make any sense. Professionalism, when it is thought of as a relational ethic of care that supports and advocates on behalf of the graduate student collective in a way that uplifts everyone, does not only show up in this one singular form. Now, suits may be how some demonstrate their commitment, but when a particular style of clothing is upheld as the primary professional standard for all, more harm is done than good. We know that behavioral, clothing, and so-called "objectivity" norms are used to discipline people of color, queer and trans folks, the differently abled, and international students (Bahrainwala, 2020; Chevrette, 2020; Nautiyal, 2020).

A particularly pernicious way the norm of objectivity often shows up is through the idea that you must somehow be detached from your work in order for it to be professional. Not so: Professional objectivity is a myth. We are who we are because of our relations with those around us, and our writing is informed by those relations, whether we understand and admit it or not. But the myth of professional objectivity persists because we invest it with power. However, by individualizing everything, this myth of professionalism makes it more difficult to support other people in the graduate program, particularly those whose race, gender, sexuality, ability, or culture does not seem to "fit" the (white, Western, heteropatriarchal, ableist) norm. Instead, I offer some ways that we can build collective professionalism within our graduate departments and communities.

First, embrace vulnerability. If you came to graduate school as a perfectionist, this might be difficult. But vulnerability is vitally important, not only to your academic work but also to growing your community. Failure is a precondition for success, not its opposite. The only way you will grow as a thinker and writer is by letting other people read your essays and tell you what did and did not work. The only way you will grow as a graduate community member is by letting people read *you* and tell you what is not working. The only way others will grow is by accepting similar feedback from you. Part of being a co-conspirator is being willing to let our comrades know where they have messed up (Carrillo Rowe, 2008): when they should have stood up against that racial microaggression (Bahrainwala, 2020), when they scoffed at an international colleague's perceived naïveté (Nautiyal, 2020), when they misgendered a colleague. Part of being a co-conspirator is also recognizing that this feedback is not a personal attack, but aimed at making sure the collective is able to reach their goals. Feedback, in this light, is an invitation to be a better community member in the future. I have failed on all of these fronts, and I will again. As my colleagues and I have written elsewhere, "We cannot be finished with failure" (Jensen et al., 2020, p. 144). The bigger failure would be responding with knee-jerk reactions of denial and fragility (Chevrette, 2020). So share your writing with other graduate students. Share your struggles with writing, with publishing, with life. Your struggles with the process may help someone else through theirs. Create a community where everyone knows that if they share their experiences they will be met with care and a determination to do better in the future.

Second, hold each other up. This one may seem particularly difficult, because some programs inculcate the belief that you need to compete with one another to get an award, get published, or get a job. But, in reality, the opposite is true. When anyone in your program gets recognition, it uplifts the reputation of the program. When someone gets published on your topic, it sends readers looking for more essays on that topic. When a communication scholar gets interviewed on national news, that's good for all of us. I know, a job is necessarily exclusive in that someone will get it and others will not. But I met some of my best friends in the discipline through jobs I did not get. The reasons I was not selected had nothing to do with "losing" any sort of competition against other candidates; rather, it was about difference in research focus, career level, or experience—that is, things over which I had no control. The more we support each other, the better we all we do. For example, pay attention to calls for special issues of journals, and send them to your colleagues working in that area. Nominate each other for awards. Create a community where people feel comfortable asking others to nominate them, because they know they will be supported. Recognize each other's victories and accomplishments.

Third, make room for self-reflection. This will mean engaging with the differential experiences and embodiments that others are starting from, as well as your own preconceived notions about them. Co-conspirators act as a bulwark for those around them, and if you are white, Western, and/or masculine-presenting in particular, you have an automatic leg up in being perceived to be professional that many of your women, LGBTQ+, BIPOC, and non-Western colleagues do not. Baharainwala (2020) makes the case that the privileged among us need to be ready to challenge racism *as it is happening*. At the same time, Nautiyal (2020) points out that sometimes standing up for others can be paternalistic, especially in regard to international students. This means you constantly need to be thinking about how your experiences and embodiment relate to those of your community. Consider the ways that you have been privileged and/or disenfranchised. Consider the different ways those around you have been privileged and/or disenfranchised. Try to educate yourself on the struggles of others that you don't yet understand. Be ready to support those around you in the very moments they need it. And be ready to take the lesson to heart without resorting to fragility if they let you know that you didn't exactly get it right. Learn, grow, and try again.

Sam on the Pressure of Time Management and Connections to Mental Health

I felt a deep sense of irony when I told Dr. Hanchey, a professor in my master's program, I would write for this chapter and found out time management was a key topic I was to write about. I had not only pushed back my master's thesis to the last possible deadline but also turned in every paper late during my first semester of the PhD. Actually, maybe this makes me the perfect person to address this topic. My experience with time mismanagement qualifies me to tell you some difficult truths. Time management may seem like a straightforward subject—but it is not. In this section, I demystify time management, discussing how time-management myths can exacerbate mental health issues and offering a framing of time management that turns toward collectivity, before concluding with practical tips.

Time management is constructed through a discourse of neoliberal rugged individualism. That is, we have told students their failure is their own fault. The myth of higher education is that if you work hard enough you can achieve success, ignoring our differential experiences and contexts. Failure has been framed as an individualized issue within higher education's culture. Focusing on time management, then, can perpetuate a myth that puts cultural responsibilities and consequences onto the individual. To demystify time management, we must first let go of the idea that we are independently in control of our success as academics. I liken this framing of time management to Gregg's (2018) ecology of the term "productivity." That is, the use of language, such as time management and productivity, carries with it a weight of histories and unequal power relations that become mystified over time. Gregg (2018) explains, "When we covet productivity in the present, we rarely consider its relationship to the manifold conditions that transformed work and home over the course of a century" (p. 19). To demystify the idea of time management as a graduate student is to critically investigate the different influences that are shaping how we use our time and whether or not we have control over them.

Procrastination is often framed as failure. Another perspective on procrastination is that procrastination denotes how we internalize the outside pressures under which we perform. The institutional system of graduate education is structured around hard-to-meet expectations that can create cycles of what feels like personal failure. These cycles are then perpetuated by norms already established in the academy and internalized within ourselves. By default we feel like we are failing as graduate students because we cannot meet all the expectations placed upon us at all times. We begin to villainize our failures rather than recognize failure as part of an important process of growing and developing our scholarly identities (Jensen et al., 2019). We cannot learn and sharpen our skill sets without learning from our failures. We must not be afraid to fail, but more importantly, we must not be afraid to embrace those failures.

I am reminded of an assignment I was given during my second semester of my PhD prompting us to write about the promise and possibilities of communication. I not only wrote about battling overwhelming feelings of self-doubt, unworthiness, and shame around my mental health issues but also about how many accomplished scholars have faced similar situations. My colleagues deeply connected to what I wrote. What normatively might seem like "failure" became a turning point for me. That's not to say that by opening up to my cohort everything became magically better, but a huge burden was lifted. I not only relieved my own burdens through sharing but also initiated a space where everyone else could too.

I had been facing struggles with my mental health from the start of my PhD program because I had not released the illusion of control. This illusion (or delusion) was that if I tried hard enough I could get through this on my own—a bootstrap mentality. However, there are just some things that rolling up your sleeves and working hard cannot solve. Upon starting my first semester, my partner went two months without full-time employment after we moved to Nebraska and then, shortly after, my father moved in to live with us. So not only did I have to work through the stresses that came with living in a new place and starting a new graduate program, but also had to deal with the complexities of switching roles from daughter to parent with my father.

It was difficult to reach out to my community of graduate students and faculty, not because they did not make themselves accessible but because of the shame I was feeling. Much of this shame was not mine, but shame I took on because there is a profound stigma around mental health—even when the circumstances make struggles perfectly reasonable. I was going through a lot; of course, I would be struggling! Yet I still felt embarrassed, and I isolated myself rather than reach out. When I finally did start talking to my community about my difficulties, there was not one faculty member I met who didn't disclose their own struggles during their first semester of doctoral work. Your struggles will look different from mine; maybe they will seem less strenuous or more—that is not the point. The point is that we are not in a vacuum during our studies. Life continues to happen, and many of us will battle with our mental health. The more honest I was about my experience, the more my colleagues were honest about their struggles and the more transparent the conversations became about how we could support each other.

Writing and sharing my struggles did not magically fix everything. I sought out resources, including therapy. I still struggle with my self-doubt, but things are getting easier. The writing assignment reminded me of the power of being open and that much of the shame, self-doubt, and pain we carry is not simply our own, but a societal burden that we must continue to work toward demystifying.

In a perfect world I would love to see a shift in how we structure graduate school, providing more space to learn at a different pace, in different ways, and without highly pressurized standards that privilege whiteness, ability, and cis-heteronormativity. While we have come a long way, we all stand witness to the distance we need to overcome. I cannot promise you that you will never procrastinate or feel defeated, but I can offer ways for you to reframe your perspective. Your procrastination and failures do not define you, and they do not mark your intelligence, capabilities, or possibilities. The pressures are actually part of a larger system of standards and benchmarks that are not working to serve you. The tips I offer you are ways to turn from individualized framing toward collectivity, as the more we work to support each other, the less power we give to the fear of failure and procrastination.

First, everyone procrastinates. Think of the person in your program who seems like they have it all together—I promise they procrastinate. However, what procrastination looks like for them may be different from what it looks like for you. And I bet you they feel just as stressed, guilty, and frustrated as you do. One good tip is to set a timer for a set period of time to work. My colleague, who to me always seems on top of her game, has told me, "Look, we all watch YouTube instead of reading that article or writing that proposal. That is why I set a timer." I do too now. A timer commits you to working for 20 minutes or whatever time frame you choose. This both helps to get you started and ensures that you take breaks in between working blocks.

Second, progress doesn't always look like studying or writing. One of my colleagues shared how they reconceptualized productivity as going to the gym, getting coffee with a friend, spending time with family. Taking care of your whole self is also an important part of finding success in your career. So schedule in time for self-care. Schedule in your walk, coffee break, dinner with family—whatever you need for you. Let go of the guilt you may feel around not doing coursework, research, teaching preparation, and other tasks that are important to your education and career by also prioritizing these other valuable components of your life. This will be a prioritization effort that will prepare you for your life after graduate studies as well.

Third, you are not alone. Often, programs (or even cohorts) create a culture of competition. One's doubts, insecurities, and moments of struggle become ways we isolate ourselves because we are afraid of seeming weak or incapable. It is important to find ways that feel safe to talk about the realities of your experience. Being open about your hardships may be a means of pioneering a new environment in your program or, on a smaller scale, helping a trusted colleague express their own difficulties. On whatever scale is comfortable, it is important that you seek out support that offers solutions beyond bootstrap advice.

Annie on the Weight of Embodiment and Connections to Physical Health

When I first announced I wanted to pursue a PhD, the responses around me varied from wondering whether I could be away from my family to making sure I understood the workload of academia. I was not concerned about anything, except how it would affect my daughter. I am an immigrant, a first-generation student, and a mom and can be almost arrogant when it comes to my workload. I did not think a PhD would be any harder than raising my daughter while working two jobs and working on a MA. I was wrong. Being a first-year doctoral student is one of the most exhausting things I have ever done. It takes a toll physically, mentally, and emotionally, which is based not only on what is required of you but also the expectations you put on yourself.

As a Mexican American woman moving to Iowa for my PhD, I armed myself with the words of Anzaldúa (2015), Carrillo-Rowe (2008), and Lorde (2015). My daughter, my dad, my dog, and I drove across the country. Channeling Anzaldúa's rebel with a deep belief in Lorde's notion that the master's tools will never dismantle the master's house, we drove without anything but a few of my daughter's toys and our clothes. To me the act of moving across country into a space that is not your own is in itself resisting. As we drove, I stared at the power lines, trusting that I would be able to create alliances, find co-conspirators, and craft spaces in our new home just as Carrillo-Rowe explained. My only desire was to survive the first semester. But survival did not quite address how I fit and saw myself in my new space.

Shome (2003) explains the way in which spatial perspectives and contextual relations need to be considered in communication studies. Shome demonstrates that power is constituted not only by identity but also the places we inhabit. In moving from my master's program in Reno to my PhD program in Iowa City, I moved from a place where the student population is more than 20% Latinx to one in which it is less than 7%—even less when it comes to graduate students. I carried my border identity from Reno to Iowa City, but the way in which I was perceived changed. In Iowa City the "student standard is still assumed to be young, white, middle-class non-disabled heterosexual women and men" (Romero, 2018, p. 62). I am a Mexican American woman in her 30s, and I was suddenly out of place.

For all the intersectional scholars I've studied, I was suddenly aware of my race and ethnicity differently. I became aware of the weight of my steps and the heaviness of the gazes on my back. I began to carry a load on my shoulders that went beyond my backpack. It was a load that was both psychological and emotional. Because I sensed myself differently, I stood and walked differently. I began to have migraines that made me lose my train of thought, my imagination, and, in essence, my voice. I could not write. As Anzaldúa (2015) reflected:

> I lack imagination you say
>
> No. I lack language.
>
> The language to clarify
>
> My resistance to the literate. (p. 165)

My stress and unrealistic expectations were now reflected on my body, and all of it came to a pinnacle in December during the final week of my first semester. But it had started long before.

Encouraged by a friend, I began applying for communication MA programs the summer my daughter Galia turned one. Instead of slowing down, I decided to forego sleep and use the little time I had to attain a degree. Into the MA program I went, and after barely sleeping for a year, I figured that not sleeping for another two years would hardly make a difference. I never imagined that I would fall in love with communication studies, become a scholar indefinitely, and never sleep again.

The lack of sleep, two jobs, and mommying around the clock started taking a toll on my body by the second year of my MA. I started gaining weight, getting migraines, and carrying an inhaler. By the time I graduated, I was exhausted, but I still did not stop. I had determined to go for my PhD, so instead of resting after I finished school, I spent the summer coordinating my daughter's custody arrangements with lawyers, preparing for our move, and finishing up work with my previous employer. By the time I arrived at University of Iowa, the migraines would make me pass out for hours. I was not taking care of my body, and for reasons I had yet to figure out, I would lose my balance and fall while walking on campus. Still, I continued to push myself to get my daughter and me settled into our new life.

That collapse that I dreaded occurred during the final week of the fall semester. Walking back from lecture on a Monday afternoon, I slipped on four concrete steps, injuring my back to the point where it was grueling to move. However, even then, I did not go to a doctor or reach out for assistance. I had an eye exam that week and did not want to miss any more time from school. It was during the eye exam, after failing multiple tests, that I was sent to the emergency room. I was told I had multiple problems, including a cyst above my kidneys, prior back injuries, and problems with my overall structure that most likely developed during my pregnancy.

Alone, each of these things could not cause much damage, but without care, they had taken a toll on my body.

With a new semester beginning, I was faced with visits to oncology, physical therapy, chiropractors, and tests, all while trying to care for my daughter. I was frustrated and was finally forced to stop and think about what I was doing to my body and what I had to do going forward. I was forced to evaluate what I had avoided for over two years. I realized it was time for me to set aside time to take care of myself and to reach out for help and rely on the community around us. I did, and I received more support than I could have imagined. By the end of the first year at the University of Iowa, I made the kinds of friendships that will last a lifetime.

Flores (1996) explains that Chicana feminist scholars have a hard time belonging in academia because we are confined geographically and rhetorically by how people respond to our bodies. Flores's resolution is to create our own spaces by embracing our heritage. In learning about our culture, we are empowered to create our own rhetorical spaces. To thrive, we must first accept and understand our differences and then create who we want to be without preimposed boundaries. In entering the program with the idea of simple survival, I set myself up to follow the rhetoric that was created for me in that space, as opposed to crafting my own identity. As a woman of color, I entered a space, and instead of making it mine, I allowed it to influence who I was, and this took a toll on my whole being. I exhausted myself with my own expectations of what others wanted me to be.

While this is my narrative, many graduate students have similar experiences, and we can learn from each other. Anzaldúa (2015) made it clear that we must embrace looking, walking, and writing differently because in doing so we confront our demons and find our voice. But beyond that, finding our voice can mean making sure that others do not have to go through what we did. As Lorde (2015) teaches, "Survival is not an academic skill. It is learning how to stand alone … and how to make common cause with others who identify outside the structures, in order to define and seek a world in which we can all flourish" (p. 95). We should be thinking beyond survival and toward thriving and creating room for others to follow.

Tupo Pamoja?

One of Jenna's favorite Swahili phrases is *tupo pamoja*, or "we are together." "Tupo pamoja" can be a declaration, indicating your support for a friend or colleague. "Tupo pamoja" can also be a statement, recognizing your inherent imbrication in networks of relation with those around you. Importantly, "tupo pamoja" is also used as a question: Are we together? By asking if we are together, "tupo pamoja" acts as an opportunity to highlight where connections have been missed, where there are misunderstandings, mistaken assumptions—where someone was lost or excluded along the way.

When we think about graduate school as a collective rather than individual endeavor, we must ask "for who?" Is it a collective endeavor for BIPOC students? Is it a collective endeavor for non-POC queer students? I think that graduate school should be a collective endeavor, but the system of higher education was never meant for some students—particularly Black students and other students of color. If the system itself was created so that some students can succeed with more ease than others, we must reconceptualize what collectivity means. If a department is comprised of predominantly privileged bodies (able bodies, cis bodies, white bodies, male bodies), then is collectivity possible? We should really pause to think about what a radical collectivity for all bodies could look like. (anonymous PhD student)

We moved through this chapter from speaking primarily in first-person singular—"I" to "you"—to speaking primarily in first-person plural—"we" to "us." We hope that we are together. We would like to speak as a collective. But it's important that we always ask "tupo pamoja?" The answer lies with you, with *us*. Together, we can do more than make graduate student life a supportive and energizing experience—we can grow a discipline that acts to facilitate camaraderie and coalition rather than individualism and competition.

For Further Thought and Reflection

1. How are we, together with our colleagues, acting as co-conspirators and providing support? How are we failing, and how might that be addressed? Try to come up with specific examples personally, as a graduate cohort, as a program, and as a discipline.

2. What are the standards of professionalism and time management to which we ascribe? How might these penalize women, queer folks, people who are disabled, or people of color? How can they be recognized, navigated, and/or changed?

3. How might we learn to see self-care as both an individual and collective endeavor in our graduate programs? What opportunities might that perspective afford?

4. How can we strengthen the support networks of our programs and discipline?

"It Was Within My Control to Max My Possibilities"

Academic Life After Graduate School

Patrice M. Buzzanell

Zhenyu Tian

Timothy Betts

Most of us dream about what life will be like after we finish our graduate degrees. For those who pursue a faculty career, we expect to have more time to research, teach students, and contribute meaningfully to our disciplines and communities. We also want full personal lives. How these dreams become actualized starts with our job search and choices we make over our first few years in academe. Some aspects are under our control, and others are not. You might be on the job market in years when the economy is great, departments are clamoring for your specialization, and positions are located at your preferred institutional types in your ideal geographic locations. More realistically, you'll have to consider what career and personal life aspects are most important to you and where you are comfortable making trade-offs.

However, your "fit" is more than a one-time judgment; it shifts and evolves after you secure employment and work to make sense of your faculty identities' fit and/or "misfit" throughout your career (Jansen & Shipp, 2019). Such reassessments are prompted not simply by your personal life and career considerations. They also emerge as a result of macro-level changes in higher education, such as changes in labor markets, university funding, advancement criteria, and institutional and/or departmental commitments to address and be accountable for safety, equity, and accessibility (Bennett, 2018).

To discuss the complexities of academic life after graduate school, we describe (a) navigating the academic job search, (b) considering different types of institutions and positions, (c) succeeding in your first academic job, (d) working toward promotion and beyond, (e) developing support networks and mentoring, (f) managing work-life balance, and (g) considering opportunities outside of the United States.

Navigating the Academic Job Search

Our job search begins long before we put our application materials together and apply for positions. When entering graduate school, we begin to articulate who we are as scholars and teachers, what we want out of life, where we want to live and work, and how we intend to integrate our professional, personal, and community engagement goals. All these considerations enter into our academic job search. These decisions are visible on our curriculum vitae (CV) and position application materials (cover letter, sample writings, and personal statements on research, teaching, service or engagement, and diversity). They also are visible in the position announcements available in the *Chronicle of Higher Education*, National Communication Association's (NCA) Career Center (https://www.natcom.org/academic-professional-resources/nca-career-center/find-job) and **COMM**Notes listserv, International Communication Association's ICA Career Center website (https://careers.icahdq.org/) and ICA Newsletter, and through other professional and regional communication associations.

Even with these common features and decisions, the job search isn't the same for everyone. Some applicants strategically maximize their options. As one new assistant professor who is international and a faculty member of color noted:

> I applied to many jobs when I was on the market. These jobs were posted by a variety of teaching and research institutions from all over the United States. I was not selective. My philosophy was that, although it was out of my control to get a job, it was within my control to max my possibilities by casting a wide net. My advisors and committee members did not miss a single deadline. I felt very supported.

Navigating the academic job search requires you to consider what you want in your academic pursuits and what kind of institutional community will foster those goals beyond the normative teaching-research dichotomy. For instance, some institutions require faith-based statements and reference checks about religious commitments. Lauren Hearit, PhD, assistant professor in the Department of Communication at Hope College (United States), talks about her experiences:

> I work at a private, faith-based institution where all faculty are of the Christian faith. When I applied, I had to write a statement in support of the mission of the college. During my on-campus interview, the dean, provost, and president all asked me to share with them about my personal faith and commitment to the college's mission during one-on-one meetings. (And, yes, small private colleges often schedule meetings with the upper administration! While nerve-racking, these meetings were some of my favorite parts of the on-campus interview and allowed me to ask questions about my potential department's reputation on campus.) ... Sitting on the other side now, I see the importance of this statement.-

As another case in point, gender relations and other forms of difference may affect your job search (and first position) experiences. According to the National Center for Education Statistics's (2019) report, the gender gap among faculty persists and is compounded by the lack of people of color in degree-granting postsecondary institutions. Moreover, the normalization of masculinity and bodies of men in organizations tend to put women in paradoxical situations where choices become difficult (Putnam & Ashcraft, 2017). As one early career assistant professor described: "I was pregnant at the time, which caused a lot of anxiety and uncertainty, but his [mentor's] advocacy and guidance helped prepare me for the challenges I faced."

You also may struggle to look and feel as though you belong given intertwined race, ethnicity, gender, nationality, language, and other differences contribute to normative assumptions of Whiteness in academe (Cruz et al., 2018). Virginia Sánchez Sánchez, PhD, assistant professor in the Department of Communication at Auburn University (United States), noted:

> One comment I have heard twice since I began my position is that I only got hired because I am Latina. This comment bothers me because of the implications it carries about the quality of my work. More importantly, it also wrongly suggests that there are a lot of Latino/a/x scholars in academia because if being Latina got me in, then it must be easy for others. In reality, I am part of a small group. I constantly wonder what I could be doing to help others from my community gain access to academic institutions, and there is never an easy answer.

Additional checks for positions may affect you if you are an international student (officially labeled "nonresident aliens"). You would want to know whether the institutions would support different categories of visa, work permit, and residency documentation amidst changing immigration regulations through sponsorship and access to specialized personnel and funds (McDonald, 2018). Your timing for pursuit of a U.S. academic career needs strategic planning so that you can transition to a sponsoring employer upon degree completion or soon afterwards.[1] As you navigate the academic job search, you would use international office/services in your affiliated institutions.

As you can see, your job search is personalized by both individual and societal factors with common decisions and starting points, such as position announcements and applications.

---

1   An ideal situation involves getting a position with a successfully negotiated immigration status transition (F1 to H1B to permanent residency) prior to graduation. If not prior to graduation, then you have to obtain the optional practical training (OPT) status allowing for up to 12 months of temporary employment in relevant fields. OPT itself is time sensitive, such as you may apply up to 90 days before and 60 days after your expected program completion date; your OPT must start within 60 days of your completion date; once OPT starts, you have up to 90 days of unemployment included in the 12 months. Finally, if you cannot acquire a sponsored position within the OPT period, you are required to leave the country after OPT.

Because navigating the academic job search feels disruptive and uncertain much of the time, you might consider adapting to and transforming your challenges using the five resilience processes that link to well-being (Buzzanell, 2010, 2018).

First, you might affirm your academic identity by reading new articles and talking to friends, faculty, and relational partners about your interests. Second, to craft normalcy during this time, you might set aside 30 minutes daily to write but also integrate new routines, such as learning how to bake or having brown bag lunches in person or virtually with colleagues to discuss their work. Third, when networking online and offline for support and insights about job searches, you might get hints about how to perform more effectively in your virtual interview not only from other grad students in your cohort but also from websites. You might decide not to access contacts and websites that speculate on who got which jobs. Fourth, during the job search, it might seem difficult to reframe experiences with humor and alternative logics, but you might say to yourself that if this search does not go in the directions you hope, that you would take up with professional improv groups or laugh, recalling how you did your job talk when electricity went off in the campus building or when the airline lost your luggage with your only business suit or favorite interview outfit. Finally, to background negative feelings while foregrounding productive action, you might vent to your advisors in person about not getting the position of your dreams, then listen to what they did when the same thing happened to them. You also could expand your search criteria, submit more and slightly different applications tailored to the positions, revise cover letters and CVs to better suit positions, revisit job talks upon getting feedback, and imagine yourself in different types of institutions and positions.

In activating these five resilience processes consciously, you can reframe your job search as opportunities to expand your professional relationships with people who learn about your work through your applications and interviews. As you go through the uncertainties and disruptions of job search activities and feelings, you might find yourself writing dissertation passages at night after getting thoughtful questions from students and faculty at the institutions. You might decide that what seemed ideal at first was not really the position and lifestyle you want. Resilience does not mean only adapting or coping with what happens but also means that you are the one in charge of making changes in your life and career.

Looking at Different Types of Institutions and Positions

Although faculty at doctoral-granting institutions sometimes act as though everyone wants a tenure-track position in a prestigious, research-intensive institution, that is not the case. There are advantages and disadvantages in different types of institutions and positions, just as there is variation in institutions themselves. We organize this section around types of institutions, then discuss promotion trajectories for positions: tenure-track (or tenure-earning), instructor or professor of practice, and adjunct positions.

Different Types of Institutions

In this section, we discuss (a) comprehensive universities, (b) community colleges, (c) liberal arts institutions, (d) residential undergraduate colleges, (e) faith-based institutions, and (f) research-intensive universities. We close by noting that (g) particular missions and interests might appeal to you—service to underserved populations and focus on international opportunities—and that these missions can be found in any of these different types of institutions.

You may enjoy and value both analytic processes in research and teaching. For a balance of both in your workload and promotion processes, you might consider a comprehensive university. These universities often have master's and some doctoral programs.

You might find that you love to teach and contribute to local communities. If so, community colleges and liberal arts institutions are a good fit. As Rebecca Todd, a tenured assistant professor at Hillsborough Community College and doctoral student at the University of South Florida, describes her work at a community college (CC) that is a unionized state public institution:

> Teaching is definitely the top priority at a community college. My teaching load is 5/5. ... The courses you teach are basic introductory level, and it is common to teach five sections of the same course each semester. Sometimes the courses require different preps depending on the instructional modality (online/face to face) and the course format (traditional/honors). This leaves little time for research while you are earning tenure, but the class sizes are much smaller than most universities (15–30 students), which allows you to really get to know your students and connect with them (and your content) in more meaningful ways. The CC I work at is an open-access institution, which means that we accept everyone with a high school diploma (or equivalent), so my students are incredibly diverse across a broad spectrum of demographics, attitudes, and beliefs. For me, this makes the entire educational process more relevant and more rewarding. ... [But another consideration is that] working at a public institution means, like it or not, you will be measured by state performance standards and requirements.

Liberal arts institutions focus on humanities and sciences (i.e., social, natural, and formal sciences, such as logic) with attention to a broad range of knowledge and skills and faculty–student interaction. If you want to focus on teaching and contribute to student life, you may find that residential undergraduate institutions (where faculty and students may live and share meals on or near campus to build community) or faith-based colleges fit your interests. For instance, Rebecca Dohrman, PhD, associate professor of communication at Maryville University (United States), writes:

Teaching a 4-4 load [four classes per semester] at a private liberal arts university has been a great fit for me. Our faculty is relatively small, so there are many opportunities for cross-disciplinary collaboration and many robust conversations about topics where my colleagues bring unique perspectives. That has enriched my own understanding of the unique value we bring in communication. I have worked on grant projects focused on developing curricula to teach young students about computing. ... Advocating for our field through participation on cross-disciplinary teams has been a wonderful part of being on a mid-sized campus.

You might want to devote time to your funded research programs, thus making research-intensive institutions with doctoral programs in your areas of expertise attractive as tenure-track faculty or as research professors of practice (also called clinical faculty). In these institutions, your professional activities and teaching are shaped by the research you do. You would work with master's and/or doctoral students as well as teaching and mentoring undergraduate students through research projects and on research teams.

Finally, regardless of the type of institution to which you aspire, there may be particular missions or interests that appeal to you and that drive your job search. As a result, you might pursue work in HBCUs (historically Black colleges and universities), HSIs (Hispanic-serving institutions), TCUs (tribal colleges and universities), or institutions emphasizing international opportunities. Alternatively, you might want to live in different parts of the world and acquire diverse language and cultural skills. Here, universities that hire and recruit for international members—faculty and students—and that offer opportunities to build study abroad, exchange, joint degree, postdocs, and other programs might offer good fits.

Different Types of Positions

What you want at one point in your career might not be what drives you later on in life, so considering the stability and flexibility offered by different career trajectories is useful (Jansen & Shipp, 2020). To follow we discuss tenure-track, adjunct faculty, professor of practice, and postdoc positions.

Tenure-track positions usually require research, teaching, service, and/or engagement with the workload percentages available in departmental and/or college promotion documents. Often, these percentages are 40% research, 40% teaching, and 20% service/engagement. There are variations in research-teaching-service ratios, depending on the type of institution in which you have your position, and at times the percentages are negotiable. If you are hired into a joint appointment, then you have these responsibilities in two different units (e.g., communication and women's and gender studies) with negotiations among unit leaderships, the dean's office, and you, of course, about what these requirements look like on a daily basis.

If you are *adjunct faculty*, then institutions pay you per course credit hours—often with no health care or other benefits—and you can seek primary or supplementary employment at another university or organization. *Visiting faculty/instructors* may be hired full- or part-time for a limited term. Although adjunct and visiting faculty positions have flexibility, they also can be stressful if you are hoping that they will be pathways to more stable and financially advantageous tenure-track lines. As one assistant professor put it:

> I was on a 2-year temporary contract where I currently work before gaining a tenure-track position. During that time, I worked incredibly hard to try and demonstrate my value in hopes I would obtain the permanent line. A lot of uncertainty came with the tenuous nature of my position, and when I look back now, I see that I worked exponentially harder than I would have during the first years of a tenure line.

Adjunct and visiting instructor positions might involve 4-4 or 5-5 teaching loads and multiple course preps; however, these positions do not involve service to the department or university unless it is written into employment contracts. Adjunct and visiting faculty are evaluated on their performance in the classroom.

For *professors of practice* (sometimes called continuing instructors or clinical faculty), these are non-tenure-leading contracts are usually around three years and are renewable, with specific teaching, research, engagement, or entrepreneurship[2] responsibilities. Professors of practice have promotion guidelines similar to that of tenure-track faculty but often without the research requirements, unless they are research professors of practice.

Postdocs or *postdoctoral fellows* is a single- to multi-year position to which new PhDs can apply to continue their training as a researcher and/or to develop their teaching skills. Postdoc opportunities vary by discipline in length, in purposes and supervision, and in pay and benefits depending on the institution and nature of the position. Postdocs are neither graduate students nor faculty, but are situated in between and often fall structurally within graduate schools and/or provost offices.

Succeeding in Your First Academic Job

Succeeding in your first academic position really depends on the type of position and institution in which you find employment. In general, most tenure-track and professor-of-practice faculty have 5- to 7-year probationary periods before they are required to go up for promotion

---

2   Professors of entrepreneurship practice often are associated with centers of entrepreneurship and teach classes for certificates, help students build business plans and start their businesses, and consult on intellectual property, such as copyrights and patents.

with career dossiers prepared and submitted to external (to your university) reviewers in your penultimate (next to last) year. Sometimes, tenure-earning faculty bring years of post-PhD work into new appointments at different universities, and sometimes, tenure-earning faculty submit materials for promotion and tenure (P&T) decisions prior to their penultimate years as they and their colleagues determine their readiness for P&T. Succeeding in your first academic position means learning about how your institution works, but it also depends on how and what you negotiate, including dual-career couple considerations, before you accept your job offer.

For all positions, universities have overall guidelines on the provost's office (vice president of academic affairs) website, while colleges and departments or schools likely have more specific promotion criteria listed. These documents contain the standards by which you will be assessed by internal and/or external evaluators for annual progress, prepromotion (often third- or fourth-year reviews), and promotion and/or tenure, if that is possible for the position you have. These documents guide you on where you should prioritize your efforts. For instance, if you have a tenure-track position at a research-intensive university, then your primary focus is on research. During your first year, you may have a course reduction or semester off teaching so that you can learn about your university, network within your department, and more broadly, connect for research teams and grants, and figure out how things get done at your institution.

If you have a joint appointment in two units, then you would probably have a central tenure or promotion home, such as in the department of communication, and another faculty home, such as in women's, gender, and sexuality studies. For joint tenure-track, professor-of-practice, or other instructional positions, you would adhere to the promotion guidelines in your home department but note that the other department or program informs and votes on your case. During the hiring process, the units will often collaborate on a shared memorandum of understanding on your requirements, and you should ask about a document like this. During your first year, this means that you would want to negotiate or clarify what you do and how your research, teaching, and/or service is valued in each space.

Your success during your first year also depends on other position negotiations. Generally speaking, you negotiate for what you need to be successful, starting when you receive an offer of employment. One international faculty member in her first position reminisced on how she negotiated her work permits and managed difference during her first year:

> I was lucky that there were tenure-track faculty jobs when I was on the market. I was able to receive an offer in early November, which was pretty early. I did a lot of preparation before calling up the department chair to negotiate the offer. I was nervous because I had never negotiated job offers before, and it was hard to get out of the "graduate-student-grateful-for-a-job" mentality and demand higher pay and more resources. My advisors and trusted mentors helped me with mental prep and strategies. I did create an excel sheet with items I wanted to ask for and even created scripts of how I would open up the conversations. In addition to regular items in job offer negotiation, I needed to make sure I

received adequate institutional support for my visa and green card application. I talked to many friends of mine who were international and had gone through the process. I took notes of their experience and tips they suggested. I wanted to make sure that I had a smooth transition from F1 to H1B visa. I also wanted sponsorship to attain a green card, which would allow me to go to international conferences without worrying about an expired visa and be able to stay in the country even if I lost my job for some reason. My negotiation was pretty successful. I remember at the very end of the conversation, the chair told me that I did well negotiating. He said, "You did everything you should be doing."

Depending on the type of position and your responsibilities, you might negotiate start-up funds for course reductions or course/certificate development, research and travel, equipment (hardware and software), graduate or undergraduate research and/or teaching assistants, moving allowances, and other resources as you negotiate the job offer. Although beyond the scope of this chapter, it is worth noting that dual-career couples face additional layers of constraints and opportunities, considering the intertwining personal career goals and family life in the unique context of the highly structured academic hiring process (Jorgenson, 2016). Usually, your doctoral mentors can advise you on negotiating position offers.

Working Toward Promotion (and Beyond)

Many institutions offer research, teaching, and engagement tracks for promotion. Your key for promotion in each is scholarship and impact consistent with the type of track. Therefore, faculty CVs would differ, or the profile when going up for promotion and tenure or promotion would be different, depending on the position. Knowing what is required for all different tracks is crucial during your probationary period so you know how to best plan your time and efforts. Working with your department chair and trusted mentors can help clarify expectations and help you plan and use your time wisely.

For promotion through research, the numbers, quality, types of publications and outlets, and impact regarding citations and article or book use is critical. There are several different indices for making cases about research quality, such as Clarivate Analytics, where you can look up whether an article is listed in the Social Sciences Citation Index (SSCI), Emerging Social Sciences Index (ESCI), or Arts and Humanities Citation Index (AHCI). Knowing what kinds of outlets are valued by your institution is important, but really, the programmatic nature and quality of your work is of utmost importance. Depending on your type of position and institution, you might find that conference presentations, chapters, white papers, and other materials "count" and are reviewed annually and for promotion.

If you are being promoted under teaching or learning, then you would want to earn high (averaged) student evaluations if your institution uses quantitative measures. Some institutions will recommend observation and review of your teaching. Additionally, indications that you are innovating and broadening your reach beyond the classroom are desirable. For example, you would document participation in teaching academies and certifications, leading workshops or preconferences about teaching materials at professional conferences, and publishing textbooks and online teaching materials.

If your institution promotes based on engagement or outreach, then you would produce scholarship of engagement (Boyer, 1996). Besides looking at provost and dean's office website materials for your institutional promotion requirements, you might check to see if your university has a founding or awarded mission (e.g., land grant, https://www.aplu.org/about-us/history-of-aplu/what-is-a-land-grant-university; sea grant, https://seagrant.noaa.gov/About; and/or space grant mission, https://www.nasa.gov/stem/spacegrant/about/index.html) or has voluntarily submitted documentation and been accepted into the Carnegie Foundation's Classification for Community Engagement (see https://www.brown.edu/swearer/carnegie). There are typically places in your P&T documents for documentation on ways you have helped to fulfill these or other missions. For instance, you may be called upon periodically via email (and in your annual reports and promotion dossier) to document community engagement, service-learning courses and impact, health campaigns, and other deliverables that would directly benefit particular groups. These CVs usually center around communication effectiveness. Your profile for engagement and outreach would include interdisciplinary teams, research funding, and publications or presentations in communication outlets, popular media, governmental fact-finding panels, and textbooks or trade publications. What works at one institution does not always work at another, so your best bet is to familiarize yourself with the expectations, requirements, and policies of each institution for which you work.

Developing Support Networks and Mentoring

Mentoring is a process whereby you and your mentor or mentee assist one another in career development, psychosocial support, advocacy, and role modeling (Buzzanell, in press). Maintaining traditional mentoring relationships—entailing reciprocal social exchange and ongoing dyadic relationship—can be beneficial to your career development; however, integrating alternative perspectives and forms may help you develop mentoring in more flexible, pragmatic, and transformative ways (Long et al., 2014). You might have mentors who oversee and provide advice about your CV and professional activities (traditional mentoring). You may have your go-to people when you have quick questions. Mentors might suggest opportunities for you, like a new grant solicitation or call for papers (CFP)(episodic or spontaneous mentoring). Nonhuman mentoring agents (e.g., books, websites, e-mentoring sites) may also offer answers and suggestions. One example is the National Center for Faculty Development and Diversity (NCFDD) website (https://www.facultydiversity.org) that hosts virtual mentoring groups organized by career developmental stage (e.g., graduate students; postdocs; and assistant, associate, and full professors). Lastly, your mentorships evolve over time as you switch roles and become mentors and as your needs for advice, support, and advocacy change. See more about mentoring and advisor-advisee relationships in Chapter 5 and Chapter 11 of this volume.

You probably will not find or want one single mentor to guide and support you. Indeed, current scholarship indicates that you would want to have a network of mentors who serve different functions, offer varied resources, and fit within different forms (Long et al., 2014). For instance, you might need advocate mentors who defend and champion your abilities, value, and research interests as marginalized group members in addition to offering spaces for emotional safety (Harris & Lee, 2019). Regardless of type and purpose, you will want mentoring relationships that help cultivate resilience for adaptation and change in departments and higher education (Buzzanell, 2010, 2018).

Faculty unions can also serve as an important resource and form of support. Unions are not only important for dispute resolution and collective bargaining but can also serve as important information sources as you make sense of your place and policies in your new institution. Rebecca, for example, had positive experiences with her community college faculty union:

> Where I work, the faculty union is very active. During my first year, I joined our union and became the secretary (a role no one ever wants), which enabled me to learn so much about the inner workings of the college. I saw firsthand the vital role they play in the faculty contract negotiation process and ensuring that our voices are heard at administrative decision-making levels.

Overall, high-quality relationships and relational resilience in organizational contexts are essential to your well-being and your institutions' effectiveness (Olekalns et al., 2020). Developing mentorships and joining the faculty union (when applicable) are two ways through which you can strengthen support networks for yourself in academe, thereby promoting resilience (Buzzanell, 2010). It is worth noting that more nuanced supportive relationships (e.g., workplace friendships, sense of family with disciplinary colleagues) also constitute important resilience resources.

Managing Work-Life Balance Over the Career

Your ability to manage work-life balance depends on your priorities and interests as well as institutional investments in your career. Knowing what you value can help you obtain a position at an institution where you feel fulfilled. For instance, Jess Pauly, PhD in the Department of Communication at Utah Valley University, wanted a more teaching-oriented or comprehensive university that she felt would better help her manage her career and personal life:

As I was navigating the job search, with husband and toddler in tow, I had many interests to consider: Will my husband be happy if I get an offer in X/Y/Z state? Will X/Y/Z state be a family-friendly place to settle down for some time? Will it be within driving distance to family, or will we have to fly home to visit parents? These thoughts didn't even hit on my personal interests to avoid R1 institutions and focus more on teaching institutions. There was plenty to consider, and it was overwhelming at times, but I buckled up for the ride and tried to trust the process. I'm quite happy with how things worked out; I'm in a tenure-track position at a large teaching-focused university. While I never imagined I'd live in Utah, I'm fairly certain I couldn't be more satisfied with the outcome.

Another new assistant professor who was not in a close personal relationship remarked that he wanted to be in a city where he could meet people whom he could date. He also wanted to work with graduate students and be within a day's drive or less from his family. Your life might seem more manageable when you have proximity to an international airport, are located close to mosques, or have access to other life aspects that you consider necessary to be happy.

The other part of managing work-life considerations is knowing what to expect from and how to use organizational policies and resources. You may want to take a position in an institution that has dual-career assistance for employment and other needs, like specialized health care or services. You may want generous parental leave policies, funds for child and pet care when you travel for conferences and talks, and credit toward course releases depending on theses or dissertations you chair and complete. You may seek a position at an institution that holds new faculty workshops on managing research teams, integrating research-teaching-service, applying for grants, handling start-up and grant funds, and learning how to respond appropriately when a colleague suffers microaggressions based on difference. You may want to be at an institution that recognizes that people from racial/ethnic minority groups are expected to do more service, with much of this work being invisible (e.g., mentoring, listening to students and faculty who have experienced microaggressions; Miller & Roksa, 2020) and exhausting (McCoy, 2020). As you continue to craft your path forward after graduate school, there are likely to be myriad disruptions, readjustments, confusions, and opportunities; finding a good fit in an academic job and a new life after graduate school is not about any one choice. Think of it, instead, as an ongoing process of crafting "new normals" and balances as you advance within your institution or find and change your academic positions over your career (Buzzanell, 2010, 2018).

Considering Opportunities Outside of the United States

As mentioned in the first section about navigating the job search, there are both similarities and differences in ways job searches are conducted, positions are labeled, and other details about academic life. The best advice is to network in the countries and regions where you would like to work. To follow, we describe the typical job search in the United States and then offer advice from an expatriate (i.e., person who lives outside of their country of origin) from the United States now living and working in the United Kingdom.

In the United States, the master narrative of the application process is that graduate students assemble materials, apply through an institutional online portal, notify individuals who have previously agreed to serve as references, and receive confirmation that applications have been received and processed. There may be one or more screening contacts via phone or virtual platforms. There may be face-to-face or virtual campus visits for three or more job candidates who make the short list based on required and preferred credentials and experiences. Then you wait for notifications about hiring decisions. If notified that an institution wants to hire you, then you negotiate salary and resources that would help you be successful in your first couple of years.

In other countries, the processes differ. Robyn V. Remke, MBA programme director in the Department of Entrepreneurship and Strategy at the Lancaster University Management School (UK) and previously at Copenhagen Business School (Denmark), provides some general guidelines:

> When considering an international career, one has to understand how different HE systems are from country to country [e.g., Higher Education System in Denmark, see https://www.euroeducation.net/prof/denmarco.htm]. ...

> Therefore, when applying for an international job, you must first talk with someone familiar with that programme—ideally someone [still] at that university. Recruitment varies greatly from system to system. If you do not know anyone at the university, make contact with the HoD [Head of Department, or Chair] or HR [Human Resources] representative and be clear that you are applying from an international position and [are] seeking advice on how best to position your application. HE is especially cliquish and not always aware of what is happening outside its own discipline. That said, disciplines can be especially ethnocentric. When applying for international positions, you must be especially transparent and explicit about your work, how you describe your research interests, etc. For example, one cannot assume that those reading the application will know about national associations or networks. ... Regarding considerations for becoming an international/expat professor, before moving abroad, it would be helpful to think about how long you want to live abroad. Also, consider the contract—do you want to be employed by a foreign university or participate in an exchange? Do you plan to live abroad for limited time (few years perhaps?), or do you see yourself returning? I appreciate that you may not know the answer to these questions at first, but there are significant consequences to how you structure your

contract and how easily you are able to return "home" depending on your position. Therefore, you will need to think through all the possibilities and make sure you are doing what you need to keep those possibilities alive. For example, if you think you may want to return to your home country to work, it would be good to maintain your network in your home country. This means traveling back to attend conferences, working with colleagues from home country universities, etc. This may be challenging as you will also be expected to establish networks in your new country—so you may have to spend some of your own money to support your travel and conference attendance.

In short, having networks of disciplinary and institutional insiders in your countries or regions of preference, plus knowing what is valued and how to project these values in your CV, are critical regardless of where you do your job search and find your academic home. By navigating the job search, selecting positions and institutions that best fit your current and hopefully future needs and interests, you have a good start to a productive and rewarding faculty life.

For Further Thought and Reflection

1. What would you like your career and personal life to look like in five years? In 10 years? What are some factors—internal and external—that might act as constraints and/or opportunities in your path to achieve your desired career/personal life? What can you do to ensure your success?

2. How do you define success for yourself? What personal and professional resources, such as dual-career couple job assistance and mentoring, do you need to be successful?

3. What are the promotion and tenure criteria at the institutions where you would like to work or where you work currently?

4. Who in the communication discipline are role models or mentors for your career and personal life? What do you learn from these role models or mentors?

5. Where might you believe you need more or more effective mentoring?

A Roadmap to Career Success

Pursuing Careers Outside of the Academy for MA Graduates

14

Stephen K. Hunt

Aimee E. Miller-Ott

Viraj Patel

We are sure by now, as a communication graduate student, or maybe even before you started graduate school, you have heard from a professor or academic advisor that a degree in communication means you can "do anything!" Maybe that is why you found yourself in a master's program—you love the study of communication but are unsure of what you can or want to do with this degree. Maybe you enrolled in a graduate program to explore and understand the link between scholarship and practical application of communication.

Whatever your reason for pursuing a master's degree in communication, your chances of employment postgraduation are excellent. A recent survey by the job site Indeed (2020a) ranks the ability to communicate effectively as the top skill that employers desire in a new employee. Importantly, your graduate education gives you much more than just good communication skills! You know the theory and research behind why and how we communicate and which variables relate to successful communication. You have applied this theoretical information to conduct research through classwork, independent studies, and internships, which provide you with firsthand experience, preparing you to demonstrate these abilities in the workplace. As one of our master's graduates told us recently, "The ability to influence people using communication strategies in general as well as specific tactics from social psychology and persuasion theory has always helped me in challenging situations. In negotiations and politics, it helps me win over people." Indeed, one of the advantages of a master's in communication is that you are exposed to and learn a wide range of communication theories and bodies of research that will be helpful to you as you begin your career. Your education and experiences in the communication discipline help you to stand out from the other applicants. In this chapter, we provide a roadmap for applying to and obtaining jobs in the field of communication after you complete your master's degree. As part of this roadmap, we also provide insights from communication master's program alumni who were eager to share stories of their successes and challenges in looking for and securing employment in the job market.

Locating Opportunities Outside of the Academy

At some point in your graduate career, if not yet, you will start to ask yourself, "So what am I going to do after my master's program?" It may be tempting to jump onto Indeed.com, LinkedIn.com, or other related job-search websites and enter "communication" in the search engine to see what appears. But wait! Doing so will be overwhelming because almost every job in your results will mention communication skills in some way and may not yield the types of results more applicable to you and your communication graduate education. As we wrote this chapter, we did that exact search on Indeed.com with "communication" as the search term and selected our hometown as the location. That search yielded nine jobs, which seemed manageable, but the actual jobs posted ranged widely, from technical writer to foreign communications analyst in the military, from corporate communication specialist to newsroom clerk. There were a broad range of jobs! So before doing a search like that, we recommend doing some soul-searching by asking yourself the following questions.

Why Did I Start in a Communication Graduate Program?

Did you want to expand your knowledge in an area of communication that piqued your interest before you finished your undergraduate education? Perhaps you did not major in communication as an undergraduate but felt that you needed to learn more about the discipline to succeed in the workplace? Did you enter graduate school with a specific career in mind and take courses to expand your skills for that end goal? Did you have a career before coming to graduate school and aim to advance in your company with a graduate degree? Whatever the reason you are pursuing a master's in communication, we urge you not to lose sight of why you came to graduate school as you think ahead to what careers you may seek after school. Throughout your graduate program, we suggest you attempt to undertake research that aligns with this end goal. Such research will help you develop and expand your professional portfolio, which will help you stand out from other candidates during the job application process.

What Type of Work Do I Want to Do?

A graduate of our master's program advised current students that "if you have not thought about what type of positions you are interested in as a current graduate student, that is something that you will need to address or else the job hunt will be very difficult for you." Communication graduates can enter a broad range of careers. From looking at just our own master's program alumni, we learned that their careers span business management, social media strategizing, human/client relations, consulting, community relations, sports management, sales, media production, public relations (PR), and marketing. While these employment areas may sound abstract, specific titles that our graduate program alumni have held are listed in Table 14.1 and may be useful as online search terms.

TABLE 14.1 Sample Job Titles for Communication Master's Alumni

Account Manager	Account Director	Client Director
Communication Specialist	Community Outreach Coordinator	Development Director
Digital Consultant	Digital Marketing Coordinator	Director of Marketing and Special Events
Faculty Development Coordinator	Freelance Photographer	Grant Writer
Human Relations Director	Instructional Design Communication Specialist	Internal Communications Lead
Marketing Coordinator	Marketing Manager	Marketing Specialist
News Director	Nonprofit Fundraiser	Political Campaign Manager
Promotions Specialist/Media Coordinator	Public Relations Client Manager	Relationship Manager
Residence Hall Coordinator	Retail Sales Consultant	Sales Specialist
Social Media Strategic Advisor	Speech Writer	Technical Communication Specialist
Training Specialist	Vice President of Public Affairs	Web Designer

At this point, you might find yourself questioning how obtaining a master's degree in communication will set you apart from those with a bachelor's degree in communication. Initially, the master's experience gives you the chance to explore communication theories and apply them to practical, real-life scenarios. As a result, most communication master's programs provide students with an opportunity to work on projects that help them practice and develop time management, writing, project management, and data analysis skills, all of which are highly sought after by employers. Communication master's students also work on a thesis or a final project, which usually entails detailed feedback from faculty who are experts on a subject matter. As a result, students learn to develop a finished project based on an original idea while taking and incorporating feedback. Communication master's students can also have an assistantship teaching a course, coaching speech or debate, or working in television or radio. Obtaining a master's degree in communication provides you the resources to explore your area of interest in depth while developing skills that are transferrable to the workplace, giving you a significant competitive advantage over those with a bachelor's degree.

As evident, the term "communication" encompasses many forms of employment, so to narrow it down for yourself, think about what area of the discipline you have studied in your program that you valued most, and consider the kinds of jobs your knowledge and skills best fit within that discipline or subdiscipline. One recent master's graduate described the challenges of breaking into the job market, especially in the areas of advertising, PR, and marketing. As most master's programs are generalist programs, this student found it difficult to secure a first-round interview with a PR agency. However, he noted that "once I started to seek more specific communication roles that aligned better with what my résumé was communicating to employers, I was then able to get a position I felt comfortable to execute." You will find additional questions that you should consider as you contemplate employment in Table 14.2.

TABLE 14.2 Key Questions to Consider as You Contemplate Employment

Do you prefer a flexible or structured schedule and/or workplace?
Are you willing to move or travel as part of this job?
Is there a minimum pay that you are comfortable accepting?
Are there ethical concerns you have about entering a particular field?
What are the benefits (i.e., medical, vision, dental, and retirement benefits) associated with the job?

The University of Michigan Human Resources (2020) department has a useful website that includes several self-assessment tools regarding job searches that will help you get started understanding your own interests and expertise. The site provides one resource, a "Needs and Wants Checklist," that we found particularly valuable and would recommend using as you consider what your future job might look like. Before you start your search, consider what criteria are essential to make the job work for you and which you would like to have but are not deal breakers. For instance, you might need to return to your hometown after graduate school, or you might need health benefits. You might want to be able to travel or work from home once a week. Thinking about these questions is important not only as you start searching for jobs but also when you receive a job offer and are determining whether the offer is a good fit for what you need and want.

Where Do I Find These Job Opportunities?

Word of mouth, personal contacts, and connections made from graduate program faculty, staff, and alumni are powerful tools to find jobs. As Rupert et al. (2016) argue, networking is rarely covered in graduate curriculum, but that skill is invaluable. As a communication master's program graduate told us, "Networking and developing relationships have also been a big part of my success to grow within current jobs or to move into a new job." However, a caveat to finding jobs through informal networks is that the information about the actual job (e.g., when they are hiring and the type of employee they are looking to employ) may not be accurate (Piercy & Lee, 2019). As a result, you will need to dedicate time to seeking additional information about the positions of interest to you.

Think about faculty mentors who might be able to give you direction and inspiration for the job search. All faculty have located and applied for jobs at some point in their careers; some likely have had experience working in the corporate and/or nonprofit sectors and can provide guidance in your search. It is very important that you have made connections with your faculty during the time in your program. Faculty with whom you have worked closely should know about your career goals and the skills you developed in their courses and projects. You can create connections in the classroom by standing out as a strong, hardworking, and dedicated student. You can also make connections with faculty outside of class, in professional contexts (e.g., by asking faculty to join their research team), or in more informal situations, such as talking in their office hours about your career aspirations.

Alumni are another resource for your job search. As a communication master's degree program graduate told us, "I think it would be great for more alumni to come speak to current graduate students about how they navigated the job market after graduation and how important it is to make the most out of a 2-year program." If your program does not help facilitate connections between you and alumni, seek them out yourself. Find out from faculty which alumni work in certain industries, and ask for their contact information, or reach out to them via LinkedIn. Seek out alumni events on campus. Attend homecoming events, and start conversations with alumni. Look for opportunities to become involved with your program's alumni advisory board. These relationships may help you land a job one day. As an alumna suggested to current graduate students, "Look for ways to connect with people who are doing the job you would like to do."

You should also consider internships and other career opportunities in graduate school that could become your first job after school. As a master's in communication program graduate we interviewed explained:

> It is important that you start job hunting before the end of your program. You might also want to start looking for internships and part-time gigs in the field you are interested in while in school because it will be extremely difficult to secure a full-time job if you only have academic training and no work experience!

Indeed (2020b) reports that having an internship can help you build your résumé, gain research experience, develop a professional network, and potentially transition to a permanent job. An alumna of a communication master's program echoed the importance of internships and noted, "In the summer between my two years of my master's program I did an internship for my current employer. I was able to stay connected with that employer and secure employment after graduation."

You can also use career websites to locate opportunities. Pew data from 2000 to 2015 show a steady increase in internet usage to search for jobs (Piercy & Lee, 2019). Most of the sites allow you to search for jobs across multiple industries. Some sites provide a more focused search. For instance, if you are looking for jobs in the nonprofit sector, sites like Indeed.com allow you to search listings of openings in nonprofit organizations. Further, the National Council of Nonprofits website (https://www.councilofnonprofits.org/) features job listings across the United States. There are some advantages and limitations to using the internet to search for jobs. As Piercy and Lee argue, "Formal sources such as job agencies and printed ads can have highly concrete and clear information about available jobs; simultaneously, formal sources are less flexible in terms of timing, access, and modifiability" (p. 1186). These formal sources also do not provide views about the job and organization from those inside the company that informal sources would be able to provide. Also, consider potential social inequality to accessibility of job information (Piercy & Lee, 2019); for instance, not everyone has the same access to computers and the internet to search for jobs online. If you are a student, use the campus library for your search, or contact the career center for help with creating documents for the application and for meeting your technology needs. Sal Navarro, a 2020 graduate of Illinois State University's communication master's program who currently serves as a PR and marketing specialist for a school district near Chicago, reflects:

> Sites like LinkedIn provide great employment opportunities. I would recommend that graduates seek out recruiters who place candidates into positions. My best piece of advice is to use your network the best you can. However, this is not a skill you can achieve overnight. You have to constantly interact with professionals in your network to show your engagement is an active commitment to your professional development. Many times, students are so caught up in classwork they do not prioritize professional development.

Initiating and maintaining connections to faculty and alumni and taking advantage of campus and online resources will help guide you on the right track for your job search.

Translating Communication Knowledge and Skills Outside of the Academy

You may have noticed that some foci on master's communication programs tend to lead graduates to follow more specific career trajectories. For instance, your classmates studying PR will likely search for jobs in PR and other related fields, like marketing, social media management, and account management. However, other classmates may be focusing on areas like interpersonal communication or family communication and may find it nearly impossible to find an opening for an "interpersonal communication specialist." However, you do have the requisite skills to succeed in many careers no matter your focus in graduate school. As a recent graduate shared, "The COM master's program helped me understand how to best articulate my skills on an application. I don't have a graphic design degree; however, I believed that I had the skills to be an exceptional designer for a company." As a result, when you begin to navigate the job search process, you must consider how you will make your knowledge and experience applicable to the position for which you are applying and understandable and impressive to those reviewing your materials and interviewing you. So how do you translate your graduate education into practical skills?

First, consider ways that your experiences in the program (e.g., internships, the process of completing a thesis, being a graduate teaching assistant [GTA] for a class, working with diverse populations) prepared you for the job. A communication master's program alumna advised current students to consider that "it's not the degree but the tools you gained in the program that will make you competitive and allow you to keep growing your career." Another graduate of a master's in communication program offered the following advice:

> Though the master's program was quite theoretical, and not so applied, I was able to make it practically relevant for a nonresearch type of job. It increased my analytical abilities in assessing situations, and communication is a very effective tool to master in most, if not all, situations involving people. Besides the ability to influence people, it also improved my interpersonal skills and my ability to work effectively in project groups, which is very common in my line of work.

Second, beyond the graduate school experience, think about materials you produced during your program. These materials might include a thesis project, a final research or analysis paper in a course, an independent study project, communication analysis documents, comprehensive exam documents, or even an IRB application! For each project you plan to discuss, make a list of your skills and qualifications that contributed to your success. Alumni shared with us many skills they believe they developed through classes and projects in graduate school, including the ability to manage multiple long-term projects; design and analyze surveys, case studies, and other assessment tools; write effectively; work well in groups; convey a message effectively; work under strict deadlines; and present ideas to a group. Consider ways to include your skills from your coursework on a résumé, and be prepared to talk about some of them in your interview. For instance, it is likely that as a student in a master's program, you have conducted research. Even if your job prospects might not ask you to research concepts in communication, you have the skills to develop an argument, collect and analyze data, find and cite credible evidence to support your claims, and present the results in a cohesive, accessible format. Walk your employers through how you would approach a problem and develop solutions using your experience with research and analysis. Similarly, as you develop application materials, consider how you can demonstrate the application of communication skills used for decision-making, problem-solving capabilities, conflict resolution, creativity, adaptability, collaboration, and critical thinking. These abilities may come from your experiences working in teams in your graduate assistantship, being involved in community engagement efforts, and completing internships that provided real-world experiences to apply communication skills, research, and theory. Keeping your training at the nexus of achieving these skills will help you bolster your résumé and fill in any gaps in experience.

In addition, those of you who were instructors and taught your own classes during graduate school (or assisted with classes), but do not want to go into a teaching career, need to consider the skills you developed in that role that you can highlight on the job search. For example, a recent graduate told us, "My master's program and graduate teaching assistantship forced me to step outside of my comfort zone almost every single day." An alumna explained, "My teaching experience in the program gave me tools I use in leadership today. Being able to think on my feet, meet people where they are, and anticipate objections are all things I use every single day." Teaching helps you gain important skills that you can translate during an interview and in your career.

Remember the Indeed.com survey of employers' desired skills for their employees that we referenced earlier? According to that survey, in addition to communication skills, employers value leadership, teamwork, interpersonal communication, self-management, organization, problem-solving skills, and an employee who is open-minded and has a strong work ethic. Similarly, in a recent conversation with employees who work in a large insurance company in our area, executives and hiring managers said they look for employees who represent a diversity of thought, culture, and experience. The executives also stressed the importance of interdisciplinary experiences, the ability to create and deliver a cogent argument, and the capacity of potential employees to enact resilience. Importantly, these are the same characteristics that our alumni have told us they developed in graduate school that they articulated on the job market and use today in their careers.

It is also important to consider the skills you developed by interacting with peers in your graduate program. For example, Krislow (2019) reports that international students "gain tremendously from the chance to experience our culture, learn from our experts, and connect with America's global leaders in industry, research, activism" (para. 2). Krislow (2019) notes that through interactions with international students, Americans can "learn to avoid stereotyping and form more informed opinions," and they are "provide[d] opportunities for unique cross-cultural experiences, whether celebrating new holidays, sampling new cuisines, or traveling to visit friends in their home countries. It forces students to confront different interpersonal and communication styles, which makes them better active listeners and critical thinkers" (para. 5). A graduate of a communication master's program described the process of learning from peers' experiences: "The program taught me how to work with people who were very different from me and how to communicate with different types of people." Another graduate noted that "we learned the value of creating an inclusive space in terms of educational benefit and personal growth. As a result, I have always tried to create inclusive spaces in my professional life as a manager or administrator." The ability to work and succeed in a diverse work environment is key. Consider ways to highlight your experiences working with diverse others when applying and interviewing for positions.

Third, developing the ability to navigate the processes of resilience is one of the most important outcomes of your graduate program. Buzzanell (2018) posits that resilience includes the following processes: (a) building a new normal, (b) anchoring identities in difficult times, (c) building and using relevant communication networks, (d) thinking beyond conventional ways of conceptualizing life and work, and (e) focusing on productive actions, strategies, and behaviors. Consider all the times you engaged in these processes during your program. You likely had to learn to operate under intense deadlines, utilize your communication networks to navigate difficult situations, learn new behaviors and skills, navigate conflict, and construct new ways of conceptualizing the discipline. As a graduate of a communication master's program told us, "My COM program experience demonstrated how challenging and competitive an academic setting can be and taught me to stay on track when it comes to meeting expectations to remain successful at what I do." In addition, you likely received a great deal of constructive feedback throughout your graduate program. Throughout that process you learned to take the criticism and move forward in a productive rather than unproductive fashion. The ability to use criticism to constructively improve performance is clearly illustrated in the following textbox. Chandler Johnson is a 2014 graduate of Illinois State University's communication master's program who is currently a graphic designer for an international nonprofit organization:

> [I had an] advantage interpreting analytics, constructing arguments and pitches, and constantly considering what the viewer wants in a design or product. The majority of my meetings are seeking to understand the data we received from a project or planning a new product for consumers. My job requires me to look at information from all angles. The master's program helped develop this flexible way of thinking through rigorous classes and discussion. The trials and tribulations of working on a thesis helped me interpret feedback, and now, I'm better at considering how to make designs better based on criticism.

Without question, the ability to navigate the processes of resilience will serve you very well in your life and professional career.

Opportunities Outside of the United States

An understanding of the differences between graduate programs in communication in the United States and abroad will give you a better idea of the diverse areas of focus and provide insight into the jobs and careers available.

Graduate programs in communication outside of the United States vary in content areas based on several factors including the "political democratization, economic prosperity, educational progress, and mass media modernization" of the host nation (Wang, 2006, p. 159). For example, mass communication, information communication, and telecommunications are the most common area of study in Taiwan (Wang, 2006). According to Bromley (2006), journalism enjoys a privileged position in communication education in the United Kingdom. Interest in multimedia studies and organizational communication has increased in France (Mattelart, 2006). In contrast, Irwin (2006) argues that because communication education was not introduced in Australia until the late 1970s, the overall teaching and research effort in those areas has been smaller compared to the United States and Europe. However, Irwin notes that approximately 75% of Australia's universities now offer coursework in communication. In Africa, Taylor et al. (2004) note that the paradigm for communication education has historically revolved around mass communication. Importantly, they also state that African universities have seen significant growth in programs in human communication (e.g., intercultural communication, speech communication, and interpersonal communication) in the last several years.

When searching for employment abroad, it might be necessary to expand the scope of your search beyond your specialization. A master's in communication program alumna recently told us about her experience working in Norway and the need for job candidates to expand their thinking about how they can apply their communication training and skills. Her communication training, as well as her experience teaching public speaking, positioned her to stand out amongst competitors in unexpected ways. Jannicke Hedum-Bakken currently serves as the vice president of communication at Telenor ASA:

> I am a prime example that the professional path you see when studying is not necessarily where you end up. I did not see myself as the mentor, coach, and expert to work with scientists with PhDs on their communication skills. I work with scientists that are deep into next-generation mobile technologies, like 5G. Others are working in artificial intelligence and analytics. I also work with colleagues from the social sciences, like economics and regulations. What has made me stand out is my training in public speaking and communication. Without that experience and knowledge, my edge would not be so unique.

The languages you speak, your experiences living abroad, and your knowledge of cross-cultural communication are factors that might influence your choice of country. Regardless, we suggest reading country-specific information compiled on https://www.hofstede-insights.com. The country comparison tool on this website provides information regarding key lifestyle factors that might affect your work experiences abroad. For instance, in India, being 15 minutes late to a meeting would be considered as being on time. In contrast, being 15 minutes late to a meeting in the United States would likely be viewed negatively. While working abroad, being open to change and new experiences is imperative. Some changes might seem miniscule while searching for employment, but remember, you are likely to have a 40-hour work week. Ask yourself what aspects of working abroad excite you the most and which of these aspects might be potential deal breakers. If you are serious about working abroad after your master's, we encourage you to take advantage of study abroad opportunities at your university. Doing so will make you more competitive in the job search process and give you a much better sense of what it would be like to live and work in another country. Additionally, while searching for jobs abroad, consider the logistics of visa processing times, the income and the cost of living, and the political stability of the country, as these factors will influence your life and work experience.

Success and Career Fulfillment

Many communication alumni shared examples of how their graduate school experiences helped them to succeed in the workplace and in life after graduate school. For instance, an alumnus shared that "holding a graduate assistant position on top of that allows you to talk about your commitments outside of the classroom and how that adversity, depending on the position, impacts your professionalism." If you are planning to enter the workforce immediately upon graduation, do not discount the option of completing a thesis in your program. We have heard from several students that they perceive writing a thesis will not help them to find a job outside of academia; however, we urge you to consider what an alumnus shared with us in the following:

> Completing a thesis will make you believe you can accomplish anything. For me, completing my thesis helped me finally see the layers of communication and scholarly research. Essentially, graduate school helps you see in 3D. You are able to look at all the angles of a problem, consider the history (i.e., literature review), and make suggestions on how to move forward. It's a powerful thing to realize problem-solving can have dimensions instead just the two: problem and solution. Every job in the world is about problem-solving. The more you can see the aspects of a problem, articulate it effectively, and provide solutions, the more you're going to be a benefit to that company. I think the COM master's program gave me those "3D" skills.

Beyond completing a thesis, he offered several valuable insights on success and career fulfillment. Initially, it is important that you look for opportunities in graduate school that will not only allow you to be competitive in the job search but also to succeed in your career. As one alumnus told us, "Ask yourself this main question: Is the current position you're in or the classes you are registered for fulfilling a purpose for the positions you desire after graduation? If not, you might be wasting your time."

When asked to provide advice about career success and fulfillment, one graduate indicated that you should "(a) be curious about everything, (b) create as much value as you can, whenever you can, and (c) choose to embrace and enjoy the experience because choosing otherwise would be silly." Several graduates also suggested that you should keep an open mind about career opportunities after you complete your master's. For example, one indicated that, since graduating, "I've started three different careers inside of my organization and taught at a small liberal arts college." Others noted the importance of continuing to participate in social and professional activities and identifying mentors and collaborators early in your career.

In a meta-analysis of the career success literature, Ng et al. (2005) found that career success is largely a function of working hard and receiving sponsorship (e.g., support from senior-level employees, participation in professional development, access to organizational resources). In another study, De Vos et al. (2011) found that participation in professional development is positively associated with self-perceived employability, which, in turn, is positively related to career satisfaction. A communication master's program alumnus Nikita Richards (employment coordinator for the city of Bloomington, Illinois, and public servant for state and local govern-ment) suggests in the following textbox that you will experience career success and fulfillment to the extent that you choose the path that is right for you.

> Become comfortable with being uncomfortable because change and trying
> new things is necessary for true growth and self-fulfillment. Whatever you
> do, please make sure that you are choosing that career path FOR YOU. All too
> often, people succumb to the pressures of what family, peers, and society says
> you should become. Remember that you can make any career lucrative if you
> think outside of the box, work smart, and network. You must also remember
> that, along with your career, you can still engage in other passions while
> working to pay the bills.

Taken together, the extant literature and the perspectives of alumni suggest that having a strong work ethic, keeping an open mind, displaying a positive attitude, being committed to lifelong learning, and enacting resilience will take you a long way toward career success and fulfillment.

Our overall objective for this chapter was to sketch out a roadmap for career success outside of the academy. Obtaining a master's in communication opens many doors, as the ability to communicate effectively is the top skill employers desire in prospective employees. Through this chapter, we have discussed strategies for setting your course in locating positions, navigating the terrain as you translate your training to new contexts, expanding your horizons by looking for positions outside of the United States, and setting your cruise control as you realize career success and fulfillment. Whatever path you choose, we wish you the best of luck in everything you do going forward!

For Further Thought and Reflection

1. What projects have you completed during your master's program that you think an employer would want to learn about during an interview, and why?

2. What skills do you think you will have gained in your master's program or hope to gain in your program that will make you stand out from others on the job search?

3. What are the needs and wants of your ideal career after graduate school? Make a list. For instance, do you need to work in a particular location in the country or world? Do you want to have a flexible schedule or something more structured?

15

Translate Your Talents

Pursuing Careers Outside of the Academy for PhD Graduates[1]

Katlyn E. Gangi

James B. Stiff

Serendipity and the Development of Career Paths

Each year, thousands of students who have completed or are nearing completion of their PhD work begin the search for gainful employment. Some students are committed to teaching and are fortunate to find a suitable employment opportunity with a college or university. Others are seeking employment in government or the private sector. Some students have no real plan at all and proceed through their final year in graduate school as though the completion of a PhD dissertation is the Holy Grail, hoping for a stroke of employment serendipity upon completion of their degree. We will begin with a brief review of our own stories.

When Katlyn graduated from University of California, Santa Barbara in 2017, she had hoped to already have a tenure-track academic position lined up. But having applied to jobs as a doctoral candidate (ABD), she had not been able to secure a job before graduation. However, during graduate school she had been working part-time at a software company in town (by the way, this wasn't a job she had actively sought out but rather an opportunity that emerged through networking). After a stint as a content writer, upper management recognized she had the skill level to manage others and communicate at a high level—so they promoted her to director of human resources. Katlyn enjoyed this job for a few years but again started longing for the intellectual discussions of academia and engaging with students. She left HR and

---

1   Quotations in this chapter were selected from participants in an informal survey conducted by the authors. The survey was sent out to members of their networks who were known to have graduate degrees in communication and work outside the academy, and these informed some of the thoughts described in this chapter. We would like to thank those who participated for sharing their experiences.

moved to Missoula just as a faculty member retired from the Communication Studies Department at University of Montana. She was hired in a non-tenure-track faculty position—teaching classes and directing the public speaking program. She decided to conduct research outside of her UM role. Then the pandemic of 2020 hit, and with university budgets slashed, Katlyn's job was drastically reduced. She realized that most employers had gone remote over the last six months, and this presented an opportunity. She sent a cover letter back to Ontraport and was recently hired remotely as lead content writer and project lead focused on improving the new user experience.

When Jim graduated from Michigan State in 1985, he had a plan to become a university professor and spend his career engaged in teaching and research. Jim was fortunate to have a number of offers and quickly accepted a position to join the faculty at Michigan State University. After several years and a reasonable amount of success in the classroom and publication arena, Jim became disenchanted with the slow pace of academic life and what he viewed as an overly politicized peer-review process. By 1990, Jim was actively seeking opportunities to engage in consulting work outside of academia, and in 1998 he made the decision to leave academia for a full-time career as a litigation consultant.

Our experiences are not unusual and reflect a common set of challenges that doctoral graduates often face. While there are a wide variety of nonacademic career opportunities for people with a PhD in communication and related social sciences and humanities, the right opportunity can be elusive. Private-sector employment may be with a small start-up company that has limited structure, few resources, and uncertain job security or with a national or multinational consulting firm with tremendous organizational resources, long hours, and consistent travel. Government and nonprofit organizations often provide considerable structure, flexible work-family schedules, and steady, but not spectacular, income.

Plan Your Career and Begin Early

One issue we noticed, both from our own experience and from the nonscientific survey we conducted in preparation for this chapter, is that most students fail to adequately plan for a career outside of academia. Often, students do not begin career preparations until their final year in graduate school. Those who intend to remain in academia may have no preparation at all when their desire to remain is confronted by the difficulty of finding ideal employment opportunities. Compounding this problem for students who lack preparation is the fact that students who were always planning for nonacademic careers may have a lengthy head start over those who are late to the party. Ideally, students who are entertaining careers outside of academia should pursue internships and apprenticeships during their graduate programs and consider methodological training that would give them other marketable skills. Just as you allocate time and resources to attend academic conferences, you should also attend professional meetings in nonacademic areas of interest. Our recommendation is to consider both academic and nonacademic career options as you navigate your way through your doctoral program. As franchisee and executive director of a tutoring center shared:

> Communication underlies everything, so your skill set will prove valuable regardless of whether you pursue a career in academia or outside of it. Think about what gets you excited—what fills your bucket—and do that. In high school we learn what to think, in college we learn how to think, and in graduate school we contribute to and shape the body of thought in our discipline. That's empowering regardless of what avenues you pursue next.

Perform a Critical Self-Assessment

Performing a thoughtful self-assessment to identify which employment characteristics are most important requires time. First, think more broadly about the tasks that make you happy in your graduate school environment, and then imagine which skills you would enjoy in a job outside the academy (and if they translate into work outside the academy). As a PhD jury consultant shared with us:

> Consider what about graduate school you really enjoy. If it's teaching, think twice about leaving academia, because most of that will go away. If it's research, consider your research style, and try to find a job that matches it. You have to be very self-aware of what you truly enjoy, and you shouldn't make the decision just because a job market is poor.

Our advice is to start by asking yourself: "What makes me feel most fulfilled? What feels draining?" People are energized by different kinds of tasks and environments, so be honest with yourself. We'd like to also give you permission to change your mind. If you started graduate school on the straight and narrow path to become a tenure-track professor but now have doubts and questions about life outside the ivory tower—that's okay! You are human.

Here's a series of questions you can ask yourself the honest answers about.

Career Self-Assessment:

- Do you want to work independently or in a team structure?

- Are you willing to accept "client-facing" responsibilities, or would you be more effective working behind the scenes?

- Do you prefer compensation based on the sales you generate or the projects that you lead? Do you want to train and/or supervise other employees?

- Are you adept at designing and conducting research?

- How are your writing skills?

- Do you want a job that involves extensive writing or public presentations?

- Will you need technology and administrative support?

- Are you a creative thinker or someone who works more effectively with well-developed procedures and protocols?

- Can you effectively manage multiple projects simultaneously?

- Are you willing to travel extensively?

- Are you looking for a career with more risk and the potential for a significant upward trajectory, or do you prefer a steady and more secure growth opportunity?

- Would you consider a career that involves an apprentice period (similar to a post-doctorate position or entry-level attorney in a law firm)?

- Are you willing to start your own business, or do you want to work for an employer?

These are just some of the factors that you should consider as you identify the best employment opportunities to pursue.

Apart from employment considerations, there are personal and family considerations.

Personal and Lifestyle Assessment:

- Are you willing to work in a job that requires you to be away from home for extended periods of time?

- Is it important to work from home several days a week or have a flexible work schedule?

- Do you work effectively in a remote situation?

- Will you need an employer that provides health insurance and retirement benefits?

- How much money do you need to make?

- How much do you want to make?

- Perhaps most important, how many hours do you want to work?

These are among the many questions that will help you decide whether you are well suited for a career outside of academia and the job characteristics that may be most important to you.

As you conduct a self-assessment, do not make the mistake of optimizing a job search around the most comfortable career path or careers you happen to know about right now. Be willing to step outside of your comfort zone and accept the challenges that you will encounter as you embark on a nonacademic career. Opportunities for professional growth depend on your ability to embrace change and manage uncertainty.

Develop Desirable Skills and Traits

Our experience leads us to conclude there are six core skills and traits that doctoral students should develop to pursue successful careers in the private sector. We list them below.

Effective Writing Skills

The inability to write clearly and concisely is the death knell for many careers. Writing skills reflect thinking skills, and people who cannot write clearly and concisely generally have difficulty thinking effectively as well. Do not mistake the ability to prepare a PowerPoint deck with the ability to write a clearly written proposal, argument, or analysis.

Effective Public Speaking Skills

It is remarkable how much difficulty professionals have with public speaking. The ability to address an audience with a clear, direct message is important, but it is equally important to develop listening skills that will enable you to respond to concerns and questions that are raised when you speak. Hone your public speaking skills as much as possible during graduate school, as the ability to communicate complex ideas adapted to your audience is a skill that will set you apart in the private sector. In her role as director of HR, Katlyn didn't feel daunted by speaking to a company of 100+ employees or adjusting a presentation for the executive team.

Research Methods and Analysis Skills

Someone who can design and direct research studies and analyze the findings is much more valuable than someone who has taken an introductory course in statistical analysis and research methods. Even if your career does not require you to conduct or analyze research, advanced training in research methods and analysis will make you an effective consumer and critic of research findings that are presented to you.

Theoretical Foundation

Communication scholars distinguish themselves in their ability to provide an explanatory level of analysis. Most consultants can describe a phenomenon, some are able to predict it, but few are able to explain it clearly. Clients are looking for clear explanations, using a layperson's language, that support specific recommendations. A cogent theoretical foundation and the ability to explain it to others are essential.

Adaptive Communication Style

Working outside of academia requires the ability to communicate with a wide variety of clients in socially appropriate ways. While eccentricities may be valued in academia, they are often shunned in the private sector. Clients want comfortable communication interactions and place the onus on consultants and service providers to adapt their styles accordingly. Becoming a social chameleon means moving outside of your comfort zone and interacting with people in a wide variety of professional settings.

Self-Motivation and the Ability to Work With Others

Two traits that are unrelated to academic training are self-motivation and the ability to work and play well with others. In many ways, academia conditions students to work independently in a structured, steady work environment. In the private sector teamwork is essential, the pace of work is accelerated, and schedules are unpredictable. The transition from academic life to work in the private sector can be difficult for people who have a low tolerance for ambiguity and are uncomfortable with constant change but can be energizing for those who seek such a dynamic environment.

Seek Out Mentors

There is a structural bias in most communication PhD programs to direct students toward careers in academia. While every PhD program has a list of alumni who have gone on to distinguished careers outside of academia, few programs are designed to specifically prepare students for work outside of academia. Jim spent five years in graduate school at ASU and MSU and never once had a conversation with a faculty member about pursuing a career outside of academia. It was always assumed that Jim would become a university professor. While many programs have adopted a broader perspective in recent years, students should be aware that in many programs the expectation that doctoral students will pursue careers in the academy persists.

Given this bias, students who are interested in nonacademic careers, and those who wish to hedge their bets, must assume full responsibility for seeking and developing mentoring relationships with nonacademic advisors. Recognize that while your academic advisors may provide outstanding counsel regarding academic careers, they may not be all that helpful when it comes to advising you about nonacademic careers. After all, most faculty advisors have limited experience outside of academia. If you're just beginning to explore the potential of a nonacademic career, you should consider checking out websites like Versatile PhD and the resources provided at the end of this chapter. Also, build relationships with academic advisors who are enthusiastic about helping you explore a career outside of academia.

> Keep your options open, and don't be afraid that your mentors might be disappointed if you don't get a faculty position. It's their job to mentor you, but it's not your job to repay them by following in their footsteps. It's okay to pursue the academic and nonacademic markets at the same time. Think about what's important to you (location, free time, salary, vacation time), and keep those things in mind when you look for a job. (Anonymous, recent PhD graduate)

When it came time for a career change, Jim was fortunate to have an extensive alumni network to tap to help him research alternative careers. Jim's first phone call was to a former PhD committee member who introduced Jim to a member of the Michigan State alumni network who owned a litigation consulting firm. After several lengthy conversations, Jim began consulting part-time with a litigation consulting firm while continuing to teach at a university.

Graduate students have access to similar networks, but students tend to underutilize these resources. When you go to academic conferences, seek out alumni of your institution, particularly those who are working in nonacademic careers. A 10-minute cup of coffee may be sufficient to begin a relationship that can be continued after the conference.

> Grow your network as much as you can. Thus far, I am hard pressed to think of anyone who got a job without the help of people who have already gone through the process. I set a goal of talking to at least one new person at each networking event I attended. Once you have a network of people, identify someone you jibe with that may be able to provide you some informal mentorship. For me, [this person] took time to sit and explain what teams are looking for in interviews, gave me insider knowledge of the way things worked at [her company], and most importantly, opened up her vast network to me. (Anonymous, recent PhD graduate)

We routinely take time to speak with graduate students who are seeking advice, and you will find that most people in your institution's alumni network will be charitable with their time. Do your homework, learn about the person you are meeting, ask meaningful questions, and be prepared to talk about your interests. When you reach a point of comfort and familiarity with a valuable resource, ask that person to serve as an informal mentor, and be available for short conversations or email exchanges a few times a year.

In addition to developing contacts in your alumni network, students seeking a career outside of academia should also attend conferences in their field of interest. Professional associations and trade groups host small and large conferences every year that provide an excellent opportunity to talk with people in your desired field of work and begin developing specialized networks with professionals in your field. Our experience has been that the smaller the conference, the more opportunities there are for meaningful encounters. It is too easy for young scholars to get lost at a large conference. During her time working at a software company, Katlyn had the opportunity to attend a small human resources conference in New York City. Although she in no way felt like an expert in HR at that point in her career, she presented a paper about processes implemented in her HR department at this conference as a way to boost her networking potential and as a way to be "seen" in the industry. Remember, the earlier you begin this process, the more opportunities you have to shop around for a desirable occupation.

Develop Your Marketing Materials

When seeking a career outside of the academy, you will want to connect with professionals and members of your program's alumni network online who may or may not come from your academic discipline. Develop an effective LinkedIn page, and model it after the pages of others in your nonacademic field of interest. Do not hesitate to reach out with alumni on job networking sites such as LinkedIn. Ideally, send them a message explaining why you're interested in connecting: "Hi, Jim. I see that you graduated from my university and work at a tech company. I'm currently working on my PhD and exploring industry career paths." With these online connections, you can interact if you have specific questions, and you can also browse profiles. A quick glance at a LinkedIn profile provides you a snapshot of someone's career trajectory—which, as we have mentioned, can sometimes be winding. From these online profiles, you can also observe how others market their skills and abilities from their doctoral work. In other words, pay attention to how people are translating their academic skills into their particular industry.

You can also use this information to develop your own elevator pitch (yes, you need one) for your skill set. In graduate school, you learn and practice your "academic" elevator pitch at conferences—the 30-second explanation about who you are in the communication discipline. This pitch often includes shortcuts that make sense to those inside our academic bubble ("quantitative relational comm researcher focused on health contexts, teaching public speaking and family comm"), but consider how you would sound if you used that same pitch to someone outside our field. Would they have any idea of what your skills mean in a broader work environment? Don't make them do the work (or make yourself sound like you're so stuck in your niche literature that you are not relevant).

Consider how to translate specific theoretical knowledge/skills you've obtained as a doctoral student to your desired career as well. When asked what knowledge/skills have translated from his graduate program to his career, a lecturer and owner of an organizational consulting firm said: "So much. Project management; theoretical understanding of organizations, teams, leadership, management, supervision, employee development, conflict; data collection and analysis skills; and writing." Think about the specific subject matter you're focusing on in your degree and how you'll communicate that as part of your unique skill set (leaving out the fancy theory names—at least for the interview).

> If you can't work in the industry [while completing your degree], read about it and follow trends and ideas in the field, and diversify your skill set as much as you can so you can be resourceful and follow any number of tracks. Being more practically informed when you enter an industry helps you apply your advanced learning more effectively and shows that you are curious and teachable. (Anonymous, director of a nonprofit)

Finally, if you are considering a career outside of academia, develop both a curriculum vitae and a résumé—even if you are yet undecided about your path. While the CV is the standard for the academy, the résumé is the document you want for a nonacademic career. There are numerous resources online that can assist you with translating a vitae to a résumé. It could be that you started graduate school knowing what your future would look like, but your vision has changed. Or perhaps you've imagined a career where you can do some teaching and some freelance or corporate work. If any of these situations describe you, you'll benefit from having both.

These two documents will be significantly different because they serve different functions and are sent to different audiences. While your curriculum vitae may be easier to assemble, the résumé will be more critical. Develop your résumé as a companion to your elevator speech. It must convey your skills and talents in language that is easily understood by professionals in your chosen nonacademic field. While you should not embellish your skills and abilities, it is important to avoid short selling your talents. While you may not consider yourself to be an expert in persuasion or organizational communication within your academic department, your knowledge may render you a subject matter expert when you join a nonacademic organization. Indeed, your employer is likely hiring you because it requires a subject matter expert. It is important to promote your skills honestly and concisely using language that will resonate with employers.

Do Not Limit Yourself to a Single, Unchangeable Career Path

In relational communication research, studies of couples and their mindsets about expectations of their partners have shown us that those who believe there is a soulmate out there for them are often setting themselves up to fail. Why? Well, they can become unsatisfied with partners who once made them happy if things get difficult because they start to believe they chose the wrong partner—and that their soulmate must still be out there.

Give yourself the grace and flexibility to mentally explore several options—even simultaneously. This is not to say that your work should become scattered as you attempt to set yourself up perfectly for multiple careers. But realize that there is no perfect soulmate when it comes to careers. In any career path you choose, you will have to deal with challenges and elements of the job that aren't perfectly aligned with your image of a dream job.

Many successful professionals have had multiple careers. Jim works with very accomplished attorneys who come from a wide variety of backgrounds: One was a professional wrestler, several were actors, and one was an officer on a submarine before entering the legal profession. Multiple careers often provide you the flexibility to adapt to your changing personal and family needs, as well as external factors beyond your control that necessitate a career change. A grad school colleague of Katlyn's landed an impressive tenure-track position at a "Research I" university straight out of her PhD. She moved across the country, hoping for the best. After a year in the position, her partner wasn't thrilled with his career trajectory, and the small town where they lived felt lonely and far from home. This motivated her to leave her academic position and utilize her data analysis skills to become a user experience researcher at a tech company. She is still in this role and thriving because she followed her intuition.

As mentioned above, Katlyn was happy in her HR position in a software company. However, her career switch back to academia was not solely motivated by nostalgia for teaching and research. In fact, she was well compensated and enjoyed tremendous benefits at the software company, including catered lunches and on-site child care. Cost of living and raising children without extended family nearby ultimately led Katlyn to quit that job and move to a place that was a better fit for those lifestyle reasons. That decision meant Katlyn was jobless for some time before she had the opportunity to rejoin academic life. But having been honest with herself about the things that were the most important to her allowed her to be flexible and a bit winding in her career path.

Expect the Unexpected

Career flexibility is critically important once you leave academia. Most professors have a tremendous amount of control over their career trajectories and enjoy considerable job security. In contrast, nonacademic careers are filled with organizational upheaval and change. Corporate downsizing and restructuring, changes in regulatory practice, political and economic cycles, and innovation combine to affect the demand for professional services. You have to adapt to survive as well as to discover opportunities for yourself. While changes in academia come at a glacial pace, change in the private sector can occur overnight.

For example, Jim started his own jury consulting firm in 2000, and by 2005, he had developed a substantial book of business. Jim's practice included conducting mock trials and focus group research, helping lawyers prepare witnesses for testimony, and developing trial themes that will resonate with jurors. Unfortunately, about 40% of Jim's business was derived from helping lawyers defend vicarious liability laws in New York and several other states. Vicarious liability laws hold a vehicle owner financially responsible for the damage caused by anyone who was given permission to drive the vehicle. Because the vicarious liability laws extended to auto companies that leased vehicles to customers, every time there was a major accident involving a leased vehicle in New York, the auto companies were sued because they held the title on the vehicle. Each year there were hundreds of lawsuits seeking billions of dollars. Then, in 2005, national legislation was enacted that eliminated these vicarious liability statutes. Overnight, Jim's business lost 40% of its revenue, and he was forced to adjust his practice and develop new clients.

In September 2008, Hurricane Ike hit the Texas Gulf Coast with devastating effects on the city of Houston, which brought an abrupt halt to litigation in the region. The next month, the stock market crashed, and a global financial crisis brought nonessential litigation to a standstill and led corporations to dramatically restructure the way they managed litigation. Decision-making authority and budgetary control that had previously been granted to outside counsel was brought back within the corporate structure of most companies, requiring Jim to develop new relationships with in-house counsel.

All of these events were unpredictable and beyond Jim's control. During the global financial crisis, Jim was confronted with the prospect of making payroll for several employees with no revenue for nine months. More recently, the COVID-19 pandemic brought a halt to jury trials and caused another significant business interruption. Indeed, it forced Katlyn to quickly shift out of academic work and back into the private sector. At the time of this writing, it is uncertain how long the COVID-19 crisis will last, but its effects have already been devastating.

When you leave academia you forfeit the safety net of a large university, with all of the benefits of a stable tenure system, health care insurance, and retirement benefits. You give up a large security blanket and assume significant economic risk. The only way to manage this risk is to plan for the unexpected, develop a strategy to protect against unforeseen circumstances, and embrace the uncertainty when it arises. While all of this sounds scary, there are wonderful benefits to careers outside of academia. For Katlyn, utilizing her high-level writing skills in developing fast-moving projects that drive a business forward has been energizing and more lucrative than academia. And she has found ways to remain connected with scholarly activity to fulfill that part of her identity. She formed a research group with other professors and has been conducting research and publishing outside of her day job. For Jim, the opportunity to conduct applied persuasion research and communication skills training in high-profile lawsuits is intellectually and financially rewarding. In the end, some people are not cut out for the risk side of the risk-reward equation, while others learn to thrive on it. The rewards are generally easy to manage; managing the risk becomes more challenging.

Expand Your Base of Experience

When you've completed your doctoral degree, don't be afraid to do something bold. If you've committed to a career outside the academy, now is your time to cut the cord with your academic comfort zone. Consider the next year your "graduate gap year"—your time to explore the world in the career you are considering. This is a great time to relocate, perhaps to an international location, and begin the work of establishing yourself as a subject matter expert for a broader audience in your chosen field.

You have the theoretical knowledge; now think about what kind of real-world experience will help you practice applying this knowledge. Having a diverse background and unique experiences will prove invaluable to you in your career, in part because it will enrich you with stories to tell. In your job search, those who can tell stories that connect their education, experience, and motivation to pursue a career will stand out in a crowd. So can you work for a multinational corporation? Work for a nonprofit? Complete an international post-doc position? Even if it's not outside the country, how can you break into the career that most interests you with an ambitious new experience? Think through how you can obtain hands-on experience and the ability to convey and apply the knowledge you've obtained—because having theoretical knowledge isn't enough.

Complete Your Degree

Failing to complete your degree is one of the biggest career mistakes you can make. Too often MA and PhD students will accept a nonacademic position and let their thesis or dissertation languish for a while before abandoning it altogether. Employers are looking for people with knowledge and skills, but they are also looking for people with credentials. According to the U.S. Census Bureau (2018), only 4.5% of adults in the United States have a PhD. Because many of those people work in academia and the federal government, a PhD is a rare commodity in the private sector. Take advantage of a great opportunity and complete your degree. It will demonstrate that you can work independently and finish important projects. But most important, it will give you a sense of accomplishment and satisfaction that no paycheck can provide.

Earning a PhD is hard work. There will be times where you will ask yourself (or maybe you've already asked yourself) "Is all this effort worth my time? Could I be doing something more worthwhile than writing a dissertation that only my committee members and my parents will read?" This is likely even more true if you've been exploring the idea of a nonacademic career. If you let your mind go down that road, you'll be able to come up with all sorts of (legitimate) excuses about why you should quit. But go ahead, list the excuses as a thought exercise ... "If I drop out of my PhD program, I won't be as stressed. If I drop out, I can start working full-time. If I drop out, I'll be able to spend more time with my partner/dog/kids/friends." For Katlyn, her advisor took a job at another university, she had a baby, and she took a part-time job at a software company while still in school. These are valid reasons for wanting to drop out. But you still shouldn't do it. Barring situations where it's absolutely necessary for you to get out of graduate school (such as caring for an ill parent), we want to implore that you remain in graduate school—despite what sometimes feels like your better judgment.

There are two solid arguments for why you should buckle up and finish your degree even if you have decided that an academic career is not in the cards for you. First, the fact that you did not finish will be a red flag for potential employers and future colleagues. Even though you have the knowledge and experience from graduate school, the fact that you did not finish creates uncertainty. Though it may seem unfair, people who begin a PhD program and fail to complete it are often viewed more negatively than those who never began a program. People who fail to complete a PhD program usually list their graduate school experience (without a degree) on their résumé, or they make no reference to it on their résumé. Either way, prospective employers will ask about the experience or gap in employment history, and both of those conversations are negative. While there are many reasonable explanations for not completing a degree, it is much more powerful to talk about the accomplishment of completing your degree than to explain why you failed to do so. In one instance, Jim was interviewing a candidate for a jury consulting position. The candidate completed a master's degree but had also been enrolled in a PhD program for several years. Failure to complete the PhD caused Jim to question the candidate's perseverance and ability to manage projects independently.

The second and most important argument for completing your PhD is that a doctorate is an ethos ticket for life. A PhD forever signals to the world that you are credible, have tremendous initiative, and are an expert in your field. As a recent graduate you may not view yourself as an expert, at least when compared with your professors who have been academia for 30 years. But outside the world of academia, a PhD will be viewed as rare and extremely valuable, particularly if you combine your academic knowledge with applied skills. Others will view you as an expert and someone who completed a very difficult task. We are not suggesting that you become pretentious or dismissive of the knowledge and ability of others who did not earn a PhD. Instead, we are suggesting that completing the degree will afford you a measure of credibility and respect that may not be apparent until you leave academia.

For Further Thought and Reflection

1. How will your life be different if you pursue a nonacademic career? What do you see as the major advantages and disadvantages of a career outside of academia?

2. After thinking about the skills necessary for a successful career outside of academia, what skills do you need to acquire or refine in order to develop a successful career?

3. Do you plan to remain connected with theory and research in communication while working outside of academia? What actions do you need to take to remain connected with the academic field?

4. List five people who have a PhD and work outside of academia. What do you admire most about their careers? If you were in their shoes, what would concern you the most about their careers?

5. What makes you the most fearful about a career outside of academia? What steps can you take to overcome your fears?

6. What do you think you would miss most if you pursued a career outside of academia? What can you do to fill that void with other projects or work?

Additional Online Resources

Cassuto, L. (2020, February 23). *Start career advising for PhD students in year 1. The Chronicle of Higher Education.* https://www.chronicle.com/article/start-career-advising-for-ph-d-students-in-year-1/

Cassuto, L. (2020, June 17). *How a postdoctoral fellowship can be a bridge to a nonacademic career, too. The Chronicle of Higher Education.* https://www.chronicle.com/article/how-a-postdoctoral-fellowship-can-be-a-bridge-to-a-nonacademic-career-too

Lodge, K. (n.d.). *3 things every PhD needs to know about getting a job outside academia.* The Muse. https://www.themuse.com/advice/3-things-phd-need-to-know-get-job-outside-academia

National Communication Association. (2019). *2018–2019 academic job listings in communication report.* https://www.natcom.org/sites/default/files/publications/NCA_JobListings_2019_REV.pdf

Polk, J., & Wood, L. M. (2018, February 14). *What can I do with a PhD in my discipline outside academe?* Inside Higher Ed. https://www.insidehighered.com/advice/2018/02/14/how-phd-students-can-find-jobs-outside-academe-appropriate-their-discipline

Stark, A. (2019, October 18). *Non-academic career paths: The dirty secret of academia?* Duck of Minerva. https://duckofminerva.com/2019/10/non-academic-career-paths-the-dirty-secret-of-academia.html

The Versatile PhD. (n.d.). *About.* https://versatilephd.com/about/

Wolgin, P. E. (2018, February 5). *An academic's guide to a non-academic job.* Medium. https://medium.com/@pwolgin/an-academics-guide-to-getting-a-non-academic-job-fa9d566b57fb

References

Afifi, T. D., & Harrison, K. (2018). Theory of resilience and relational load (TRRL): Understanding families as systems of stress and calibration. In D.O. Braithwaite, E.A. Suter, & K. Floyd (Eds.), *Engaging theories in family communication: Multiple Perspectives* (pp. 324–336). Routledge.

Allen, B. J., Orbe, M. P., & Olivas, M. R. (2006). The complexity of our tears: Dis/enchantment and (in)difference in the academy. *Communication Theory, 9*(4), 402–429. https://doi.org/10.1111/j.1468-2885.1999.tb00206.x

Amienne, K. A. (2017, November 2). Abusers and enablers in faculty culture. *The Chronicle of Higher Education.* www.chronicle.com/article/abusers-and-enablers-in-faculty-culture/

Anzaldúa, G. (2015). Speaking in tongues: A letter to third world women writers. In C. Moraga & G. Anzaldúa (Eds.), *This bridge called my back: Writings by radical women of color* (4th ed., pp. 163–172). SUNY Press.

Asante, M. K. (2009, April 13). *Afrocentricity.* https://www.asante.net/articles/1/afrocentricity/

Azar, B. (2010, November). Sink or skim? Tackle that endless pile of books and journal articles with the help of these reading tips. *gradPSYCH.* https://www.apa.org/gradpsych/2010/11/skim

Bach, B. W., Braithwaite, D. O., & Bullis, C. A. (2008). Selecting the right graduate program and maximizing chances for admission to that program. In S. Morreale & P. Arneson (Eds.), *Getting the most from your graduate education in communication: A student's handbook* (pp. 17–28). National Communication Association.

Badenhorst, C., Moloney, C., Rosales, J., & Dyer, J. (2012). Graduate research writing: A pedagogy of possibility. *Learning Landscapes Journal, 6*(1), 63–80. https://doi.org/10.36510/learnland.v6i1.576

Bahrainwala, L. (2020, March 11). Precarity, citizenship, and the "traditional" student. *Communication Education, 69*(2), 250–260. https://doi.org/10.1080/03634523.2020.1723805

Bahrainwala, L. (2020). The web of white disengagement. *Women & Language, 43,* 135–140. https://doi:org/10.34036/WL.2020.013

Bain, K. (2004). *What the best college teachers do.* Harvard University Press.

Baird, L. L., Clark, M. J., & Hartnett, R. T. (1973). *The Graduates.* Educational Testing Service.

Ballard, D., Allen, B., Ashcraft, K., Ganesh, S., McLeod, P., & Zoller, H. (2020). When words do not matter: Identifying actions to effect diversity, equity, and inclusion in the academy. *Management Communication Quarterly, 34*(4), 590–616. https://doi.org/10.1177/0893318920951643

Barkley, E. F. (2009). *Student engagement techniques: A handbook for college faculty.* Jossey-Bass.

Bastalich, W. (2017). Content and context in knowledge production: A critical review of doctoral supervision literature. *Studies in Higher Education, 42*(7), 1145–1157.

Baxter, L. A. (2014). Theorizing the communicative construction of "family": The three R's. In L. A. Baxter (Ed.), *Remaking "family" communicatively* (pp. 33–50). Peter Lang.

Bazerman, C. (2009). Genre and cognitive development: Beyond writing to learn. In C. Bazerman, A. Bonini, & D. Figueiredo (Eds.), *Genre in a changing world* (pp. 279–294). The WAC Clearinghouse.

Belcher, W. (2009). *Writing your journal article in 12 weeks*. SAGE.

Bennett, D. (2018, July), Graduate employability and higher education: Past, present and future. *HERDSA Review of Higher Education, 5*, 31–61. www.herdsa.org.au/herdsa-review-higher-education-vol-5/31-61

Bhattacharya, K. (2009). Negotiating shuttling between transnational experiences: A de/colonizing approach to performance ethnography. *Qualitative Inquiry, 15*(6), 1061–1083. https://doi.org/10.1177/1077800409332746

Blake, C. (2009). *The African origins of rhetoric*. Routledge.

Boettcher, J. V., & Conrad, R.-M. (2016). *The online teaching survival guide: Simple and practical pedagogical tips* (2nd ed.). Jossey-Bass.

Boice, R. (1989). Procrastination, busyness and bingeing. *Behaviour Research and Therapy, 27*(6), 605–611. https://doi.org/10.1016/0005-7967(89)90144-7

Boice, R. (1997). Which is more productive, writing in binge patterns of creative illness or in moderation? *Written Communication, 14*(4), 435–459. https://doi.org/10.1177/0741088397014004001

Boice, R. (2000). *Advice for new faculty members: Nihil Nimus*. Pearson.

Bolker, J. (1998). *Writing your dissertation in fifteen minutes a day: A guide to starting, revising, and finishing your doctoral thesis*. Owl Books.

Booth, W. C., Colomb, G. G., & Williams, J. M. (2008). *The craft of research* (3rd ed.). University of Chicago Press.

Bovill, C., Cook-Sather, A., Felten, P., Millard, L., & Moore-Cherry, N. (2016). Addressing potential challenges in co-creating learning and teaching: Overcoming resistance, navigating institutional norms and ensuring inclusivity in student–staff partnerships. *Higher Education, 71*, 195–208. https://doi.org/10.1007/s10734-015-9896-4

Boyer, E. L. (1996). The scholarship of engagement. *Journal of Public Service and Outreach, 1*(1), 11–20.

Braithwaite, D. O. (2010). *Discourses of stability and change: Presidential address* [Video]. National Communication Association YouTube. https://www.youtube.com/watch?v=CjbbvOurNVQ&feature=youtu.be

Braithwaite, D. O. (2014). "Opening the door": The history and future of qualitative scholarship in interpersonal communication. *Communication Studies, 65*(4), 441–445. https://doi.org/10.1080/10510974.2014.927295

Braithwaite, D. O., & Suter, E. (in press). Family communication. In K. Adamsons, A. Few-Demo, C. Proulx, & K. Roy (Eds.), *Sourcebook of family theories and methodologies* (2nd ed.). SAGE.

Brenneise, A. D. (2020). Presuming competence: Troubling the ideal student. *Communication Education. 69*(3), 317–334. https://doi.org/10.1080/03634523.2020.1770307

Bromley, M. (2006). One journalism or many? Confronting the contradictions in the education and training of journalists in the United Kingdom. In K. W. Y. Leung, J. Kenny, & P. S. N. Lee (Eds.), *Global trends in communication education and research* (pp. 53–71). Hampton Press.

Brookfield, S. D., & Preskill, S. (2005). *Discussion as a way of teaching: Tools and techniques for democratic classrooms* (2nd ed.). Jossey-Bass.

Buber, M. (1958). *I and thou.* Macmillan Publishing.

Burke, K. (1969). *A rhetoric of motives.* University of California Press.

Buzzanell, P. M. (2010). Resilience: Talking, resisting, and imagining new normalcies into being. *Journal of Communication, 60*(1), 1–14. https://doi.org/10.1111/j.1460-2466.2009.01469.x

Buzzanell, P. M. (2017). Communication theory of resilience: Enacting adaptive-transformative processes when families experience loss and disruption. In D. O. Braithwaite, E. A. Suter, & K. Floyd (Eds.), *Engaging theories in family communication: Multiple perspectives* (2nd ed., pp. 98–109). Routledge. https://doi.org/10.4324/9781315204321-9

Buzzanell, P. M. (2018). Organizing resilience as adaptive-transformational tensions. *Journal of Applied Communication Research, 46*(1), 14–18. https://doi.org/10.1080/00909882.2018.1426711

Buzzanell, P. M. (in press). Mentoring. In F. Cooren & P. Stücheli-Herlach (Eds.), *Handbook of management communication.* de Gruyter-Mouton.

Buzzanell, P. M., & Carbaugh, D. (2009). *Distinctive qualities in communication research.* Routledge.

Calvente, L. B. Y., Calafell, B. M., & Chávez, K. R. (2020). Here is something you can't understand: The suffocating whiteness of communication studies. *Communication and Critical/Cultural Studies, 17*(2), 202–209.

Carpenter, S., Makhadmeh, N., & Thornton, L.-J. (2015). Mentorship on the doctoral level: An examination of communication faculty mentors' traits and functions. *Communication Education, 64*(3), 366–384. https://doi.org/10.1080/03634523.2015.1041997

Carrillo Rowe, A. (2008). *Power lines: On the subject of feminist alliances.* Duke University Press.

Cassuto, L. (2013, July 1). Ph.D. attrition: How much is too much? *The Chronicle of Higher Education.* https://www.chronicle.com/article/PhD-Attrition-How-Much-Is/140045

Chakravartty, P., Kuo, R., Grubbs, V., & McIlwain, C. (2018, April). #CommunicationSoWhite. *Journal of Communication, 68*(2), 254–266. https://doi.org/10.1093/joc/jqy003

Chamorro-Premuzic, T. (2020, January 7). Should you go to graduate school? *Harvard Business Review.* https://hbr.org/2020/01/should-you-go-to-graduate-school

Charland, M. (1987). Constitutive rhetoric: The case of the *Peuple Québéois. Quarterly Journal of Speech, 73*(2), 133–150. https://doi.org/10.1080/00335638709383799

Chevrette, R. (2020). Blinded by acceptance: Straight fragility, shame, and the dangers of postqueer politics. *QED: A Journal in Queer Worldmaking, 7*(1), 100–107. https://doi.org/10.14321/qed.7.1.0105

Cirillo, F. (2018). *The Pomodoro technique: The acclaimed time-management system that has transformed how we work.* Crown. (Original work published 2006)

Cohen, H. (1994). *The history of speech communication: The emergence of a discipline, 1914–1945.* National Communication Association.

Committee on Publication Ethics. (2019). *Discussion document: Authorship.* https://publicationethics.org/files/COPE_DD_A4_Authorship_SEPT19_SCREEN_AW.pdf

Craig, R. T. (1999). Communication theory as a field. *Communication Theory, 9*(2), 119–161.

Cruz, J. (2014). Memories of trauma and organizing: Market women's susu groups in postconflict Liberia. *Organization, 21*(4), 447–462. https://doi.org/10.1177/1350508414527254

Cruz, J., McDonald, J., Broadfoot, K., Chuang, A., & Ganesh, S. (2018, September 2). "Aliens" in the United States: A collaborative autoethnography of foreign-born faculty. *Journal of Management Inquiry, 29*(3), 272–285. https://doi.org/10.1177/1056492618796561

Deetz, S. (1998). Discursive formations, strategized subordination and self-surveillance. In A. McKinlay & K. Starkey (Eds.), *Foucault, management and organization theory: From panopticon to technologies of self* (pp. 151–172). SAGE.

Deetz, S. (2001). Conceptual foundations. In F. M. Jablin & L. L. Putnam (Eds.), *The new handbook of organizational communication: Advances in theory, research, and methods* (pp. 3–46). SAGE.

Denis, C., Colet, N. R., & Lison, C. (2019). Doctoral supervision in North America: Perception and challenges of supervisor and supervisee. *Higher Education Studies, 9*(1), 30–39.

Devine, K., & Hunter, K. H. (2017). PhD student emotional exhaustion: The role of supportive supervision and self-presentation behaviours. *Innovations in Education and Teaching International, 54*(4), 335–344.

De Vos, A., De Hauw, S., & Van der Heijden, I. J. M. (2011, October). Competency development and career success: The mediating role of employability. *Journal of Vocational Behavior, 79*(2), 438–447. https://doi.org/10.1016/j.jvb.2011.05.010

Dreyfus, H. L., & Dreyfus, S. E. (2005, May 1). Peripheral vision: Expertise in real world contexts. *Organization Studies, 26*(5), 779–792. https://doi.org/10.1177/0170840605053102

Durham, M. G. (2011). Critical and cultural studies. *Oxford Bibliographies.* https://www.oxfordbibliographies.com/view/document/obo-9780199756841/obo-9780199756841-0041.xml

Eadie, W. F. (2008). Understanding the communication discipline and deciding to go to graduate school. In S. Morreale & P. Arneson (Eds.), *Getting the most from your graduate education in communication: A student's handbook* (pp. 1–16). National Communication Association.

Educational Testing Service. (2020). *The GRE General Test.* https://www.ets.org/gre

Ehninger, D. (1968). On systems of rhetoric. *Philosophy & Rhetoric, 1*(3), 131–144.

Elfenbein, M. (2015, November 5). Take it easy: The wisdom of Robert Boice. *GradHacker.* https://www.insidehighered.com/blogs/gradhacker/take-it-easy-wisdom-robert-boice

Fine, M. A., & Kurdek, L. A. (1993). Reflections on determining authorship credit and authorship order on faculty-student collaborations. *American Psychologist, 48*(11), 1141–1147. https://doi.org/10.1037/0003-066X.48.11.1141

Flores, L. A. (1996). Creating discursive space through a rhetoric of difference: Chicana feminists craft a homeland. *Quarterly Journal of Speech, 82*(2), 142–156. https://doi.org/10.1080/00335639609384147

Flores, L. A. (2016). Between abundance and marginalization: The imperative of racial rhetorical criticism. *Review of Communication, 16*(1), 4–24. https://doi.org/10.1080/15358593.2016.1183871

Flyvbjerg, B. (2001). *Making social science matter: Why social inquiry fails and how it can succeed again.* Cambridge University Press.

Foss, S. K., & Griffin, C. L. (1995). Beyond persuasion: A proposal for an invitational rhetoric. *Communication Monographs, 62*(1), 2–18. https://doi.org/10.1080/03637759509376345

Foss, S. K., & Waters, W. (2007). *Destination dissertation: A traveler's guide to a done dissertation.* Rowman & Littlefield.

Frey, L. R. (2009). What a difference more difference-making communication scholarship might make: Making a difference from and through communication research. *Journal of Applied Communication, 37*(2), 205–214. https://doi.org/10.1080/00909880902792321

Fuchs, C. (2016). *Critical theory of communication.* University of Westminster Press.

Gardner, S. K. (2013). The challenges of first-generation doctoral students. *New Directions for Higher Education, 163*, 43–54. https://doi.org/10.1002/he.20064

Gehrke, P. J., & Keith, W. M. (2014). A brief history of the National Communication Association. In P. J. Gehrke & W. M. Keith (Eds.), *The unfinished conversation: 100 years of communication studies* (pp. 1–25). Routledge.

Germano, W. (2013). *From dissertation to book* (2nd ed.). University of Chicago Press.

González, M. C. (2000, September). The four seasons of ethnography: A creation-centered ontology for ethnography. *International Journal of Intercultural Relations, 24*(5), 623–650. https://doi.org/10.1016/S0147-1767(00)00020-1

Graff, G., Birkenstein, C., & Durst, R. (2016). *"They say/I say": The moves that matter in academic writing* (3rd ed.). W. W. Norton.

Gregg, M. (2018). *Counterproductive: Time management in the knowledge economy*. Duke University Press.

GSI Teaching & Resource Center. (2020). *Grading student work.* https://gsi.berkeley.edu/gsi-guide-contents/grading-intro

Hackman, R. (2015, June 26). "We need co-conspirators, not allies": How white Americans can fight racism. *The Guardian.* https://www.theguardian.com/world/2015/jun/26/how-white-americans-can-fight-racism

Harris, T., & Lee, C. (2019). Advocate-mentoring: A communicative response to diversity in higher education. *Communication Education, 68*(1), 103–113. https://doi.org/10.1080/03634523.2018.1536272

Herrmann, A. F. (2008). *Narratives and sensemaking in the new corporate university: The socialization of first year communication faculty* [Doctoral dissertation, University of South Florida]. Scholar Commons.

Hoops, J., & Drzewiecka, J. (2017, July 27). Critical perspectives toward cultural and communication research. *Oxford Research Encyclopedia of Communication.* https://oxfordre.com/communication/view/10.1093/acrefore/9780190228613.001.0001/acrefore-9780190228613-e-175

Huffman, T., & Tracy, S. J. (2017, December 11). Making claims that matter: Heuristics for theoretical and social impact in qualitative research. *Qualitative Inquiry, 24*(8), 558–570. https://doi.org/10.1177/1077800417742411

Indeed. (2020a, December 1). *Top 11 skills employers look for in candidates.* https://www.indeed.com/career-advice/resumes-cover-letters/skills-employers-look-for

Indeed. (2020b, December 28). *10 benefits of doing an internship.* https://www.indeed.com/career-advice/career-development/benefits-of-internships

Inglis, L. L., & Steinfeld, P. K. (2000). *Old dead white men's philosophy.* Humanity Books.

International Labour Organization. (2020). *ILO Monitor: COVID-19 and the world of work* (3rd ed.). International Labour Organization.

Irwin, H. (2006). Australian communication studies: Achievements and immediate challenges. In K. W. Y. Leung, J. Kenny, & P. S. N. Lee (Eds.), *Global trends in communication education and research* (pp. 97–113). Hampton Press.

Jansen, K., & Shipp, A. (2019). Fitting as a temporal sensemaking process: Shifting trajectories and stable themes. *Human Relations, 72*(7), 1154–1186. https://doi.org/10.1177/0018726718794268

Jensen, P. R., Cruz, J., Eger, E. K., Hanchey, J. N., Gist-Mackey, A. N., Ruiz-Mesa, K., & Villamil, A. (2020). Pushing beyond positionalities and through "failures" in qualitative organizational communication:

Experiences and lessons on identities in ethnographic praxis. *Management Communication Quarterly,* *34*(1), 121–151. https://doi:org/10.1177/0893318919885654

Jorgenson, J. (2016). Performing the "two-body problem": An analysis of academic couples' career sensemaking as revealed through joint storytelling. *Journal of Family Communication, 16*(4), 403–418. https://doi.org/10.1080/15267431.2016.1215985

Kapitan, A. (2016, September 21). Ask a radical copy editor: Black with a capital "B." *Radical Copy Editor.* https://radicalcopyeditor.com/2016/09/21/black-with-a-capital-b/

Kearns, H., & Gardiner, M. (2013). *Time for research: Time management for academics, researchers and research students.* Thinkwell.

Kehm, B. M. (2006). Doctoral education in Europe and North America: A comparative analysis. In U. Teichler (Ed.), *The formative years of scholars* (pp. 67–78). Portland Press.

Kim, H. (2018). The mutual constitution of social media use and status hierarchies in global organizing. *Management Communication Quarterly, 32*(4), 471–503. https://doi.org/10.1177/0893318918779135

Kinsley, K., Besara, R., Scheel, A., Colvin, G., Brady, J. E., & Burel, M. (2015). Graduate conversations: Assessing the space needs of graduate students. *College & Research Libraries, 76*(6), 756–770. https://doi.org/10.5860/crl.76.6.756

Krislow, M. (2019, March 22). Why international students are good for colleges, universities, and America. *Forbes.* https://www.forbes.com/sites/marvinkrislov/2019/03/22/why-international-students-are-good-for-colleges-universities-and-america/#19c2248af496

Lewis, C. S. (1973). *The great divorce.* Macmillan.

Long, Z., Buzzanell, P. M., Anderson, L., Batra, J., Kokini, K., & Wilson, R. (2014). Episodic, network, and intersectional perspectives taking a communication stance on mentoring in the workplace. *Annals of the International Communication Association, 38*(1), 388–422. https://doi.org/10.1080/23808985.2014.11679169

Lorde, A. (2015). The master's tools will never dismantle the master's house. In C. Moraga & G. Anzaldúa (Eds.), *This bridge called my back: Writings by radical women of color* (4th ed., pp. 94–102). SUNY Press.

Lunsford, L. G. (2011). Psychology of mentoring: The case of talented college students. *Journal of Advanced Academics, 22*(3), 474–498. https://doi.org/10.1177/1932202X1102200305

Marte, L. (2008). *El reino de la imagen: Memoria, comida y representación.* Isla Negra Editores.

Mattelart, A. (2006). Toward the end of the French exception in communication research? In K. W. Y. Leung, J. Kenny, & P. S. N. Lee (Eds.), *Global trends in communication education and research* (pp. 73–95). Hampton Press.

Mazer, J. P., & Hess, J. A. (Eds.). (2016). Instructional communication and millennial students [Special issue]. *Communication Education, 65*(3) (pp. 356).

McCoy, H. (2020). The life of a Black academic: Tired and terrorized. *Inside Higher Education.* https://www.insidehighered.com/advice/2020/06/12/terror-many-black-academics-are-experiencing-has-left-them-absolutely-exhausted?utm_source=Inside+Higher+Ed&utm_campaign=4753b0d402-DiversityMatters_COPY_01&utm_medium=email&utm_term=0_1fc-bc04421-4753b0d402-233780849&mc_cid=4753b0d402&mc_eid=20a7214035

McCulloch, A., Kumar, V., van Schalkwyk, S., & Wisker, G. (2016). Excellence in doctoral supervision: An examination of authoritative sources across four countries in search of performance higher than competence. *Quality in Higher Education*, *22*(1), 64–77.

McDonald, J. (2018). Negotiating the "closet" in US academia: Foreign scholars on the job market. *Management Communication Quarterly*, *32*(2), 287–291. https://doi.org/10.1177/0893318917740428

McKerrow, R. E. (1989). Critical rhetoric: Theory and praxis. *Communication Monographs*, *56*(2), 91–111. https://doi.org/10.1080/03637758909390253

McPhail, M. L. (1991). Complicity: The theory of negative difference. *Howard Journal of Communications*, *3*(1–2), 1–13.

Miller, C., & Roksa, J. (2020). Balancing research and service in academia: Gender, race, and laboratory tasks. *Gender & Society*, *34*(1), 131–152. https://doi.org/10.1177/0891243219867917

Miller, G. R. (1976). Foreword. In G. R. Miller (Ed.), *Explorations in interpersonal communication* (pp. 9–16). SAGE.

Moon, J. (1999). *Reflection in learning and professional development: Theory and practice.* Kogan Page.

Moore, J. (2017). Where is the critical empirical interpersonal communication research? A roadmap for future inquiry into discourse and power. *Communication Theory*, *27*(1), 1–20. https://doi.org/10.1111/comt.12107

Murthy, D. (2020). From hashtag activism to inclusion and diversity in a discipline. *Communication, Culture & Critique*, *13*(2). https://doi.org/10.1093/ccc/tcaa014

Nautiyal, J. (2020). Tease and persist: A scratchy note to white "allies." *Women & Language*, *43*(1), 141–145. https://doi:org/10.34036/WL.2020.014

Ng, T. W. H., Eby, L. T., Sorensen, K. L., & Feldman, D. C. (2005). Predictors of objective and subjective career success: A meta-analysis. *Personnel Psychology*, *58*(2), 367–408. https://doi.org/10.1111/j.1744-6570.2005.00515.x

Olekalns, M., Caza, B., & Vogus, T. (2020). Gradual drifts, abrupt shocks: From relationship fractures to relational resilience. *Academy of Management Annals*, *14*(1), 1–28. https://doi.org/10.5465/annals.2017.0111

O'Neill, J. (1989). A message from James O'Neill, First President. In W. W. Work & R. C. Jeffrey (Eds.), *The past is prologue: A 75th-anniversary history of the Speech Communication Association* (p. 3). Speech Communication Association.

Orbe, M., & Harris, T. M. (2015). *Interracial communication: Theory to practice* (3rd ed.). SAGE.

Payne, M., & Barbera, J. R. (2010). *A dictionary of cultural and critical theory* (2nd ed.). Blackwell.

Peterson, P. (1993). *Peterson's guides to graduate study.* Peterson's.

Piercy, C., & Lee, S. (2019). A typology of job search sources: Exploring the changing nature of job search networks. *New Media & Society*, *21*(6), 1173–1191. https://doi.org/10.1177/1461444818808071

Pope-Ruark, R. (2017). *Agile faculty: Practical strategies for managing research, service, and teaching.* University of Chicago.

Pratt, D. D., Collins, J., & Jarvis-Selinger, S. (2020). *Teaching perspectives inventory.* http://www.teachingperspectives.com/tpi/

Pratt, D. D., Smulers, D., & Associates (2016). *Five perspectives on teaching: Mapping a plurality of the good* (2nd ed.). Krieger Publishing.

Putnam, L., & Ashcraft, K. (2017). Gender and organizational paradox. In W. Smith, M. Lewis, P. Jarzab-kowski, & A. Langley (Eds.), *The Oxford handbook of organizational paradox* (pp. 333–352). Oxford University Press.

Race, P. (2019). *The lecturer's toolkit: A practical guide to assessment, learning and teaching* (5th ed.). Routledge.

Robertson, M. J. (2017). Team modes and power: Supervision of doctoral students. *Higher Education Research & Development, 36*(2), 358–371.

Robinson, S. J. (2013). Spoke*tokenism*: Black women *talking back* about graduate school experiences. *Race Ethnicity and Education, 16*(2), 155–181. https://doi.org/10.1080/13613324.2011.645567

Rogers, E. M., & Hart, W. B. (2001). The histories of intercultural, international, and development communication. In W. B. Gudykunst & B. Mody (Eds.), *The handbook of international and intercultural communication* (2nd ed., pp. 1–18). SAGE.

Roig, M. (2015). Avoiding plagiarism, self-plagiarism, and other questionable writing practices: A guide to ethical writing. U.S. Office of Research Integrity, Department of Health and Human Services, https://ori.hhs.gov/avoiding-plagiarism-self-plagiarism-and-other-questionable-writing-practices-guide-ethical-writing

Romero, M. (2018). *Introducing intersectionality.* Polity Press.

Rupert, D., Dillon, E., Teitelbaum, A., & Ray, S. (2016). Succeeding as a master's degree health communication professional: Six key skills and characteristics. *Journal of Communication in Healthcare, 9*(3), 146–150. https://doi.org/10.1080/17538068.2016.1239343

Seeger, M. (2009). Does communication research make a difference: Reconsidering the impact of our work. *Communication Monographs, 76*(1), 12–19.

Shome, R. (1996). Postcolonial interventions in the rhetorical canon: An "other" view. *Communication Theory, 6*(1), 40–59. https://doi.org/10.1111/j.1468-2885.1996.tb00119.x

Shome, R. (2003). Space matters: The power and practice of space. *Communication Theory, 13*(1), 39–56. https://doi.org/10.1111/j.1468-2885.2003.tb00281.x

Smith, T. C., & Virtue, E. E. (2019). It's time to unite: A collaborative approach to addressing the needs of graduate students of colour. *Journal of Student Affairs in Africa, 7*(1), 101–110. https://doi.org/10.24085/jsaa.v7i1.3695

Southwick, S. M., & Charney, D. S. (2012). *Resilience: The science of mastering life's greatest challenges.* Cambridge University Press.

Svinicki, M., & McKeachie, W. J. (2010). *McKeachie's teaching tips: Strategies, research, and theory for college and university teachers* (13th ed.). Cengage Learning.

Swedberg, R. (2016). Before theory comes theorizing or how to make social science more interesting. *The British Journal of Sociology, 67*(1), 5–22. https://doi.org/10.1111/1468-4446.12184

Sweeney, M. E. (2012, June 20). How to read for grad school. *Miriam E. Sweeney: Feminist Research in Critical Information Studies.* https://miriamsweeney.net/2012/06/20/readforgradschool/

Sword, H. (2016). "Write every day!": A mantra dismantled. *International Journal for Academic Development, 21*(4), 312–322. https://doi.org/10.1080/1360144X.2016.1210153

Taylor, D. S., Nwosu, P. O., & Mutua-Kombo, E. (2004). Communication studies in Africa: The case for a paradigm shift for the 21st century. *Africa Media Review, 12*(2), 1–23.

Taylor, S., Kiley, M., & Humphrey, R. (2018). *A handbook for doctoral supervisors.* Routledge.

Thornberg, R., & Charmaz, K. (2014). Grounded theory and theoretical coding. In U. Flick (Ed.), *The SAGE handbook of qualitative data analysis* (pp. 153–169). SAGE.

Tracy, S. J. (2010). Qualitative quality: Eight "big-tent" criteria for excellent qualitative research. *Qualitative Inquiry, 16*(10), 837–851. https://doi.org/10.1177/1077800410383121

Tracy, S. J. (2020). *Qualitative research methods: Collecting evidence, crafting analysis, communicating impact* (2nd ed.). Wiley-Blackwell.

Tracy, S. J., & Donovan, M. C. J. (2018). Moving from practical application to expert craft practice in organizational communication: A review of the past and OPPT-ing into the future. In P. J. Salem & E. Timmerman (Eds.), *Transformative practice and research in organizational communication* (pp. 202–220). IGI Global.

United States Census Bureau. (2018). *Educational attainment in the United States.* https://www.census.gov/data/tables/2018/demo/education-attainment/cps-detailed-tables.html

University of Michigan Human Resources. (2020). *Self-assessment tools and readiness for change.* Regents of the University of Michigan. https://hr.umich.edu/working-u-m/professional-development/professional-development-courses/additional-career-development-resources/self-assessment-tools-readiness-change

UT Austin graduate student/worker open letter: COVID-19 demands. (2020, May 13). https://docs.google.com/document/d/1gegVWFWd1SSEUd6g4EJi6yn3Bv1yd0hHfdXH2FZic7E/edit

Wang, S. S. (2006). Journalism and communication education in Taiwan: An observation in a transitional society. In K. W. Y. Leung, J. Kenny, & P. S. N. Lee (Eds.), *Global trends in communication education and research* (pp. 159–176). Hampton Press.

Wethington, E., Herman, H., & Pillemer, K. (2012). Introduction: Translational research in the social and behavioral sciences. In E. Wethington & R. E. Dunifon (Eds.), *Research for the public good: Applying the methods of translational research to improve human health and well-being* (pp. 3–19). American Psychological Association.

Wood, J. (2004). *Communication theories in action: An introduction.* Wadsworth.

About the Editors

Betsy Wackernagel Bach (PhD, University of Washington) is professor emerita at the University of Montana, where she spent her career. She is past president of the National Communication Association and the Western States Communication Association and also worked for two years as director of research initiatives at NCA. She studies organizational socialization/identification, has published one book and 40 articles and chapters, and received WSCA's Distinguished Service Award and NCA's Eckroyd Award for Teaching Excellence.

Dawn O. Braithwaite (PhD, University of Minnesota) is a Willa Cather professor of communication, University of Nebraska–Lincoln. She studies discourse dependent relationships, dialectics of relating, and communication in step- and voluntary families. She has published six books and 130 articles and chapters. A distinguished scholar of the National Communication Association and Western States Communication Association, Braithwaite received NCA's Brommel Family Communication and Becker Distinguished Service Awards. She is a past president of WSCA and NCA.

Shiv Ganesh (PhD, Purdue University) is professor in the Department of Communication Studies at the University of Texas at Austin. He writes about communication and collective action issues in the context of global and technological processes. He has worked in the United States, Aotearoa New Zealand, and India and has held leadership positions in both the National Communication Association as well as the International Communication Association.

About the Authors

Brianna Avalos (MA, San Diego State University) is a PhD student at the Hugh Downs School of Human Communication at Arizona State University. Brianna is interested in interpersonal communication, specifically social support and preservation of authentic relationships.

Kendyl Barney (MA, University of Montana) graduated with her MA from the University of Montana. She plans to apply for PhD programs in the coming years, with the ultimate goal of being a professor of communication studies. In the meantime, Kendyl is investing in her research. She studies interpersonal and family communication, primarily exploring grief in families. Kendyl hopes this research will be impactful for nonprofit organizations and counselors to support grieving communities.

Timothy Betts (MS, Texas Christian University) is a doctoral student in the Department of Communication at the University of South Florida where he studies organizational communication. His work examines the communicative construction and organization of economic systems and institutions.

Emma Frances Bloomfield (PhD, University of Southern California) is assistant professor of communication studies at the University of Nevada, Las Vegas. She studies the rhetoric of science, environmental communication, and public controversy, especially on topics of climate change and evolution. Her book *Communication Strategies for Engaging Climate Skeptics: Religion and the Environment* was published in Routledge's Advances in Climate Change Research series in 2019 and provides both theoretical and practical insights into climate communication.

Beth L. Boser (PhD, University of Southern California) is assistant professor of communication studies at the University of Wisconsin–La Crosse. She studies rhetorics of motherhood and birth and constructions of agency therein. Some of her prior work appears in *Rhetoric & Public Affairs* and the edited volumes *Mediated Moms: Contemporary Challenges to the Motherhood Myth, Interrogating Gendered Pathologies*, and *Nasty Women and Bad Hombres: Gender and Race in the 2016 US Presidential Election*.

Patrice M. Buzzanell (PhD, Purdue University) is professor and chair of the University of South Florida's Department of Communication and endowed visiting professor for Shanghai Jiao Tong University's School of Media and Design. She has published four books and 260 articles, chapters, and engineering education proceedings on careers, design, equity, and resilience. She is an ICA fellow and past president; NCA Distinguished Scholar; and past president of the Organization for the Study of Communication, Language and Gender.

Megan E. Cardwell (MA, University of Nebraska–Lincoln) is a doctoral student in the Department of Communication Studies at the University of Nebraska–Lincoln. She studies communicative aspects of (multi)ethnic-racial identity, race, and racism(s), and well-being. Her research is published in the *Journal of Social and Personal Relationships*, *Identity: An International Journal of Theory and Research*, and the *Journal of Nonverbal Behavior*.

C. L. Dangerfield (MA, Penn State University) is a doctoral candidate at the University of Memphis. She applies a critical lens to the study of rhetoric, gender, race, and religion. Dangerfield has published her work in numerous journals and anthologies, including *Journal of Communication* and the book *Understanding African American Rhetoric: Classical Origins to Contemporary Innovations*. She has presented her work widely at national and regional conferences and serves as a board member for the Rhetoric Society of America.

Uttaran Dutta (PhD, Purdue University) is associate professor in the Hugh Downs School of Human Communication at Arizona State University, United States. His research focuses on sustainable development and social change in marginalized communities, specifically on the importance of culture, communication, design, and innovation in transforming the lives of people who are socially, politically, and economically underserved.

Katlyn E. Gangi (PhD, University of California, Santa Barbara) is manager of the product education team at Ontraport, a software company. She writes educational content and directs the communication of written and live-taught content aimed at employees and clients. Her scholarly interests are in relational communication, focusing on stressful and uncertain events in relationships. She is researching loss and grief during the COVID-19 pandemic and has served as visiting assistant professor at University of Montana.

Samantha Gillespie (MA, University of Nevada, Reno) is a doctoral student at the University of Nebraska–Lincoln, studying communication studies, rhetoric, and public culture. After finishing her thesis project about eating and gender politics within YouTube eating shows, Samantha is continuing her critical rhetorical research of online spaces focused on the intersections of gender, subjectivity, and neoliberalism. She is both excited and proud to be part of this book, which constitutes her first published work.

Andrew Gilmore (MA, University of Colorado Denver) is a doctoral candidate at Colorado State University. He studies rhetorical theory and criticism, focusing on Hong Kong's complex relationship with mainland China and addressing issues surrounding protest, national identity, cultural preservation, censorship, governmentality, and democracy. His work on the Umbrella Revolution explores the use of buildings, transportation, and everyday items as tools of protest that can also be utilized to maintain hegemonic structures of inequality and power.

Jenna N. Hanchey (PhD, University of Texas at Austin) is assistant professor of communication studies at the University of Nevada, Reno. Her award-winning research is premised on a politics of decolonization and attends to the intersections of rhetoric, women of color feminisms, African studies, and critical development studies. She is currently working on a book titled *The Center Cannot Hold: Haunted Reflexivity, Fugitive Rhetorical Agency, and Decolonial Dreamwork in the Ruination of a Tanzanian NGO.*

Tina M. Harris (PhD, University of Kentucky) is the inaugural Douglas L. Manship Sr.–Dori Maynard Race, Media, and Cultural Literacy Endowed Chair at Louisiana State University. She is an internationally renowned interracial communication scholar with particular interests in race, media representations, and racial social justice. Dr. Harris has received multiple awards, including the University of Georgia's 2017 Engaged Scholar Award and the National Communication Association's Robert J. Kibler Award for service.

Stephen K. Hunt (PhD, Southern Illinois University, Carbondale) is professor and director of the School of Communication at Illinois State University. As an AASCU Civic Fellow for Political Engagement, he helps lead national efforts to sharpen the political and civic leadership skills of today's college students. He is the author of over 30 scholarly articles, many focused on civic and political engagement. He is also past president of the Central States Communication Association.

Ronald L. Jackson II (PhD, Howard University) is professor of communication, past president of the National Communication Association, and previous Dean of Arts & Sciences at the University of Cincinnati. His research explores empirical, conceptual, and critical approaches to masculinity, identity negotiation, and race. He is the author of 15 books, including *Scripting the Black Masculine Body in Popular Media* and the 2014 Comic-Con Eisner Award-winning book *Black Comics: Politics of Race and Representation.*

Trevor Kauer (MA, Texas State University) is a communication studies doctoral student at the University of Nebraska–Lincoln. From a service-oriented and applied perspective, he studies the communication and participation in (un)healthy extremes (e.g., excessive behaviors/situations; stressful/hazardous work, over-parenting/teaching, etc.) and communicated meaning-making in personal relationships and work/life experiences. His expertise focuses on job stress/coping of first responders and military, helicopter teaching, emerging adults and nontraditional students in the classroom, family storytelling, and body image/weight.

Lisa Keränen (PhD, University of Pittsburgh) is associate professor and chair of the Department of Communication at the University of Colorado Denver. She studies the rhetorics of health and medicine. Her books include *Scientific Characters: Rhetoric, Politics, and Trust in Breast Cancer Research* and *Imagining China*. She received the Karl R. Wallace Memorial Research Award and the Marie Hochmuth Nichols Award and is past president of the Association for the Rhetoric of Science, Technology, and Medicine.

Dayna N. Kloeber (MA, Arizona State University) is a doctoral candidate at ASU's Hugh Downs School of Human Communication. Dayna's dissertation research focuses on how the communication of forgiveness helps advance the theoretical distinctions between forgiveness and reconciliation. She has coauthored a number of journal articles, book chapters, and most recently a 2018 book titled *A Communicative Approach to Conflict, Forgiveness, and Reconciliation: Reimagining Our Relationships,* with Douglas Kelley and Vincent Waldron.

Randall A. Lake (PhD, University of Kansas) is associate professor of communication in the Annenberg School for Communication and Journalism at the University of Southern California; a faculty affiliate of the USC Race and Equity Center; and former director of the Annenberg Doctoral Program. He researches and teaches in rhetorical theory, history, and criticism; argumentation; race and gender in public controversies; and movements for and against social, political, and cultural change.

Simon Mallette (PhD student, Université de Montréal, Canada) is lecturer in the Department of Communication at the Université de Montréal and the Department of Communication at the Université de Sherbrooke, Canada. He studies organizational communication, discourse, and ICT-mediated collaboration. His doctoral thesis explores the communicative and relational nature of entrepreneurship in a digital society.

Laura V. Martinez (MA, California State University, Fullerton) is a doctoral student in the Hugh Downs School of Human Communication at Arizona State University–Tempe. Her research interests include identity work, organizational- and group-level identification, resilience in the face of trauma, sensemaking, qualitative methods, and the intersection between organizational and health communication.

Kirstie McAllum (PhD, University of Waikato, New Zealand) is associate professor in the Department of Communication at the Université de Montréal, Canada. Her research examines topics related to volunteering, nonprofit organizing, care, and the occupational identities of nonstandard workers, particularly in health care contexts.

Aimee E. Miller-Ott (PhD, University of Nebraska–Lincoln) is professor and graduate program coordinator in the School of Communication at Illinois State University. She teaches a variety of courses, including family communication, interpersonal communication, and research methods. Her research centers on ways that people communicatively manage identity and information in various personal relationships. She is the author of over 20 scholarly articles, many recently focused on co-present cell phone usage in interpersonal relationships.

Mackensie Minniear (PhD, University of Nebraska–Lincoln) is assistant professor in the Department of Communication Studies at the University of Georgia. Her research focuses on race in the family. She studies how communication can create a stronger connection to ethnic-racial identity in Black, Indigenous, and Families of Color as well as integrating social systems that disenfranchise these same families. Her research can be found in the *Journal of Family Communication* and *Communication Reports*.

Jessy J. Ohl (PhD, University of Nebraska–Lincoln) is associate professor of communication studies at the University of Alabama, where he specializes in rhetoric and political discourse. His research and teaching focus on the relationship between rhetoric, violence, and democracy. His scholarship has been featured in *Communication and Critical Cultural Studies*; *Argumentation, Advocacy, Rhetoric and Public Affairs*; and *The Quarterly Journal of Speech*, among others.

Ana-Luisa Ortiz-Martinez (MA, University of Nevada, Reno) is a PhD student at Texas A&M University in communication studies. She studies colonialism, immigration, and Latin American social movements through a rhetorical lens. Her work explores the vernacular uses of Latin American music in social movements. Some of her projects implement autoethnographic methods. Her story as an immigrant forms the foundation of her research and her passion to help others, teach, and write for her community.

Viraj Patel (MS, Illinois State University) is a master's graduate from the School of Communication at Illinois State University. At the 2019 National Communication Association Conference, he presented a poster regarding the #UniteTheRight and Charlottesville protests. His graduate thesis examined the role of media richness in increasing student participation with student government associations. He was named an All-American by the American Forensics Association in 2018.

Barbara A. Pickering (PhD, University of Southern California) is assistant director of the School of Communication at the University of Nebraska Omaha. Her research in political communication, gender and communication, and rhetorical criticism has been published in national and international journals. She was honored at UNO in 2007 with the College of Communication, Fine Arts and Media Excellence in Teaching award, and in 2011 she received the NCA-Master's Education Division Outstanding Graduate Mentor award.

Bridget Reynolds Sheffer (PhD, University of Waikato) completed her MA in professional communication at Southern Utah University. She has experience in the United States and the European models of graduate work and has worked to understand the value of both experiences. She has been teaching for 11 years and currently teaches part-time at Brigham Young University, Utah.

Tyler S. Rife (PhD candidate, Arizona State University) is a graduate teaching associate in the Hugh Downs School of Human Communication at Arizona State University. He studies critical/cultural communication, rhetoric, performance, art, media, and environment. He is currently developing a rhetoric and performance-focused dissertation on the ecological organization of necropolitics in the urban desert landscape of Phoenix, Arizona.

Andrea Shute Zorn (PGDip) is a PhD student and assistant lecturer in the School of Communication, Journalism and Marketing at Massey University in Auckland, Aotearoa New Zealand. She is interested in studying positive social change for marginalized communities, and her thesis is on the meaning of work for women entrepreneurs who started their businesses during a time of hardship. She teaches a first-year communication course in Massey Business School, with a focus on intercultural communication and diversity in the workplace.

Jordan Soliz (PhD, University of Kansas) is professor of communication studies at the University of Nebraska–Lincoln. His research centers primarily on identity and difference in personal relationships, families, and communities especially as it relates to race-ethnicity and religious orientations. He is a previous editor of the *Journal of Family Communication* and past chair of the Intergroup Communication Interest Group of the International Communication Association.

James B. Stiff (PhD, Michigan State University) is the founder of Trial Strategies and has been a jury consultant for almost 30 years. Clients engage Jim in a wide variety of consulting activities, including case strategy, jury research (focus groups, mock trials, and community attitude surveys), witness preparation, and jury selection. Prior to being a jury consultant, Jim was a tenured university professor specializing in graduate-level courses in persuasion, interpersonal communication, and scientific research methods.

Jameien R. Taylor (PhD, Arizona State University) is lecturer in the School of Social and Behavioral Sciences at Arizona State University. Jameien is interested in ethics, broadly. Specifically, they study the implication of care, kindness, and compassion in intimate and in-acquainted interactions. Phenomenology, philology, and grounded theory approaches assist in their address of these phenomena.

Zhenyu Tian (MA, San Diego State University) is a doctoral candidate in the Department of Communication at the University of South Florida. His current research interests focus on gender and organizing, gender identities, and resilience. His work can be found in the *Journal of Applied Communication Research.*

Cris J. Tietsort (MA, Whitworth University) is a doctoral student in the Hugh Downs School of Human Communication at Arizona State University–Tempe. His scholarly interests lie in leadership communication, compassion, practical wisdom, and transformative approaches to communication skill development.

Sarah J. Tracy (PhD, University of Colorado Boulder) is professor and director of the Transformation Project in the Hugh Downs School of Human Communication at Arizona State University–Tempe. She researches, writes, speaks, and teaches in the areas of organizational communication, well-being at work, compassion, conversation, leadership, and qualitative research methods. She is author of more than 90 scholarly essays and two books. More information: www.SarahJTracy.com and Twitter handle @SarahJTracy.

Vincent R. Waldron (PhD, Ohio State University) is professor of communication and Lincoln Professor of Relational Ethics at Arizona State University. He studies communication in personal and work relationships, with particular interest in such topics as the communication of forgiveness and relational resilience. Vince is author or editor of eight books, including *Communicating Forgiveness* (with Douglas Kelley) and *Negotiating Work Relationships* (with Jeffrey Kassing).

C. Kay Weaver (PhD, University of Stirling, Scotland) is professor and dean of the School of Graduate Research at the University of Waikato in New Zealand. She researches strategic communication from critical theory perspectives, has coauthored and coedited several books, and published in, among other journals, *Public Relations Review*, *Journal of Public Relations Research*, *Media Culture & Society*, *New Media and Society*, and the *Journal of Applied Communication Research.*

Index

Review of Communication (National Communication Association), 7
rhetoric
 constitutive, 10
 critical, 10
 diversifying and decolonizing, 11
 invitational, 10
 study of, 10
rhetorical and humanistic approaches, 10–11
Robertson, M. J., 66
Robinson, S. J., 35
Rogers, E. M., 5
Rupert, D., 180

S
scholarly process, 84–85
scholarly traditions for inquiry, 72–73
self-assessment, 192–194
self-motivation, 195
Shome, R., 212
skills
 development, 73–75
 effective public speaking, 194
 effective writing, 194
 research methods and analysis, 194
social science, 4, 10–11
Social Science Research Council (SSRC), 1
Social Sciences Citation Index (SSCI), 171
Southern Communication Journal (Southern States Communication Association), 8
style manuals, 93
submission considerations, 101–102
supervision agreements, 63

T
Taylor, D. S., 186
teacher, 111–123
 appraisals and improving one's practice, 119–120
 "failures" in, 116–118
 meanings and purpose, 112–113
 navigating landscapes of teaching, 112–113
 resilient, 116–121
 teaching environment, 112–115
 team work, 122–123
team work, 122–123

tenure-track positions, 168–169
Text and Performance Quarterly (National Communication Association), 7
theoretical foundation, 195–196
thesis/dissertation, 44–45, 50–53
thesis/dissertation defenses, 54
time management, 156–159
Todd, R., 167
topic development, 73
trustworthy relationships, 131
tupo pamoja, 161

U
unchangeable career path, 198–199
U.S. Census Bureau, 201

V
Vietnam War, 4
visit F2F or virtually, 17–19
visiting faculty/instructors, 169
voice as scholar and writer, 87–88

W
Waters, W., 88, 92
Western Journal of Communication (Western Communication Association), 8
work-life balance, 173–174
workload, 47–48
writer, 83–96, 87–88
 abstract writing, 90–91
 citation styles, 93–94
 developing tools as, 84–89
 key terms writing, 90–91
 literature, 92
 making arguments in writing, 89
 rationale for study, 91–92
 sources, 92
 writing collaboratively, 95–96
 writing hacks, 96
writerly attitude, 84–85
writing hacks, 96

Z
Zhang, Rudong, 85
Zotero, 95

CPSIA information can be obtained
at www.ICGtesting.com
Printed in the USA
LVHW060451280522
719949LV00001B/4